The Vagaries of Swing

(Footprints on the M … Time)

ISBN 978-1-291-38135-1

Cover design by Sian Dodkins

My thanks to John B, Sue F, Ant and Brian for their encouragement and patience in reading the draft versions and of course to Andi

I should also mention my admiration for local historians generally who work tirelessly to bring the past to life and particularly those in the Isle of Thanet, without whom this would not have been possible.

Synopsis

The BBC TV series "True Love" was the catalyst for this tale, portraying various romantic encounters, all set by the Margate seaside. True love has many forms. A passion for cricket can also be a manifestation of love. Yet it is impossible to discuss cricket, with its broad themes, without reflecting on life itself. I have set my story broadly in 1965, when a girl lost her life. At the time, her death meant little to us but such are the vagaries of writing, that the more I researched the subject, the greater I became drawn in. Any discussion on the circumstances surrounding her murder led inevitably to the inclusion of another theme, which I have encountered in life, violence towards women. I still return to Margate regularly and regard it with deep affection. It was in danger of becoming a wasteland. There are those now, some famous, some often unsung, trying to fashion a resurgence. Another form of true love. May their guardian angels help them succeed.

A man destined for high rank in the law once referred to the author in words borrowed from 'All's Well That Ends Well':

"He is a most notable coward, an infinite and endless liar, an hourly promise-breaker, the owner of no one good quality".

He then tried to repair the damage with a quote from the 'Two Gentleman of Verona' which is irrelevant in this context. Most of the characters in this story are or were real but anyone taking offence at the content or the quality of the writing should re-read the above. As Kingsley Amis once said, "If you can't annoy someone, there is little point in writing".

"I tend to think that cricket is the greatest thing that God created on earth, certainly greater than sex, although sex isn't too bad either."

Harold Pinter

Biff was wearing his thick green woollen crew-cut sweater. He actually only had two sweaters, one green and one yellow, which he wore alternately and without any sign of embarrassment. Not much of a social wardrobe. We always assumed that his mother had knitted them as Christmas presents as none of us would have been seen dead buying or wearing them. She must have lovingly and painstakingly washed them whilst he was at work, as they never seemed to show the marks of the copious beer-stains which would have accurately reflected his way of life. Yet there again, my sight was not particularly good. Friends would tell me that they had often passed me by in the street and smiled, without receiving any sign of mutual recognition, so how could I tell. Biff must have had a suit of sorts as he worked as a civil servant for the Ministry of Defence by day, in an age when drones could only be found leaning over a garden fence. He was a lovely shambles of a man and by night had an amusing habit of curling an arm around his beer mug and cradling it gently on his ample belly. The Ruby Lounge, with its crusty and eccentric host Les, was our most frequent haunt in those days, from whence we could spill out afterwards to Don's Oyster Bar for a plate of cockles or whelks before staggering home. Shellfish are a pretty amazing food, the food of the Gods and my brother's best friends, Keith and Bruce, had started that trend one glorious night and it kind of stuck. Bruce was apparently the most senior petty officer in the Navy at that time, but they made a mistake one Christmas when they left him in charge of a frigate in Chatham dockyard. The naval hospitality to my brother and me in the mess was miraculous and if we had not had the little Citroen Dyane on the quayside, we could have walked back to Margate across the water, our guardian angels hovering on high. Mind you, it was the only water we had seen for some hours.

In a different era the Ruby Lounge directly opposite the little harbour had begun life as the Black Horse, before transforming itself into the New Inn, 'the principal house of entertainment in Margate'. Its proprietor enterprisingly dug a channel to the sea to create the first seawater baths in the country and ladies would queue to use them. Now the only liquid which might swirl around your feet in the cellars would be the remnants of beer or urine. Biff would always drive everywhere. His internal satnav seemed automatically to point his battered Vauxhall Viva in the right direction up past the police station above the harbour where the Fort used to stand, the seven or eight pints of best bitter barely registering on his ability to peer out through the windscreen. The seagulls wheeling above would have been proud of his homing instincts, although his build did tend to suggest a closer bonding to a rather large and plump pigeon. It was the year though when government announcements on blood alcohol testing were first proposed. Biff would soon have something other to fear than closing time.

He had been a ladies' man in his youth but according to legend was jilted by his first love. Perhaps she ran off with one of the donkey men who strode manfully across the sands. Donkeys were a permanent feature in the area, said to have borne 'angels by day and spirits by night', an amusing hint at the long association with smuggling on the coast. Biff had abandoned women when true love receded and thereafter tended to treat most of them with scant regard. I doubt that he would have been able to verify the second part of Harold Pinter's theory on the pleasures of sex, except as a solitary pursuit. The Ruby was largely a man's pub. Biff could tolerate a barmaid, but nothing on his side of the counter. There would be no secretaries, office girls or waitresses here. The 'principal house of entertainment' did not even possess a dartboard. He put on weight fairly steadily, developing a ruddy blotched complexion. He was not quite the 'fat boy' from Pickwick Papers but he might have had a roll of flannel down each leg. Not for lack of exercise, for he loved sport and had a wonderful eye for a ball. It was just that he could not really run. Cricket was his first love, but he played in the winter for Cliftonville's second and third hockey teams at centre half. He could stop anything within arm's reach and maybe two steps away. Beyond that he was soon breathing hard and toiling manfully to keep up. This would never be surprising, because his match preparation for hockey and cricket - slightly at odds with today's science - was to drink four pints at lunchtime and then have an occasional cigarette. His only concession would be, on away matches, to stop halfway up the Thanet Way and urinate by one of the rubbish bins just past the Roman Galley, thus lightening his bulk considerably. Warming up or stretching any part of the anatomy would have been regarded with scorn. If he only had one good sprint, why would he want to waste it before the game started? Yet he had great hands and they rarely lost matches, probably because most of the opposition trained in the same old way.

Urination has its own protocol, a process, a flow. Militant women in Germany and Scandinavia have fought bitterly in recent years to keep seats in toilets down. Nothing to do with sexual preferences, purely to reduce male random spraying. They surely cannot understand that a seated male will always have residue, possibly half as much again as you begin ageing. A close examination of any set of y-fronts would prove conclusive and would separate the men from the boys. German girls were once said to have the most ample bosoms in Europe, but boys that cannot compensate for toilet seats where the position is mandatorily set to horizontal. Stand up to these Amazons and against their toilets and become men. Let 'uber alles' become your watchword, although 'alles' should not be seen as giving free expression to the popular male custom of watering the floor around the toilet base. Invading Poland is also out of bounds of course, although these days to successfully conquer the Poles you would need to capture most of Lincolnshire as well. In public houses, the protocol largely consists of men, often in a line, standing against a wall. They will always be looking down but rarely to the side. A furtive glance is allowed but any suggestion that you are contemplating your neighbour's member can be explosive. In any case why would you want to do that, on the basis that your pride might then be permanently scarred by the comparison.

You can handle your own appendage, lightly with one hand, proudly with two hands and occasionally, as a smart ass, letting it fire independently. You are not permitted, certainly in the urinals that I frequent, to reach out and hold anyone else's appendage. One of my great discoveries, when pissed and pissing, was that if you stood with friends on either side, it was possible to swing your tool to the left or right and send a flow past two comrades and hit the third cleanly on the shoes. You would hold this position briefly and then swing back. Your colleague at the end would suddenly notice the steam rising from his shoes without being at all sure how this had happened. Childish, immature? Absolutely. Do we ever grow up? I think not. Urination of course can take place anywhere in natural surroundings, depending on the urgency of the call. At the seaside you should always test the water, not just because of the proximity of sewerage pipes, but because excess drinking tends to take place when most of the public urinals are closed. If you are not cocooned in a Vauxhall Viva, and who would be these days, then sometimes you have a long way to walk home. Beaches are always close to hand, but preferably not those festooned with blue flags. Yellow flags are the flags of convenience. Parks where there are bushes and trees are also natural havens. Yet, under all circumstances, stay well away from the cricket field, that holiest of places. Do not relieve yourself on the square.

“Women playing cricket should treat it as a matter between consenting females in private”

Michael Parkinson

Biff had learned to bowl fast at the grammar school under a maths master called Jacobson, pronounced as you would the biscuit. Crackers might be a safer guide. Jake was a single man who had managed to save enough from his teacher’s salary to run an old Jaguar, but had an unfortunate tendency to lisp in a most exaggerated fashion. Nonetheless he was saved the normal schoolboy taunting, beyond the constant mimicry, by his innate sense of humour and his dedication to coaching the first eleven at cricket. Even when Biff lost his speed he had learnt enough to retain his subtlety and ability to swing. He could move the ball both ways, although often the movement was unexpected, and his length was always impeccable. When he joined us the next season, after the club split, he could drop the ball just short of a length at Dane Park. Roughly about the spot where we thought and joked that she had died. None of us at the time had really paid much attention to the details of the murder. The park was in the area down from the main town and from the heights of Cliftonville, sometimes known as The Dane. The Danes were said to have been involved in a fierce battle with the English at the Bank of Hackendown in the reign of King Ethelwolf. Many of them had been thrown off the cliff, tossed off, legend has it, without mercy. Just another routine day at the seaside. Centuries later, roads were named after them, Dane Road, Upper Dane Road, Dane Valley Road. Imagination was rarely a strength in our council chambers. A station halt was built in anticipation of a railway line that never came and became an inn, the Dane Valley Arms. Housing estates grew around it. In Dane Park, George would turn up weekly in the early evening during the summer after work to roll the cricket pitch. True love and dedication. Park groundsmen were employed by the council and that enabled a cricket festival of some repute each year down in the valley. Marquees like those at Dingley Dell were set up. A Kent team of sorts used to turn up, including very occasionally the likes of Derek Underwood and Brian Luckhurst. Guest players were invited in to strengthen the local side, often schoolmasters, like Ken and Tommy.

Our school was fortunate then to have a number of inspirational teachers and sport was particularly strong. Their presence was reflected in the enthusiasm and skill of our local teams, whether in cricket, hockey or rugby and the hospitality to visitors was also normally overflowing. In the summer, touring sides would willingly come down to visit for a day at the seaside and bring their families. Rachel Hayhoe Flint two or three times brought her team of England ladies to play at the Margate Festival. Did Michael Parkinson really say that about women playing cricket? He used to write such humorous sporting prose as a journalist. Promoting life insurance must have dulled his brain, those persistent and annoying television advertisements certainly dulling mine. Maybe it was the effect of the emu attacks and dyno-rod. Just how many free Parker Pens do you need in life anyway? The offer of a free Parka might make a difference, bringing back the memories, but another bloody pen? Why do so many of our celebrities sell themselves cheap, for what are to them just a few dollars more?

In any case, in the park itself the games were popular and competition immensely fierce to be included in the mixed events. Apart from the illusion of post-match sex in the bar or in the bike sheds after the match - we were all dreamers and eternal optimists - the lady bowlers were not fast and were there in theory to be knocked about. Perhaps the fate of ladies throughout the ages and certainly not just on Ilkey Moor. In those unreconstructed days we would vie to field at short leg to peer more closely at any shapely legs and buttocks and our Mike even asked one of them if he could adjust the coconut shells he assumed she wore for protection. Must have been a Caribbean tradition. In our defence, we groaned in unison. Mike was a handsome young man with great charm and a winning smile and could get away with murder. Not everyone could get away with murder in this park. Any children, brought reluctantly along as an after-thought to the cricket, would be sent away up to the newly refurbished playground. The swing had been there for many years enjoying the laughter, when it was not in motion. The roundabout was gentle and less discerning. It was newly installed in such a way as to ensure a steady rotation. You would not lose consciousness in its embrace.

Julie, let's call her, was only sixteen and even then might have been used to the occasional blow, but the anger and aggression must have taken her by surprise. It just took her breath away. The pitch was further down the slope and slightly to the right of where her body was actually found. The main path that drove through the centre of the park was on higher ground and then there was a smaller path, lined with trees, which turned up in the direction of the windmill. On the opposite side where the pavilion stood, on a good day people would hire deckchairs and we would often have a collection for the club. The cricket was of a decent enough standard, although the team sadly declined after the great split. The sea air would help the ball swing, often without explanation, and a really quick bowler could make the ball lift. This was beyond Biff now although his run-up, more of a trundle, remained substantial.

Willie though was a different matter. Willie was tall, slim, had a wicked grin and hair cropped short. It was as if Lee Van Cleef and Lee Marvin had fathered a son together, an awkward left-handed child. The Marvin of Point Blank though, not Cat Ballou, which was playing at Dreamland cinema that very week. Willie worked in a factory, a physical repetitive job, and also lived for his sport. He would say that, “if my wife and girls are clothed, there is food on the table, enough for a pint or two and the cricket is good, then what else is there on God’s earth”. What indeed? He was a lovely funny gentle man - until he opened the bowling. He liked to run down from the Hastings Avenue end, where my grandparents lived in their small terraced house, sitting under the gas lights on either side of the kitchen stove, and would usually bowl round the wicket. This allowed him to bring the ball back into right-handed batsmen and then try to move it away on the seam. He was quite intimidating - his hair even bristled - and he had played with some decent sides in his youth. He could make the ball rear wickedly. Arms would jerk upwards in defence. If only she had reached the swing or had run down for the cricket square. So close to the road and home. Her arms must have instinctively shot up too. Run for your life, little girl, if you can.

"His guns were loaded with poison bait, as they hung and swung at his side,
Tonight you'll be drinking your drinks with the dead, there'll be blood a-running in town by night".

'A Cowboy's song of fate', from the 1934 film 'Riders of Destiny'

As "Singin' Sandy" Saunders rode into town you can just imagine the outlaws trembling, particularly as he was prone to break into song before each gunfight. Just one verse and they would be face down in the dust, begging for mercy. 'Riders of Destiny' was only the second movie at that time to feature a singing cowboy and John Wayne, who played "Singin' Sandy", not surprisingly refused ever to sign up for anything similar again. To cap it all, the words don't even rhyme. However I have always been fascinated by the part fate plays in history, how people come to arrive at a certain place and time, even if in Wayne's case the method of transport tended to be on the lines of "All the world's a stage". The first record that I bought with my pocket money was actually 'Davy Crockett, King of the Wild Frontier', who of course died at the Alamo surrounded by dead Mexicans. Like part of my family, the Crocketts claimed to be descended from the Huguenots but they turned left and sailed for the States instead of London. In 1960 John Wayne played the fifty year old Crockett, complete with coonskin hat, but never sang, not even to Jim Bowie. In the earlier Disney film with Fess Parker, the song was sung by the Wellingtons, no relation though that I know to the Iron Duke. Was there ever a Black and White Minstrel song about Crockett's coonskin hat, even a comical one that Alf Garnett could have enjoyed? Can't recall one on the radio on 'Sing Something Simple', as we stood and washed the dishes on a Sunday evening.

There has always been a persistent story that Davy did not die in the onslaught, had actually surrendered at the Alamo and been one of those ruthlessly and secretly executed by General Santa Anna for their part in the resistance. Never quite gone away, that rumour. The first Americans we encountered in Margate as youngsters, were when we sang as choirboys to some American airmen at their airbase and were rewarded with our first iconic bottles of Coca Cola. Our bedroom had a clear outlook over the fields to Manston Aerodrome in the far distance, but as kids my brother and I had not Spitfires and Mustangs but cowboys on the wallpaper in our shared room. I guess I grew up dreaming of the Wild West and once I had disposed of The Faraway Tree and Mr Saucepan Man, westerns were my novels of choice.

One Xmas my grandmother gave me a model Winchester rifle which I treasured for at least one day, until on Boxing Day I climbed on to the coal bunker to fend off the Indian attacks at the back of the house. I smashed it down hard on Crazy Horse but he moved slightly to the right and the rifle smashed in two on the bunker edge. I was inconsolable. Fortunately there was no such coal bunker at the back of James Stewart's cabin in the film Winchester 73 or the story would have ended prematurely.

I still devour stories of the West and, for instance, have long been intrigued by the events at the Little Big Horn in 1876 and the fate of other riders of destiny, the various men who either fell with George Armstrong Custer or who escaped a similar grisly fate. The sheer element of chance that seems to emerge as you delve down into the detail. Some men, like Custer himself, the Canadian Cooke and Keogh, might have thought themselves immortal. Custer certainly did. Cooke with his long-flowing side whiskers did have a premonition that the next battle might be his last, but was the best shot and the fastest runner in the troop, fearing no-one. Keogh, who is thought to have suggested 'Garryowen' to the Seventh Cavalry as their regimental song, had made his way from his native Limerick to Africa, had fought with the Papal Army in Italy and then through the American Civil War. The Cross of the Order of St Gregory which Pope Pius the Ninth hung round his neck, for bravery against the Piedmontese, is believed to be the sole reason why his body was not mutilated by the Indians, who recognised some sort of sacred symbol. Yet I doubt if Keogh would have guessed that the long and diverse journey he had already taken in life was to end that day in that very place. There were men who should have died that day but were just lucky. Custer's regular orderly, Burkman, was ordered back to guard the pack train that very morning and actually resented his survival to his dying day. His temporary replacement, Giovanni Martin, had been a drummer boy with Garibaldi's Army in Italy and had emigrated to the States for a better life. Custer gave Martin the piece of paper to take to Benteen, 'Come quick', but Martin could not explain the reasoning behind the request because his English was so poor. He survived because he stayed with Benteen and did not ride back.

Charles de Rudio had been imprisoned for life after an abortive attempt in Paris on Louis Napoleon's life and was one of the few men ever to escape from Devil's Island. He sailed from British Guiana to London, sadly no cricketer, and then on to America where he enlisted. He even served with a coloured regiment before joining Custer. His life should have ended that day as he was assigned to E company but as the troops fatally split, Custer sent him with Reno. The Indians reported two soldiers wielding sabres that day, unauthorised swords of course, and De Rudio was one of them. Private

Thompson's horse broke down and he continued on foot and never caught up the main body. He survived. Yet the newspaper correspondent Mark Kellogg was not so fortunate, so lucky. He wasn't even meant to be there as General Sheridan had strictly forbidden newspaper reporters, but Custer wanted the exposure for a possible future political career in Washington. He saw no real danger in this campaign. He invited the Bismark Tribune's publisher to accompany them but at the last moment his wife fell ill. Young Kellogg was sent as a replacement and wrote that it was the trip of a lifetime. His body was found mutilated on a slope at the edge of a gully. In Dane Park, Julie's was found on a slope under the fifth tree. Had the boy from the previous evening responded more gently, had he rather welcomed her or at least softened his apparent rejection, then she would not have reacted in a manner that was to end her life. Their discussion was the catalyst that triggered her death. Similarly had she only listened to her young friend Tara, we'll call her, and headed for home with her sorrow and pain, then there would have been no story to tell. Was it just destiny that night, drawing her to the park? Is there such a thing, a song of fate,that merely records or warns of a journey that was always pre-destined? Can the gods be that cruel?

Julie was easily identified, as the doctor summoned to attend recognised her as one of his patients. So there was no need to analyse the scattered clothing for her identity or to pay more than passing attention to the single button lying nearby on the path. It had come from her white cardigan. And yes, sadly, there was some blood a runnin' in town that night, from her nose and mouth. At the Little Big Horn they needed more skill to identify the victims. Custer's interpreter Isaiah was black so even the vicious mutilation was no barrier. He had personally known Sitting Bull and had married a Santee Squaw but his treatment had been more brutal as they thought he had betrayed them. His colour though gave him identity. You might have thought they would readily find Lieutenant McIntosh. The year before, a new Lieutenant had gone to pay his compliments at the McIntosh home. "Well", his wife said, "you are the first man I ever saw that is uglier than my husband". Tosh had been unlucky, his boot slipping through his stirrup when he went to mount his horse. His features were unrecognisable but fortunately there was a single button besides his body. His sister had given him a set of unusual buttons for his tunic so that had to be him.

Some of the others were never recognised in the general savagery following Custer's Last Stand. However it is always worth remembering the words some time later of William Cody, Buffalo Bill, when we need to put this into some sort of context. "Every Indian outbreak that I have ever seen has been caused by the broken promises and broken treaties of the government". In other words, he thought the Indians were nearly always being provoked. The theme of perceived provocation and how you respond seems to be an eternal debate. Can even surface in a park near a cricket square.

"The first blow is half the battle"

Oliver Goldsmith – 'She Stoops To Conquer'

The Hippodrome had been the major theatre in Margate but the Theatre Royal had the quality. 'She Stoops To Conquer' was the first play ever staged there, just a short walk down from the park. Charles Dickens visited the theatre there twice. Some women would be glad to know, after the first blow, that it was half the battle, that there was only one more to come. All too frequently it may unleash an unrelenting torrent, Bill Sykes springing to mind. How did he first meet Nancy, do you think? At an inn or some sort of guest house? In Margate they had only met briefly and visually the evening before at the house, the 'Mad House' everyone called it. He was six foot at least, tall and very slim with clear blue eyes and had slept that first night in a chair. A jobbing mechanic by trade, down in his van with James and Clive for the weekend. He and James had met in the Robin Hood pub at St Mary Cray, not far from where he had gone to school. The 'Croydon' guest house might have sounded like home from home, familiar in name at least. Unusual landlady. Not quite sure what sort of house she ran. Like most of the lads, he liked a drink. Alcohol makes people talkative with its feel-good factor. The tablets helped as well, eased the boredom and made him relax. As a young teenager he had boxed in the Kent Junior Championships. Men were entitled to hit their ladies in those days, weren't they, but he had no intention at first of hitting her. For most men it was just a natural instinct, hard wired into the subconscious.

What did it matter if women got the odd back-hander? If they were fast and elusive enough, they could duck a really wild swing. But a swing that was unexpected, which came out of nowhere, was the ideal way to discipline. It imposed an order to your relationship and established your place in the pecking order. A dog would understand and would accept the blow and then return wagging its tail. Why not a woman? The swing in the playground had never witnessed violence before. It had seen children fight and push each other and parents who would clip their errant children round the ear or shake them. On occasions it had noticed people sitting on the benches outside the wire and sometimes they might shout at each other. Its purpose in life was merely to move rhythmically to and fro, backwards and forwards. A swing like that might be a refuge, a place of calm where you could rest and get your breath. A children's playground, a place of innocence. If she had only headed for there, perching on the swing. The chains would have tightened, but then the swing would have eased back. He might have paused, perhaps he would have relented. But she was on the grass under the trees some distance away and even though the swing willed her to approach with all its might, she was unable to turn her head towards it ever again. The safety of the swing and the playground had eluded her. All it could do was to groan and creak in the night breeze, in some form of resigned acceptance of its part, its inability to save her.

Why do men do this? Are we all capable of murder and is it just chance that stops the red mist, the anger, before it is too late? It was true that my father had never hit my mother, but then he was gentle and kind. Alcohol though does seem to change some men's souls. My grandfather used to think the world of my grandmother, briefly becoming a bus driver in London to woo her. He had been a blacksmith in the beginning and soon reverted to being a master carpenter. Proud of never being out of work, even after he had brought the young family down to the seaside to live. Seven of them in all, living in that small terraced two bed-roomed house with its outside privy, where they never used to use the sitting room except on Sundays and for best. They even in the summer took in lodgers, seaside holidaymakers - where the hell did they all sleep? The kids mostly prospered, although two of them died from the rampant tuberculosis which also later nearly took my sister. Yet in that modest over-crowded setting how could there be space for an elephant in the room? But there was.

It was only very late in their lives that my mother and aunt could bring themselves to talk about the bad days - about the elephant. My grandfather would return from a drinking session and lose his temper. My aunt told me that the girls would sit silently on the stairs outside the bedroom, waiting for the storm to blow over. It was an occasional event, not a regular one, but it stayed with them to the end. How can people who love each other ever behave in this way. My mother always hated the effects of excess alcohol and worried endlessly that my brother and I were doomed for an early grave. It is not the alcohol, although it can have its place. There are countries where alcohol is banned where the treatment of women is abhorrent and abuse prevalent. It is an attitude of mind, often embedded in cultures and sometimes encouraged by mindless conformity based on a set of beliefs. You are my God-given property. Mine to control. It is always the men who should have to answer, who bear the shame. Men in power, men in authority, both secular and religious. Bullies, cowards, tossers.

My grandfather was like so many other men. Yet in many ways he was better than that. A proud man, a great craftsman, good enough to work through the depression. He was always faithful, devoted to Nellie and distraught when she died. In his case, it was just the drink. He liked a beer and occasionally couldn't handle it. I never remember speaking much to him when I was young as he always seemed austere, dressed often in black but always smart. However the memories of my grandmother are wonderfully warm. The John Bull magazines were stacked on the windowsill as reading material and the biscuit tin always contained an inexhaustible store of digestive biscuits for dunking. My mother and my grandfather were desolated at the loss when she died. To make the grief worse we would begin to get the calls from the Margate police station just after closing time. My father would have to get on his bicycle to collect the old boy from the station or Cecil Square and get him home. He was lonely, had gone to the pub and couldn't take the drink any longer. My father would have to cycle back and still be up at 6.00 am to be at the shop at Coffin House Corner to catch the workmen. He was always upset if he missed them. The grocer's shop has gone now, swept away to make the crossing safer. There is a picture of the Salmestone Stores in 1911 at the time of Lord Sanger's funeral procession, the crowds milling round in their hundreds. My other grandfather, down from London, bought it in 1913 with his army gratuity. The original owner of Gwendoline House had built it in the shape of a coffin in mourning for his daughter who died young. Five roads converging and near the cemetery too. Useful when accidents occurred, not far to drag the bodies. The actor Jack Warner used to pop into the shop on his way home from the film studios - evening all.

Good living once until Edward Heath abolished retail price maintenance in the grocery trade. All those times I sang in the school choir in Cliftonville when as an 'old boy' he conducted the annual Christmas carol concert. If only I had known what effect he would have on my father's livelihood. A weaker man would have crumbled. My father never lost his smile. I could at the very least have urinated on Heath's shoes. I used to see him from time to time in the Tartar Frigate in Broadstairs. I could have raised my fists. I could have grasped him by the throat, taking his private bodyguard by surprise, squeezing that fat neck. One of our more eccentric history masters, Curzon, was quoted as saying, "I wouldn't place Teddy with the brilliant ones.... His abilities were really developed after school". Enough said. The year Julie died was the year he began to lead the Conservatives, shoulders shaking when he laughed, his French accent later wonderfully illustrated by Officer Crabtree, the gendarme in 'Allo Allo'. Pass off Heath, at the helm of your Good Moaning Cloud.

"In the dark I stand, In the dark I cry, In the dark I run, In the dark I hide, In the dark I die"

Bryer Rose

Julie had no time to cry, to run, to hide. If only she had been able to run. As it was she must have lost consciousness quickly in the park she knew so well. The first fumbling attempts though were on the grass near the path. He suggested moving to a bench but she was impatient and cavalier. If only she had come to her senses and run, if not up for the swing, then down for the square, for the wicket, even just short of a length. No-one would have dared touch her there. If you had thoughts of sex, the last place on earth should be on the cricket square, a sacred place. In her mind she pulled herself away and was up running, anyway, anyhow, anywhere. The playground, the swing, even the roundabout could have provided respite. Her head was certainly spinning. She had not expected this of all things, firmly squeezing the young life out of her.

"A crime scene" the plod said. "Our investigations could take some time. The park is shut until further notice". Well for Christ's sake, restrict yourselves to the area where she died? How can the whole park be a crime scene? I was a junior member of the cricket committee, organising the 'A' team, and can remember their anger. Round at Don's house on the Monday night. Who cares about the girl? The police must be in league with the Corporation. Useless. Refused to help when the vandalism threatened our festival and now this. Where were the police when we needed them? We're not just talking murder here, but a week-long campaign by several mindless yobs. Police Constable Dixon on his bike would have sufficed. Now this. We lost our game on the Sunday and now the ones at the next weekend are threatened. Listen, you boys in blue, you thin blue line. We have games to play. Our opponents have planned to travel for weeks, coaches booked, Chas and Dave as their guide. 'Well I've been working hard to reach me target, to earn a few bob for a day trip down to Margit'.

Families in tow for a day on the sands. Mr Punch would be throttling Judy as usual on the front at Marine Parade. Too late to cancel the coaches, so because of some stupid police rule, the men might actually have to spend time with their wives and children. A few more ladies might be battered before the sun set. The following Saturday and Sunday were forecast to be good.

There were twenty two of us raring to play cricket on each day and they had marked off the pitch and the park! When we take guard we just tap the bat lightly, religiously, to leave an indentation. Murder is a simple crime. You know who did it. Why do you need to search the park, marking and scarring the cricket pitch with your large size twelve police boots? Why on earth do you need to keep the public away and rope off the square? Think of the damage you will cause. And all for what? It was only a girl anyway and we all thought we knew what had happened. A waitress wearing a short skirt, miniskirt for all we knew. Girls are always asking for it, aren't they? Halfway through the park, they had begun to argue, maybe about his manhood. We had joked in the pavilion the next week that they had stumbled on to the pitch, down towards the end where Willie could land the ball on a sixpence. Just short of a length. That was it we said - she had laughed about his dick. "Call that a length", she had said. "That's well short of a length". You didn't need to be Dixon of Dock Green to work that one out. Then she should have run. Should have been in my family. She would have out-run him then.

My parents are to blame for our genetic mix, our DNA. We have always been runners rather than fighters in our family. We can all shift a bit. In the days of Marlborough, who sometimes used Margate for embarkation to the continent, they used to keep stocks of armaments and ammunition in the Fort above the harbour. They had watchmen, two brass cannon and a strong gate. In our house we kept the ammunition hidden under the shoes in the closet. My mother never knew. My brother had brought the thunder-flashes back from the military academy and kept them in the wardrobe. I had seen them there but thought they would be like the small premiums you got free in the Wizard comic. You waved your arm vigorously and they would crack and bang. When the thunder-flashes went off in Hawley Square, the noise apparently was rather louder. The town came to a standstill, in mild shock. Fortunately this was well before the Irish began to treat us to their own sort of brutal fireworks campaign, so there was no sinister association. My brother ran the fastest that night when his friends scattered, then hid under a car. Fortunately the police weren't as quick. The Z cars must have been down by the harbour or maybe they were always up in Liverpool.

Police cars did arrive on the scene, probably Detective Chief Superintendent Lockhart, bell jangling. No hiding place. Don't think Ted Willis ever wrote for them or for Fancy Smith and Bert Lynch. He was a Blue Lamp and Dock Green man. 1965 did have an episode called 'Act of Violence' which P C Dixon had to help his son-in-law solve, before retreating back to his small terraced house. Dixon's house could have been in Hastings Avenue. Got the violence right though Ted, but who would have guessed that it would be in the park. It was such a quiet neighbourhood. My aunt said one of her fondest memories of Hastings Avenue and my grandfather during the First World War was seeing him sprint down the alleyway to avoid some sort of military police at the front door. That was a major event. This running lark must run in the family. Elite sprint squad, see, and that was only my daughter. The bangs from the thunder-flashes hit the headlines in the local papers. The Isle of Thanet Gazette had a field day. That was the week that was, it's over, let it go. Bet the security people didn't find that out when they later vetted my brother - maybe the job description required a good turn of foot. There may still be a forgotten box of thunder-flashes under a pair of shoes in some dusty office filing cabinet in Brussels to this day. About as many armaments as they found in Saddam's wardrobe. WMD. Can everything in life be reduced to three letters?

"Girls. Jesus Christ. They can drive you crazy. They really can".

J D Salinger – 'Catcher in the Rye'

Girls and horses can drive you crazy. George, who opened the batting for Margate, was a real gambler and would take us all to the dogs at Dumpton Greyhound track on a Saturday. He was usually lucky and when he was, he used to treat us to the Chinese restaurant in King Street, the Golden Coin I think. He and Mike liked dogs and horses and I began my training under them. We won at Dumpton by assuming that the trainers were bent. If they ran two dogs, back the outsider. Worked a treat. Not every cricketer likes the horses, although I am sure I have seen Sir Gary Sobers in the betting tent at Lords, more than once. My friend Fred was a fine cricketer and a linguist, but knew little about dogs or horses. He nearly parted with his whole term's funds when Mike encouraged him out of the library to Newmarket for an afternoon at the races. We had travelled up for the weekend and saw Brigadier Gerard win the 2000 Guineas there impressively, but none of us backed it. Plus ca change.

Gerard was supposed to have lured the Prussians away after Waterloo to allow Napoleon to escape. Nine Prussians to be correct. I noticed that Conan Doyle originally placed him in a Forest Inn so he presumably wanted to engage the Guards in a drinking match. Pure fiction, I'm sure, if he reckoned the French could out-drink the Guards. As it turned out Gerard had to make a run for it, then grabbed Napoleon's cloak and hat and rode off to draw them after him. Gambled that he could out-run them all. Mike was a gambler too, gambling large, in that wonderful laid-back Caribbean style. Thank Christ that Lester saved the day. 'Lester' is six letters. Meant more to us than DNA ever did and three letters more. Did they give Piggott a Nobel prize? No indeed, the establishment actually jailed him for tax evasion. Now we knight people or send them to the Lords for avoiding tax, millions more than he ever earned. I saw him win one of his last big races at York on Rodrigo de Triano, scything his way effortlessly past the rest of the field. Mind you, how is he still alive when Mike, Biff and Willie are all gone? Jockeys merely waste, whilst cricketers get wasted? That must be it. Yet what a celestial team they will make, the boys. Probably in one of heaven's many cricket sides right now. Gabriel will have turned the Milky Way floodlights on. Hope he has remembered to unlock the bar.

Cricketers surely don't go to hell. Just show your cricket whites to St Peter. Automatic pass through the Pearly Gates. Just don't bat with William the Silent, he's crap at calling. Harold Pinter would be hanging around there somewhere, angling for a game. He'd be looking after the pavilion. He'd be the caretaker. Actually played for a wandering cricket side called the Gaieties. My friend Willoughby played for the Grannies. Said he was often top scorer even in his seventies. If they were all like Carl Giles' grandma, no wonder. You can see all the grannies in the Griffin pub in Sussex, Willoughby the only one in a blazer. Maybe there is a new team up there called the Wine Tasters. What a great writer's team they would have in heaven, assuming they all got there. Pinter, Wodehouse, Barrie, Conan Doyle, Beckett, Hazlitt, Lamb. Prose and poetry in motion. All devotees of the noble game. Do souls have legs? Or would the shouts for lbw be imaginary? Maybe there is some form of electronic hawkeye, fashioned by Leonardo Da Vinci and Steve Jobs, which allows you to follow the virtual ball past the imaginary bat, pinging loudly as it hits the stumps. Crowds of guardian angels cheering round the boundaries, some playing instruments, maybe a swing band. Plenty of trumpets and the occasional harp. Or would the religious police, bearded and unsmiling, have confiscated them at the gates? There would be pearly gates everywhere, of course, smaller models of those standing at the Day of Judgment Passage.

My friend Ant was a bearded purple Games Maker at the Olympics and Paralympics, checking ID's. What a triumph. Seventy thousand gold medals won, all for smiling. All the volunteers smiled. They and that Danny Boy with his opening ceremony turned public opinion right round. Even a cricket game in there at the beginning and then the closing ceremony celebrating our ancient heritage. The Spice Girls, George Michael. Not my bloody heritage. Mind you, thank God they mainly put the Services on security rather than those G4S boys. Forget any bombs and suicide vests. They were initially going to go for after the can of coke, the wrong packet of crisps or an unauthorised logo. Hogwash, I hear you say. Have you ever written or read a sponsorship contract? Forced to back off though. They were even forced to let in branded T shirts with 'Jesus saves, but Lineker scores from the rebound'. Did you catch those? Mind you, Gary was a bit of a cricketer. Would have seen Ken Higgs play. Let him in when he comes, but confiscate the crisps. Sorry about the ties and the bag over the head, sir. Standard security practice now abroad if you are a private defence contractor. In any case the bags are environmentally friendly and bio-degradable. Too good a sponsoring opportunity and might help the share price recover. Made you feel as if you couldn't breathe? Quite normal in any park, let alone an Olympic one. Have a nice day, sir.

She was murdered on the Sunday, early in the morning, and as we had left the pub at closing time the night before, it was much too late for us. The park would have been about a mile away, yet in the night air noise could travel far. You would have heard any screams, if she only had been able to move her broken jaw. Petite and not strong at all. Slim build again, all five foot five of her. A not un-attractive girl with a small almost snub nose, freckles and the ginger hair which made her stand out. Would we have cared in this kiss-me-quick sprawl of a town? 'Fuck off and die, you slag' as Tracey puts it. Julie was no slag. Just another youngster looking for excitement who had fallen into the wrong company. When Tracey Emin first revealed her blue tent of names, the reaction of most of the men in Thanet might well not have been one of disapproval, but a breathless scramble to check that their name was not included. Yet that is maybe a little unfair. Not all of my friends were sexual athletes, just one or two. There were always the boys who now would be regarded as babe magnets. How did they do it?

The rest of us mostly put our hands down our trousers, but only our own. As grammar school boys we might have thought briefly of arse, but breasts kept bouncing up as a welcome accompaniment, leaving the field open for our public school neighbours. That has to be the answer to so much of our political condition. If the formative years of the establishment are spent in being buggered, then it becomes a natural reaction, once in power, to want to practise on your public. There was mild pornography about by then and once the following year, when his wife was away, our left arm quickie brought a bag load of magazines for the team to rifle through in the changing room. Mayfair was around by then. I was batting number five that day and the third wicket partnership lasted for half an hour. The opposition pace-man was mighty quick. A wicket eventually fell and I strode out and took guard. Middle, thanks. I saw his arm come over and all I could see were two naked breasts. I played for the left one, in the hope that it might be larger. Somehow the bowler speared the ball right through the breasts and took my stump away. Not literally, of course. I guess I had discovered the bosom particle.

Long way to walk back up that incline to the dressing room. Girls, they can drive you crazy. Yet on the Day of Reckoning, when the four horsemen of the Apocalypse ride out, please don't judge me on that innings. I'm not boasting, but I was a long-handled man. Well not in every detail, of course. I know I don't believe in all this religious stuff, but I can field OK. I could hit the birdbath in the garden regularly with a tennis ball. Mind you Peter Davison once threw a cricket ball at the Raston Warrior Robot, deflecting the javelin and he got back to the Tardis by catching the rebound from the Monarch's ship in 'Four to Domesday'. Impressive business. Cricket balls featured with a few of the Doctor's, but he was the only one to keep one in his pocket. He was the fifth Doctor Who and wore, if you recall, a sort of Edwardian cricket uniform. Wouldn't get into heaven with those plimsolls though. Just as in the wonderful beer advert when the astronauts approach the end of the universe, God doesn't really do plimsolls or trainers. Peter, our 'Molesworth', wore plimsolls and in one match failed miserably to try and flick the ball to the wicketkeeper with his foot when the batsmen were running. I practiced a lot at home near the apple trees and twice later ran people out in our matches. You approached the ball from a ninety degree angle, put your right foot by the ball and then pirouetted on it, trying to flick the ball up in an arc. Once it did trickle on to the bottom of the stumps but the second time it flicked up and travelled the six yards to the keeper in a perfect fashion. Just over the bails. Batsman had no chance. Julie at least, was in the middle of the park, under the trees but close to the open spaces. She could have run on the level along the path. Don't think he had ever been there before. If she could only have got away, she would have some sort of a chance.

"On Margate Sands.
I can connect, Nothing with nothing."

T S Eliot

You and me both, TS. Never had much joy in connecting on the sands. Apparently you can get an App of 'Wasteland' now so you can reprise the bits Eliot wrote on Margate front. Margate in my era was already in firm decline, a million miles away from its heady days of hosting Conservative Party Conferences and good old Winston. Strangely he died in exactly the same year as Julie. No state funeral for her. Ferries like the Royal Sovereign and Royal Daffodil used to dock at the jetty, and in the last party conference year of 1953, despite the severe winter storms and floods, you could still walk along it to the end. Margate in 1965 even then had some two million visitors a year, but the conference now was the National Union of Miners, the lower orders. Don't worry about the police, lads. Batons and riot shields are for the Mods. Except in those days the police had to get by just with their courage. See the old footage of them chasing the boys across the sands. Just hands and only occasionally a truncheon. Ah, but then the Mods and Rockers wouldn't have hidden behind masks or thrown stones from twenty yards away like the lads you see nowadays. Not cricket, see. No-one in cricket wore a mask or a helmet. Not the done thing.

No crash helmets either, until 1973. Lawrence of Arabia wasn't wearing one when he came off his Brough Supreme motor bike and look what happened to him. No helmets at all until April 1916 in the First World War and then only on general issue that summer. Brodie helmets, tin hats, 'clumsy', Wilfred Owen called them. There was a strong antipathy to soldiers wearing helmets from generals largely sat behind desks. It might encourage the soldiers to be defensive. Reduces head injuries drastically? Don't worry about the casualties Lord Kitchener. Remember Agincourt and Rorke's Drift. It's the spirit of the men that counts. Straight bats boys. Then when it's our turn, bowl at the enemy with fortitude and let the swing do the rest.

Top entertainers came down to Margate for the summer season. Arthur Askey began his career here and, as a busy bee, frequently buzzed back and forth. Ted Ray, Arthur Haynes, Billy Cotton and his band, the latter throwing hundreds of soft balls at the audience to end the show, all were regulars. Family entertainment see. Wakey, wakey. Don't think the Brough Supreme was that successful, people fell off them, and I think the firm went into ventriloquism. Their most famous product, Educating Archie, had come off the radio by 1965, although returned briefly the following year. Peter Brough's doll had somehow even been on television for two years and Marty Feldman had helped write the scripts. A great emphasis on word play and innuendo, as the blue pencil brigade were still very powerful. Controlled what we could see and hear. Paid to do it by the establishment, who didn't care, because they could afford to pay for the blue stuff themselves outside of the system. Strange the words they banned. Surely if you had been to public school, the first word you would ban would be broomstick? Mind you, perhaps they enjoyed it, all that waving wands and casting spells on each other? Young Harry has made millions from it. Comedians then were rarely outrageous, tending for the wonderful double-entendres which had been the hallmark of Max Miller. Mind you, watch out if he moved to his other book. Blue book, please. I didn't know whether to block her passage or toss myself off. We've all been there.

Max Miller had trained as a motor mechanic too. Now there's a funny thing. I read that he left his white trilby to Tommy Cooper. Doesn't sound right? Cooper would have fumbled and dropped it, or filled it with props. Another one who liked a drink and couldn't handle the consequences. You can never tell, can you? Morecambe and Wise, the great family entertainers, did a session at the Windmill with all the nude dancers. Get out of that. Ernie even started with the Nig Nogs, a minstrel troupe. Eric married a Miss Margate, celebrating briefly at the Fort Lodge hotel opposite the Winter Gardens. My sister had her reception there. Posh then. They didn't need to ask, "What do you think of it so far?" Had to be silver service. With vision and courage they probably should have compulsory purchased part of the sea front and pulled down most of the tacky amusement centres. Nothing much they could do about the decline in British seaside towns, which is about timing, but the Thanet landlords seem to have meticulously stripped out the guest houses and hotels, converted them to flats and filled them with short term tenants.

If you compare how parts of Lyme Regis or say Llandudno in North Wales have been carefully refurbished and then walk along the front by the Winter Gardens, you can easily despair. Obviously down in the harbour there are groups who are trying very hard to change the image of Margate but you need landlords who have an interest in their home town and not just a love of profit. Now so many of these hotels and guest houses are faded and peeling, turned into shabby apartments. I am sure that, inside, tenants try to make a difference but most of the landlords seem not to care. Even back then the Theatre Royal had an Indian owner who closed it down and turned it into a bingo club. Just for the money. Pathetic. The secret of life, eh. Make as many bucks as you can. Anything for a few dollars more. Where's Clint when you need him? He'd like the Margate donkeys. He was with that Shirley MacLaine in 'Two Mules for Sister Sara', so he knows a thing about pack animals. Dynamite Shirley and certainly no nun. Interesting DNA and starring in Downton Abbey right now, in the senior wing. No country for old men? Don't you believe it. Upstairs or downstairs.

So which of our genes tells us to control women, to knock them about? Is it a genetic instinct or are we influenced by the acts of our fathers? Forgive me father for I have sinned. I found these old tablets and scrolls buried in the ground, in a cave or up the mountain and I have used them ever since to beat the shit out of my women. I am the sole interpreter, the judge, the umpire. Control, power, authority. These so-called commandments were written in a different time and universe, before we had begun to understand how old our world really is, to unravel the heavens, to communicate in real time across the globe. We thought then that the sun revolved around the earth and the authorities ruthlessly suppressed anyone who begged to differ. Advances in medical science will now one day make dying an option that we choose rather than one that advances relentlessly. Human nature will of course be broadly the same and individual men and women from groups of various colours will continue to seek power and wealth for reasons of ego, of control. Ten per cent of what we all earn and you can be rich, fists full of dollars. Easier than being a landlord. Whatever happened to all the men who wrote gospels that weren't on message, like Basilides? Someone decided that their version of the truth was inconvenient so they were air-brushed out of history. They edited out all the ones that didn't fit the message, the mission statement. Perhaps we could have a complete new bible based on the gospels that were divinely inspired but which were politically incorrect.

Basilides provoked a fair amount of fury. You never know what triggers anger and aggression do you? In 1972 a BBC survey found that Doctor Who was the most violent of all the programmes the Corporation produced. Mary Whitehouse even objected. Did our mechanic use to watch Doctor Who when he was young? Are the Daleks to blame for what happened in Dane Park? I used to watch old William Hartnell, the first Doctor Who. Liked him in the Army Game as well. Did I go out and terrorise the neighbourhood, exterminating all about me? Absolutely not. The good Doctor anyway would always be saving the world, provided the cardboard scenery didn't fall down on him. It did use to wobble around a bit, didn't it, more dangerous than the Cybermen. In January 1966 the Doctor managed to land the Tardis at the Oval during an England Australia test. Earlier in August 1965 he was on a break, so no chance of any random night landings in our park to save her. If only she had had a cricket ball that night. Always put one in your pocket when you go out to a party. What do you mean you don't? Julie could have bounced it off the fountain on to the back of his head, although not easy in the dark. Do you think Time Lords have guardian angels? Only angels I've ever seen in Doctor Who are those boring stone ones that move about when your back is turned and then kill you. Need to be eternally on your guard.

"The answer to the ultimate question of life, the universe, and everything"

"Forty Two"

Deep Thought, 'Hitchhiker's Guide to the Galaxy'

There was no trace of any scuffing or blood when Bert next took guard on the Saturday following the park re-opening. For the record, he tried to score forty two but fifty four appeared on the scorecard. There had been blood on the guy's clothes from the bleeding from her mouth and nose, but in those days before blogging, tweeting and twittering we didn't know that. We only knew that she had died. We didn't know how or exactly where. We did fool around, pretending we could see blood on the edge of the crease, but we didn't really care. The cricket was the thing. We didn't even know her name then, just that she was a waitress. Nearly missed our bloody cricket because of her. Mind you, not much would have shifted Bert in any case. The more established members of the team thought he was a bit common but he had his own guardian angel. True love, you see.

True love. Good name for a BBC television series. Set it by the seaside - nine miles of golden sands. First up, girl comes back for boy. Get Dr Who, or the one before Matt Smith, to play the lead, driving her to Ramsgate for a night of passion. Have you ever been to Ramsgate? For a night of passion? Really? Strangely he had driven Judy back to Ramsgate after the sex in the early afternoon that fatal Saturday, which at least shows a caring streak. That's real life, not like the television show. Come on Tennant, most boys in Margate that I knew wouldn't have ponced off to a hotel. They'd have bought her half of lager and tried to give her one under the Sundeck. I know it's not there now but come on, local knowledge. Plenty of shelters on the cliffs. You were the tenth doctor. Doesn't this sort of information survive the regeneration? Bet you can see for miles and miles. So could the real Who. If you really want to know, they played in Dreamland Ballroom on the 12th August, ten days before she died. Was Julie there? She was a member of the Dreamland Rendezvous Club, so very possibly. Talking about my generation. Girls whose movement suggested they knew how to use their squeezebox. Our Bert did have a guardian angel. It wore large hobnail boots and a dirty old white coat. It was his dad, old Bert, who used to follow him everywhere. He umpired in all the games that Bert played. The opposition would thunder in, the ball would spear into Bert's pads, the slips would rise and appeal in unison. Fat chance. Bert was never lbw, not when his dad was umpiring. LBW. Now there are three letters which do encompass the secret of life.

The Scenic Railway at Dreamland is a wooden roller coaster, requires a brakeman and is one of the oldest in the world. It's listed. Douglas Adams would have probably said it had fifty four seats. Terrific joke that. The meaning of life is forty two only because the Earth computer malfunctioned and miscalculates six by nine. Did you know that fifty four is exactly how many runs All-Muggleton scored in their first innings against Dingley Dell in the Pickwick Papers. Perhaps Dickens was in on it too. He was fond of all sorts of twists. One of our local clergy has just been charged with thirty eight sexual offences, so don't think they ever got the joke though. At least sixteen gropings short. Anyway if you rode on the Scenic Railway with its twenty eight seats I think, round the twists and turns, you felt you had answered the ultimate questions of life. The origins of roller coasters are a little obscure, although it is said that a forerunner was trialled in Margate back in the 1820's. The ride was essentially a static circuit with carriages on wheels hauled up by hand and then moving independently by gravity and was apparently known as the Russian Mountains. The French had them first. At about the same time they do know that a similar Russian Mountains' attraction was built in City Road, London by the proprietor of The Eagle. The very same pub as in the nursery rhyme, although the verse about the Eagle was added later for the theatre. Pop goes the weasel. Weasels obviously can't handle the twists and turns of roller coasters. Must be their genetic structure as they seem to explode into bits of tupenny rice.

James Naughtie on the radio recently described how in 1953 Crick and Watson ran into the Eagle to announce their discovery of genetic structure, the discovery of DNA. Their journey must have been some roller coaster ride. This pub though wasn't in London but in Benet Street, Cambridge. They had stumbled across three small letters denoting the secret of life. Worth a Nobel prize. Do me a favour! Running into the Eagle is worth all that? Try running out of the Eagle, after a two hour session with the Swallows. The Swallows were a sort of social drinking club, where you met each Thursday to loosely discuss and minute the week's events. Often after the sessions we noticed that our co-ordination and balance seemed to have deteriorated. At the time we thought that it was probably down to those parts of our body which had been too well refreshed, although one or two of the lads put it down to some sort of junk DNA. They never bothered to apply for any sort of prize, let alone write to Alfred Nobel. Now it turns out that this junk stuff actually plays rather a vital role in deciding who becomes ill after serious drinking, but we wouldn't want to claim any credit now. If the Swallows met in the Eagle, why were they called the Swallows? Don't go there, we really don't have the time. In the bar stories would be told usually with an element of comedy - I use the word loosely - so the answer could change every week. Mostly you would listen to Peter with his Black Country stories, or Fred with tales from the North East which never ended. You were doomed to listen to them until you fell unconscious. DNA? DAN more likely, a touch of the desperates.

Who on earth would run into the Eagle anyway? Jonathan King used to drink there. Bet he didn't run into the main bar crying 'Everyone's Gone To The Moon'. Great song so why don't we hear it anymore? I know the politically correct answer but Frank Sinatra used to hit people and we still hear lots of his standards. Let us return to Crick and Watson. Watson must have been the trusty sidekick, ex-Army, carried a pearl-handled service revolver. Crick would have played the violin, injecting himself with all sorts of drugs and taking tablets, attempting to change his DNA. Wasn't there too some sort of token woman? Rosalind Franklin. Typical Newnham type, probably ex-public school, hanging around the boys. Lucky she wasn't found strangled on Parker's Piece wearing nothing but blue stockings, but no children's playgrounds there then. Not a swing in sight when you need one. Can you imagine Rosalind trying to tell someone in Margate that they had one helix too many? If you told them they really only needed a double helix, they'd have tried to order one at the bar in the happy hour. Even in Betjeman's Cliftonville, they would have punched you or grabbed you by the throat. Squeezed hard until your legs buckled.

My mother lived in Cliftonville in her last years and I walked up Northdown Road recently to where I thought the Parakeet was, where Jude worked as a waitress. Cool, the Parakeet. I never learnt how to be cool as we often had hand-me-downs. It's called recycling now. My kids wouldn't be seen dead in my old clothes. They've no idea they're living with a style guru, I lived through the Sixties. In those heady days we had Mary Quant and Carnaby Street. I remember paper dresses. One girl even had the temerity to wear one at a party I went to and it lasted two hours. Must have been a page three girl. Showed her knickers quicker than she intended, but I suppose that's one of the qualifications. The area of Cliftonville is much changed, although probably not in that way. Fortunately I was able to use my knowledge of Klingon, Klingonese to those in the know, to order a coffee. Good decision. Some of the inhabitants now only speak Klingonese. Probably some mechanics amongst them.

"Certain women should be struck regularly, like gongs".

Noel Coward

Discussion today on the radio with women depressed by the turn of events after the Arab Spring. Women are being oppressed and threatened by men who have yet to move beyond the seventh century. Good sound-bite anyway. Religious fundamentalists from hell. Tom Holland seems to think they are in denial. They're after him now, bullying, threatening, after what was a pretty inoffensive recent documentary on Islam. Yes, I have watched it. My mother used to say, "Your trouble is that you think that anyone who plays sport is alright". What's wrong with that? Playing a bit of cricket would sort these boys out, make the stonings a bit more accurate. Did our man in Dane Park play cricket? He must surely have played sport at school and if he boxed would have had fast hands. Forty seven years ago we knew nothing about men from the seventh century and their methods. He didn't throw acid in her eyes. He didn't try to mutilate her genitals. He just thought he was provoked and strangled her. I bet he really liked her that night, cheeky and sparky. Mind you she didn't look too well, "white as a ghost" one witness said. Had to be the drugs she took. Just not used to taking them or the quantity. But she was angry with that Wally, let's call him. They had slept together and then he seems not to have wanted to know. Sorry she died, our guy said, when he finally changed his statement. Surely that is progress? Look how far we men have come. I like the girls who do, I like the girls who don't. Yeah, we even like the girls who don't.

As my mate John R used to say, "There are them that do and them that haven't been asked right". He was from Yorkshire so he knew a bit about women, did John, so he told us. He didn't have to hit them though. Bowled, naturally enough, like 'Fiery Fred'. Fred learnt to swing the ball both ways from Cyril at the Sheffield United Club. Swing isn't something that is easy, it's elusive, unpredictable. John was a Sheffield lad and, as far as I knew, he only learnt to swing one way. Bowlers need power and control. Is it the same in life? Why is it so hard to treat women equally and with respect? Is it just because all the scholars and interpreters, the umpires, were and are men? Look at the spirit of cricket. The umpires are the sole judges of fair and unfair play. Unlike some of the churches, they are even appointing women umpires these days. How much longer can you use the good Lord as an excuse? Did he tell you personally, in a vision perhaps? Ah, you read the scrolls. If women in days gone by were permitted to read, then was it only in a context that men judged to be uncontroversial - religion and the Virgin Mary, housekeeping tips and manuals, how to cook dog and fricassee rat during a siege, knit balaclavas? Balaclavas are topical today. For a long time too they tried to keep the girls well away from the Articles of cricket. If you're not careful they used to say, the women will be playing the damn game and they won't be happy just fielding. Bit of a problem right from the start. States very clearly in the Articles that there is no place for violence on the field of play. Not quite like life then.

Until merchants and financiers arrived on the scene, power resided exclusively with the clergy and the king and his lords. Each group battled to establish rules and precedents that would allow them to remain in power and then pass that down to their kin or to people of their persuasion. They created myths that they had been selected by divine influence and then set out ruthlessly to enforce that interpretation and exclude their rivals. If the sources were unclear, they would engage scholars to discover and magic new evidence, falsifying documents with impunity. They would have discovered proof of WMD in an afternoon, not so much golden days but maybe a touch of scarlet. If they grew wealthy, then was that not just a sign that God, whichever god they had chosen, favoured them? They resisted any spread towards literacy and the distribution of copies of sacred documents, particularly with the advent of printing, because that would inevitably lead to their sources being re-interpreted and challenged. Some of them still can't stand challenge or open discussion. And that's just the men. Dissenting and being a heretic were never good career choices. Priests and kings were the judges, the umpires. Never question the integrity of an umpire. Their eyesight, possibly.

I once called an umpire, "a short-sighted old git" as I lay face down with my bat yards over the line. Not one of my finest hours, against the spirit, but in hindsight he was just another guardian angel, he was their umpire. Just came with the territory. I occasionally drive briefly through Birchington and cannot help glancing up to the clouds, looking for some old angel sat on a cloud shaking his head. Never question an umpire's decision. It's not cricket. Unless of course you're Mike Gatting and he's from Pakistan. Or you're from Yorkshire. Umpired once up there in a league match. Made the mistake of giving the batsman not out. The ball had hit his pad, was sliding miles down the leg-side but the fielders appealed. The captain came up to his bowler and said about me, "If he does that again, I'll effing have him replaced". Fortunately the bowler, who hadn't appealed, assured him that everything was OK, that it was missing the wicket. I felt I needed to establish my knowledge of the laws of cricket, explained that I was from Kent, a strong cricketing county, and that he could replace me at any time. He might however have trouble running around on the field with a stump up his arse. Inappropriate? Absolutely. Successful strategy? I finished the match. I've never liked bullies, male or female.

"Life is just an elaborate metaphor for cricket"

Marvin Cohen

Is life like cricket, or is cricket like life? No-one got struck or beaten in the True Love television series. Obviously not based on the Noel Coward song-book, designed for piano, women and gongs. Multi-cultural society now. Need to balance the ethnic mix. Must have a coloured man in a love series on television. True love stories written by romantics. We weren't used to that in Thanet, the romance or coloured men. Mind you the press reports for bank holiday August of that year, 1965, claimed that two thousand young people had visited Margate, one hundred and forty five of them being a party of West Indians down for the day. We had all seen the Black and White Minstrels. We knew how to behave. Sunday evening wasn't complete without 'Sing Something Simple' and a few choruses of 'Swanee River' as we did the washing up in the kitchen. Doctor Who was once in an episode called the 'Black and White Guardians', wonder if that included singing and blacking up. Mike was one of the few coloured men in the area and I know he had his problems. He certainly couldn't sing and he definitely never needed to black up.

Did you know that in 1965, NBC in the States objected for a long time to Gene Roddenberry's insistence that the crew of the 'Enterprise' in Star Trek should be racially diverse. He eventually won. Good for him, brave man. You may also recall that Alfred Jingle in the Pickwick Papers claimed to have played his cricket in the West Indies. He scored five hundred and seventy runs until Quanko Samba, who then died from exhaustion, bowled him out. No Quanko Samba, Mike. He had left Berbice in Guyana for London, had begun to play cricket socially and found he had a natural skill. He eventually settled in Thanet, living with George and June. By coincidence my brother and I had sung in the choir when they married at All Saints Church, Westbrook. Singing was a regular part of our lives for many years on Sundays and as choristers we were paid to do it. George worked at the Rovex factory and June and cricket were his primary focus. Harold Larwood said that cricket was his life, even in the mines he would bowl imaginary balls in the dark. George was the same, that plus the gambling. No children sadly. Lived and eventually died for cricket, the heart attack taking him whilst he was tending a school wicket in Westgate. After the club break-up George went off to play for Broadstairs. Mike joined him briefly but missed the social scene and soon returned.

In cricketing terms, Broadstairs liked to think they were John Cleese in that great class sketch in the Frost Report. Part-written by Marty Feldman, it went out the year after she died. Margate they regarded as being somewhere between Ronnie Barker and Ronnie Corbett. Did we look up to them? To borrow again from our Tracey, is anal sex legal? Is the Pope a Catholic? Actually the book I am reading currently is about the Popes and I have learned that the answer was not always what you would expect. Mike's first game was actually against a very good West Indian side, Caribbean CC they called themselves. Ten coloured guys and one white guy from Jamaica, Sammy. They chose to bat and Broadstairs fielded, Mike being sent to the boundary. The West Indians loved to strike the ball and sure enough it was quickly clipped in his direction. He ran in, gathered the ball in one hand and threw expertly over the stumps. He was a cousin of Rohan Kanhai, young Mike. The old Broadstairs umpire, Beagley, signalled four. You're wrong said the skipper, he's one of ours. "Ridiculous" said Beagley, "it's bad enough having to play them. We can't have the buggers running on and fielding". Margate used to play a second team of West Indians as well as the Caribbean and our normal landlord for teas and beer, running the Dane Valley Arms by chance, on learning their colour conveniently found that he was double booked. I had to find an alternative pub for them, forty in all including women and children. The Cricketers Arms would have done. They serve food and have a black owner and chef. Only one governor though? Four pubs I tried before the landlord of The Hussar in Garlinge came to the rescue. We bought them lots of beer and had a great night. Their cricket was so exciting. They loved to strike the ball. Plenty of room for you in heaven, man.

In 1965 the Margate town promotional video showed the natural beauty of the sea and beaches. Our other opening bowler, a young lad called Roger, was in the Entertainments Department at the Council and I think he moved to a bigger job down at Bournemouth on the strength of the video. Our loss, made harder by the removal of his young lady called Maureen, because he bowled like the future Darren Gough. Mind you, after a few pints, we might have suggested he bowled like Van Gogh. No-one stood on ceremony in our world. The Butlin's hotels, including the Queen's at Highcliffe, got a mention too in the video, along with Thornton Bobby's. Our Department store at that time had several outlets, including a separate music section across the road where you could listen to records in the booths. Sadly once Bobby's had closed you had to travel to Canterbury for the nearest large department store, where you could enjoy tea and teacakes whilst an ageing trio performed in the background. A music troupe, I hasten to add, not anything saucy.

The promotional video mentioned Dane Park as being a place where good cricket was played. Kenneth Horne did the voice-over. Never knew he played tennis for Cambridge with Bunny Austen before being sent down, at Magdalene with all the toffs. He left the London School of Economics to go there. If only he had completed the LSE course. Those three letters after his name and he could have been in a rock band, rather than beyond our ken. He never did get a degree. We had our own Bunny. He was in his late sixties and kept wicket for the Second Eleven. Bet Austen didn't ride to Wimbledon matches on a ladies bike with his kit sticking out of a wicker basket on the front. Kenneth Horne said that Dane Park had grassy green slopes, a bowling green and fountains. A top spot. Controversial video that. Tracey Emin's 2004 'Top Spot' video, not the Margate Entertainment's promotional one. Teenage girls who cut school, hung out in the amusement park, had casual sex and got raped in alleyways. Her themes were 'the loss of virginity, desire for escape, hopeless search for love and promiscuity'. So it's not all fun and sticks of rock in Margate. Not one mention of Dane Park or the children's playground. I can't explain.

Boys used to hang out in Dreamland too, walking down past the Cinque Ports for all the fun of the fair. Jim, who played occasionally for us, used to be the landlord there and the barmaids were always beautiful. They only had to smile and we would buy them a drink. When you are young and pissed you fall in love at the drop of a beer mat. Not true love though. There were fights and gangs to avoid. Down from North Kent or London for the day, from the Midlands sometimes for the summer. You looking at me son? You staring at my girl? They were looking for trouble, occasionally knuckle-dusters and knives. Keep talking, smiling, sphinx-like, hope there is one decent one amongst them. Then when they move on, leg it helter skelter. Oh boy, thank your lucky stars and head for the River Caves, the Ghost Train or the Hall of Mirrors. Everyone's confused in that attraction. Never flash in a Hall of Mirrors. There are at least two restaurants in London which have distorting mirrors in the gents' toilets and after a bottle of wine or two that can cause great distress and often alarm. If the mirror reduces your status you find yourself pitching forward into the urinal. If it increases your size, you sway back and urinate on your shoes. Showmen. Never trust them. In the old days they would have been working for the church or the monarchy, trying to make the public believe in the flummery. PT Barnum rightly said "'there's a sucker born every minute". However against that, as a politician in his later years, he did also speak out to say, "That all souls of whatever ethnic mix are immortal spirits". All souls? Treat them all equal? What was he thinking of? Must have made him unpopular in his home town of Connecticut. Even worse in the far south. They'd have hanged him from a tree as strange fruit. Barnum couldn't surely have meant to include the souls of women, as well as black people. Another elephant in the room. Jumbo was his elephant, I believe.

"Rather a tough customer in an argeyment, Joe, if anybody was to try and tackle him".

Charles Dickens – 'Barnaby Rudge'

We used to pretend we could fight, could handle ourselves. Rowdy Yates in 'Rawhide' or Robert Horton in 'Wagon Train' would take a couple of heavy punches, then be quickly back on their feet. Would block the next two, avoid the chair smashing down and then knock the bad guy to the ground. Darbs was no John Wayne, although he might have had the build in those days, but was selected to play in a Kent schools cricket team in London. Bob Woolmer was the captain. He was a Skinner's boy, a year younger than us and we came across him at cricket and hockey. I went as scorer and Darbs and I stayed that night at my brother's flat in the East End. Took us to one of the Friends' Chinese restaurants, possibly the New Friends. Pretty special then, although he had to pay the kids outside to mind the car. Best to pay he had discovered. Moved on to some famous Whitechapel pub, perhaps The Blind Beggar, the molls all sitting at the tables, the men at the bar. All dressed in suits. Suits were part of the ritual. Strange. Neither of the Krays were there. They had been arrested in January that year, 1965, but the trial collapsed in February. Ray's dad was a friend of theirs, so he said in a recent article. "Just don't look at anyone in a suit" my brother whispered. "Don't stare. It's their manor. They let me live, long hair and all, because I teach their kids. Think when you've had a few, you could take them? They'll smash you with a bottle or glass and you won't get back to your feet". Reggie used to break jaws just with a left hook. If you're lucky they won't kick you more than once. Best to talk and apologise. Runners not fighters. More Wishbone than Rowdy. They're replaying 'Rawhide' on TCM with Wishbone, Rowdy and Gil Favor. Sadly Gil, Eric Fleming, died in 1966, when his canoe over-turned whilst filming in Peru. It was one year after Julie's jaw was broken. Probably a single punch.

Mike said he had been in his under-sixteen sprint team. Went to visit him often when he was old and grey and living in the Midlands. We would swap cricketing stories, always the same identical ones, Biff, Willie and George in the starring roles. We never tired of them. Once he was lodging with a girl who had left her abusive husband. Wimbledon week just starting but we're not just talking back-handers here. He thought Mike was doing more than just lodging and blocked our passage from the pub, accompanied by his brother, built like a brick shithouse. Mike was almost blind by then from the diabetes but Guiana would have been proud of him. He had lived in the neighbourhood for twenty years and was off down the street from a standing start. Dwain Chambers wouldn't have seen him for dust. Funny at the time, although the other lads couldn't see it. Thought for a moment about taking it out on me, but I had grown up hanging around in amusement parks. Talk and smile. The bastards got him later I found out, gave him a kicking, although he deliberately never told me. I'd have gone after them. God knows how because I haven't fought anyone for years, not since I stopped playing sport. Who would ambush a blind man for heaven's sake? Even the hard men from the East End wouldn't have beaten up a blind beggar. Never a guardian angel in sight when you need one.

Most of my friends have at some time or other made the great pilgrimage to the Isle of Thanet. Very occasionally I would get a call on a Sunday morning asking if I knew of anyone who wanted to play cricket if there had been an unexpected injury on the Saturday and we were one short. This never seemed to happen when my visitors were actually cricketers, as at least two of them would have graced any of the local sides, but always when the visitor was not that proficient. On one occasion a young Swiss friend agreed to stand in, despite knowing nothing of what this would entail. We found him some spare whites and put him out to field in the deep. Naturally enough the ball then proceeded to follow him around and as a final insult was smashed at him waist high by one of the batsmen. We had tried to explain the articles of cricket but the art of catching eluded him and the ball hit him painfully somewhere around the middle of the solar plexus, knocking him over. It certainly saved a boundary but by the time the pain stopped and he was back on his feet, they had already run four. When it was our turn to bat, he very gamely wanted to take his chance and the excitement mounted as his turn approached. Sadly stumps were drawn with him padded up but not able to get on, so we never actually knew whether or not the Swiss could play cricket.

In a second incident, my friend Alan was asked to fill in. He was a notable rugby player, mentioned on the television as being a future England star, before a couple of teams decided to target him by kicking him in the head. Alan was literally larger than life and was always supremely confident about his sporting prowess in any game. Indeed I had first witnessed that at close hand when the two of us were teamed together in a college three-legged race. I think it was William Cowper who wrote that "a noisy man is always in the right" and at first I was not sure that I wished to be bound closely together with this man, whom I knew only vaguely and mainly by sound. However rather a lot of Pimms had been consumed, we were students, the cocktail in the tin bath seemed to be never-ending, so any prejudices tended to quickly fade away. We very quickly sailed through the preliminary rounds and would clearly have won the final had not skulduggery of the worst type, reminiscent of the Borgias, been practised. Someone had sabotaged our handkerchief and as the gun went we rose from the sprint position and fell in opposite directions. The gold medals had been lost but a friendship had begun which has happily endured.

However I had seen Alan play cricket and if you were a captain in a playground you would not have been too ready to choose him for your team. I did tell the Margate captain at the time that Alan was very happy to fill in to make up the numbers one weekend but warned them that he was not really a cricketer as I understood the term. We fielded first and they put Alan at second slip and of course he proceeded to take two quite brilliant catches. To my great annoyance the skipper then even asked him if he could bowl. Thank Christ he refused. However by now the Margate team were convinced that Alan was a star cricketer, a belief that he did nothing to dispel, and put him at number six, just after me. I of course was out cheaply and Alan proceeded to score freely before being bowled. We won the match and in the changing room and bar afterwards I kept saying to my colleagues that Alan was not really a cricketer and had just had a good day, whereas they feted him as some sort of superstar. The skipper even asked him if he would be down again from the Midlands and to let us know. Alan didn't bat an eyelid and then told me that he unfortunately could not stay and drink because he needed to be on the road home. I was totally sympathetic until later it transpired that he had driven off with one of my girlfriends, whom I was hoping to know better, and that they had gone to watch the sunset over the bay before he eventually drove the three hours back home. For weeks after that I kept being asked when Alan was returning to Thanet to play again for the team. 'Whom the gods would destroy they first make mad' was actually an episode of Star Trek. Beam me up, Scotty.

Friday evening and "the weekend starts here", according to 'Ready, Steady Go'. The Surfaris 'Wipe Out', which Brian and his Decoys used to open with in our local venues, originally saw the TV show in and later was replaced by Manfred Mann's '5-4-3-2-1'. Julie would have been watching at home before setting out. It was compulsory viewing. In the film Quadrophenia, the show was on the television screen that Jimmy was watching and the following year The Who had an episode all to themselves entitled 'Ready Steady Who'. At about that time the boys were meeting up in the St Cray pub. They didn't get to the Excel Bowl in Margate until 11.00 and that was where James first took them. Our guy had a black and white dog and it was allowed in the Bowling

Alley when they all met the Birmingham crowd there. After a brief chat they ate in a café, probably the Parakeet, and on to the 'Mad House'. The other James took his suitcase to look after and he would have seen Julie head off at around 1.00 with Wally.

The group at the Croydon Guest House were about twenty in number and all in the one room. It was Michael's birthday, not sure where he was from, but his room on the top floor was too small. So they had gone into his friend Noel's room, next door, Room two. They were all 'blocked', high on drugs, except the newcomers from the St Mary Cray pub who were just warming up. Nearly all boys but there were at least three girls in evidence. The landlady didn't seem to care. Most of them seemed to be always there but they must have slipped her something from time to time. She never seemed too keen to discuss the financial arrangements. Would rent out the rooms when they were needed. He had rented one the next day, the Saturday, because he had found a girl, this Judy from Ramsgate. She had been on the tablets and out for a good time. He was capable enough. Had come to Margate partly for the fun but also as there might just be some work down there.

The house was not the greatest though, certainly not the pick of the pops. Do you want to dance? Dance, dance, dance. Julie would have gone to the Dance Cavern near the Lido. Dancing or flailing without moving the feet in crowded dark rooms. Just like this. 1965. The sound of music. Music to die for. Love was everywhere, baby love, the price of love, true love. All you need is love. Blame Cole Porter. Baby can I take you home? For your love. Stop in the name of love. He's still squeezing. So this will be the last time. Then blackness. Will he know, will he feel, the minute you're gone. The minute I've gone. Her feet buckled or maybe just her knees. Her body went limp. I got you babe. I sure got you.

"April is the cruellest month"

TS Eliot

Eliot also by sheer coincidence died in 1965. Actually August has a better claim to be the cruellest month, particularly if someone has you by the throat. They say he partly wrote some of 'The Wasteland' sitting in the entrance to the Halls by the Sea road and some in the Nayland Rock shelter at Margate, not far from where the 'Friends of All Nations' surf-boat had capsized in the great storm of 1897, with the sad loss of nine lives. Maybe sitting all day on a hard bench looking out to sea had numbed his brain. Perhaps he was trying to catch sight of any nude bathers. There was a huge market in telescopes at the seaside, don't you know. No internet porn for the Edwardians or Victorians, just large telescopes. Was 'The Wasteland' actually a visionary poem about what Margate might become? If so it's a pretty sharp observation. He must have been sniffing the seaweed. It's a sad sad situation for those of us who are fond of the old place as parts of it are a wasteland, but the Turner/Emin recovery is at least a beginning. TS was almost right but hopefully the cavalry have arrived just in time. Perhaps the Seventh cavalry.

Queues now to get into the elegant white building, the Turner centre, where in the past we queued to walk down the jetty. Confusingly that actually looked just like a pier and there are wonderful photos of the old structure, one in my living room. Londoners have always travelled down by hoy, yacht or steamship to the golden sands, quite the fashion. Another Eagle, Eagle Steamers, operated from the pier and then the jetty. Plenty of crime in those days and men seeking a good time. The 'Husband's Boat' on a Friday night might have sounded romantic, but it was the source of many a brief encounter. Francesca and Paolo are fairly typical, embraced in their Rodin kiss. True love. Except that apparently her husband turns up later and drags them down an alleyway. He would have pulled them as far as the park before he killed them, but you know what these Italians are like. Strolling around like Pirlo, using as little energy as possible. Rodin's off soon anyway, I hear. Just check out Dane Park if he's gone from the Turner. No museum or even a sundeck in Turner's day, or a Ruby Lounge, where he and Sophie could hang out. They certainly went to Ye Foy Boat Inn where Turner could enjoy his beer mulled with a red-hot poker. Wonder how well he knew her whilst Mr Booth was still alive. Lodgers and pokers is surely the stuff that Charles and Fiona used to embrace in 'Round The Horne'. Hanging out of Sophie's boarding house window, Turner swore that they were the finest skies in

Europe. After four pints of brown and cider I would have sworn that they were the finest in the galaxy.

1965 saw the first episode of the radio programme 'Round the Horne'. Everything stopped for J Peasemold Gruntfuttock, the world's dirtiest old man. Even later at college, we used to gather in reverence to listen. Took and Feldman were brilliant. Maybe missed a trick on the Western front though. I remember spoofs on Apache Story and The Palone Ranger, but where was Round the Little Big Horn? Rain in the Face would have been there with his red and white warpaint. The Wild Bunch and the Hole in the Wall Gang were also a shoe-in for Kenneth Williams. I know Sundance died in Bolivia but Butch Cassidy actually lived until 1937. Butch Williams? Has a fine ring, or had. Butch liked cars too, but not as a mechanic. Marty Feldman had actually spent one summer at Dreamland with Mitch and Morty, arriving for work each day in an open-topped sports car. Come to think of it he always looked as if he had been grabbed by the throat, his eyes bulging. They said it was a medical condition. Could he ever have been in Dane Park? If you saw him in his poncy car, you might have wanted to throttle him. No wonder his eyes had popped out. He'd have been faster though. He would have made it back to the fountains. When I was a boy the Park had those, along with a fine pond and a bridge from where you could observe the ducks. I still have a photo of the pond on my wall.

Mike used to take some of the young kids down there from the home where he worked to the children's playground. Fair old walk down the Approach Road hill. Even harder going home. They would have sat on the swings, maybe tucking their chins behind the chains. Don't get caught out, the metal cold on your throat. No clinking chains in prison though only handcuffs, moving to and fro in transit. You have to do time for murder now because 1965 is the year they effectively abolished the death penalty. Mike loved those kids. One of them became an English high jumper. Not true love though, just tender loving care. Mike was good like that. He was a formidable batsman and occasionally they would throw him the ball as well. He bowled slow medium innocuous deliveries but on his day he could run through a side. Afterwards he would try and run through their ladies. On his day he might have gone close.

Round the Horne's Julian and Sandy on the radio talking Polari to Kenneth Horne, who was in every way their straight man. Billie Piper would have been more than welcome in our pavilion changing rooms amongst the boxes and the jock-straps, but we would have been banging on the desks ourselves, like her pupils on television, if we knew she had a 'True Love' lesbian secret.

“Nobody loves a fairy when she’s forty” might have been understood in Soho, but never in the suburbs. As she was sitting on the cliffs above the harbour with her new schoolgirl friend, Billie might have been looking out to sea at the lifeboat station. The first lifeboat was bought for Margate by Angela Burdett-Coutts, who was then the wealthiest woman in the UK. You can even see her likeness in the St George’s Cape Town Cathedral where Desmond Tutu heroically served as Archbishop, so she spread her charms and fortune widely. She was friend to both Wellington and Dickens, but not in the way you might think. The boat was quickly taken over by the Royal National Lifeboat Institution and was named ‘Angela & Hannah’. That’s an odd name for a boat you might say.

Angela refused many offers of marriage, succumbing only when she was sixty seven. However every year she spent part of her time at the Royal Albion Hotel in Brighton with her long-standing friend Mrs Hannah Brown, ‘the companion and sunshine of my life for fifty two years’. I hope it does not detract from the bravery of the lifeboat men of that period to mention that amongst the vessels the ‘Angela & Hannah’ gallantly saved were ships such as ‘Lady Anne’ and ‘Susan West’ off Long Nose; ‘Sarah’ and ‘Eliza Harrison’ off Margate Sands; and best of all, ‘Fanny’ off Tongue Sands. You could not make it up. There is an old picture in Margate Library of ‘Angela and Hannah’ relieving ‘Fanny’ off Tongue Sands. It’s filed away in brown paper and you have to ask for it specially. To cap it all, when the ‘Angela & Hannah’ was replaced, they named its successor ‘Quiver No 1’. That’s a whole new series of True Love. Billie, you have a role for life. You could make all of us quiver, whichever side we dress.

Gay was then just a respectable adjective to describe a jolly day. In 1965 one of the features on Margate beach was the appearance of Miss Milko from the ‘drinka pinta milka day’ campaign. If you were lucky to come across Miss Milko she would give you a Ten Shilling note or a gay beach bag. If you were lucky and she was at hand, you could use the ten shillings to buy medical supplies, perhaps pain-killers or diet pills. Perhaps the gay beach bag might catch your attention. Remember the star pianist, Russ Conway? He had a house in Broadstairs. In 1958 he was actually able to appear in a show called ‘Let’s Go Gay’ without adverse comment. We never knew if he was side saddle or western saddle. Viking Bay was no Brokeback Mountain, not even a small mound. Wasn’t a cricketer though, no gaieties for him. In any case, bona love was something we didn’t understand, particularly amongst women. Sportsmen and salesmen alike were united in their abhorrence - no-one came out lightly in our presence. No-one came out at all voluntarily that I can remember. We were focused on wogglers and nadgers. Rambling Syd

Rumpo was our hero. We just thought the effeminate Kenneth Williams voice was part of the fun. Queer - stop messing about.

When women began to figure large in my education I was reduced to reading my mother's magazines for clues on behaviour. I also liked to look at the underwear adverts, but then mine was a sad life. What do women want? What do young women of sixteen want? The romantic stories, all written by women, had broadly the same plot. Couple meet, couple chat, brief encounter. Trevor Howard of 'Brief Encounter' fame was born in Margate, same year as my mother. Man tries to kiss the girl. She is coy, resistant. He persists, she resists. No is a request for further information, I was taught. What arsehole of a sales trainer dreamed that up? When you try to produce your dick and she says no, don't be concerned. She doesn't really mean it, she's just requesting further information. She really wants to know your girth and length, that you're not short of a length. All the romantic stories encourage girls to resist, but then there will be some sort of magical moment when she feels a warm glow and the heart beats faster. Is he the one? Her eyes glisten and she melts into his arms. The girls all give way in the end. They all want it. You just have to push harder. Women mainly write this stuff. Fifty shades of it apparently, all the way to the bank. Use a pyjama cord or maybe a curtain pull. Find a deserted alleyway. Plenty of those where I lived.

"When roses are red, They're ready for plucking
When a girl is sixteen, She's ready for.... Err"

Max Miller

Blue book again eh, Max? 'I'm Alive' by the Hollies was playing at the 'Mad House' birthday party. They got that wrong then. So was Help, fourth week in the charts at number one. Why not scream for Help? Won't you please, please help me? 'Help!' was back for a second week in August at the Dreamland cinema because the film had been so popular. John and Paul maybe running to save her. Had Julie only died two years earlier, they might have heard her, exiting from the back of a restaurant near the Winter Gardens at about that time of night. We all went to see the Beatles live, but you could hardly hear the music over the screaming. Nothing to do with murder then. They were nowhere men in August 1965, visiting the good old US of A. No respite there. Hang on though. Well can't technically hang anyone now. It's been abolished, remember. John Lennon liked to treat his women mean, they say. If you were an eggman, a walrus, you had to be hard, even with your women. Keep them in order. Solid middle class values. Not sure about Russell Brand at the closing ceremony, he's more of a walrus, but in those days we had our own eggman.

Tall gentle funny giant whose family managed the Hennesseys pub in Ramsgate. He was a rebel. He would lead us in choruses of the Marcel's Blue Moon, *bom-ba-ba-bom,ba-bom ba-bom bom* echoing down the narrow corridors. Our school had a head who everyone considered outstanding although he never really liked me and the feeling was mutual. But I wasn't brave and was disruptive from the back and side of the class, waiting until teachers had turned their backs. My friend Andrew seems to be convinced that whenever I caused trouble, that he was the one who would be ordered out. I have to confess that the words "Thorpe, get out" do have a sort of familiar ring to them. Eggleton however would take the teachers on face to face and he was eventually beaten down. He had a mental breakdown of some sort and I last saw him at Dumpton dog track, wearing a long brown institutional coat. You could wear a coat like that and skulk in the bushes, opening it wide at each passer-by, although that wasn't his style. Egg smiled and nodded. I hope he came through as he was a bright guy. We had come third earlier that year, 1965, in the five-a-side indoor football league played twice a week at Dreamland. We played as boys against the men. We were fit and fast and used the walls to beat the opposition, thus reducing the opportunity for physical challenge. We were good and when they chose us the following year to represent Thanet in a regional tournament at Folkestone, Egg lent us his battered Ford Anglia. Baby, you can drive my car. A Ford Prefect was out of his price range, probably wrong galaxy. Seven of us got into it, including two girl supporters, and the car was so crowded that I failed to notice the red oil light which displayed brightly somewhere on our return journey. The car sadly never recovered from the dearth of oil although it did get us back, before grinding to a halt the next morning. Maybe for his Ford Anglia the cruellest month.

The Lido and the Winter Gardens in Cliftonville could attract decent performers then. At one time there was a theatre, a mini-zoo, a puppet theatre, a bathing pool and a regular organist. Henry Hudson who played the piano for Wilfred Pickles in 'Have a Go', just before Ena Sharples, used to play the organ. Is there anyone still alive who remembers Wilfred Pickles, or who doesn't think 'Have a Go' is the name of a programme to encourage the public to tackle criminals. Very few major villains down in Margate in my time, as they were beginning to head for Spain, but always been some serious animals on display. When Lord Sanger opened Dreamland, one of the lion tamers apparently used to walk around town with a revolver in his waistband. Indeed Sanger's wife was said to have been the very first woman lion tamer in the UK. There is also a story of a thirty four ton yacht being built in the town, called the Miss Rose. The steam roller towing it to the harbour broke down and Sanger lent them his team of elephants to finish the job. Clowns walked behind with shovels. And you wonder why the bungalows all had good rose gardens.

Terry Scott and Hugh Lloyd were the attraction that summer at the Winter Gardens, fresh from their TV comedy series 'Hugh and I'. Two guys living together but no funny business, not even intentionally. Kathy Kirby was the attraction on Sundays, reportedly the highest-paid female singer of her generation, a Marilyn Monroe look-alike who became a gay icon. Her biggest hit was 'Secret Love' and in 1965 she had appeared for Britain at the Eurovision Song Contest. Bill Maynard, best known later for Selwyn Froggitt and his part in 'Heartbeat', was on at the Lido. Benny Hill had previously worked at the Lido for a season, mainly with slapstick comedy, and was also a regular visitor to the Winter Gardens. In his early days he had even formed a partnership with Reg Varney from 'On the Buses'. Benny is another one who had trained as a mechanic, despite starting life as a milkman. Not the fastest milkman in the west though, which is presumably why he changed career.

Further down the line, Ben Elton accused Benny Hill of being largely responsible for the incidences of rape in England during a later period in question. Fortunately he didn't accuse our Benny of dumbing down, bit difficult when you yourself were responsible for the 'Thin Blue Line'. In 1965 Benny's troupe of Hill's Angels was well in the future. It's a good debate anyway. Does programme content contribute to violence against women? If I watch repeats of the 'Young Ones' am I more likely to go and beat the shit out of people and treat them with disrespect. If you stereotype people in traditional ways, does that encourage lazy thinking? Surely most comedy writers create comic stereotypes, that is their stock in trade. I hate political correctness with a vengeance anyway, as I am sure does our Ben. If they watch the Chippendales regularly, do women try and savage the next man they see? Actually men apparently go to strip shows singly or in ones and twos, whereas women go in groups. So they wouldn't rape, just gang-bang. In any case what do mechanics watch? Did the Pirelli calendars on the garage walls make them all dangerous?

It might certainly create a culture which cheapens the role of women but then who writes most of the romantic novels? We've all misread signs and sometimes people do change their minds. Max Miller used to say, "The girls that I like most of all, and boys you know I'm right, are the girls who say they never will but look as though they might". When you had had a few beers could you tell the difference, Max? Did you care? Thought for a musical, Ben. What about one based on the story of the Black and White Minstrels? In 1965 eighteen million used to watch the programme and the albums were often number one in the charts. Great singing and in the early days for black and white television, they blacked up in red. So if you called it the Red and White Minstrels you could be politically correct. I can see Tonto ringing the BBC to complain on his celestial phone. We'll get Ray in to play a historical character called the daddy. Thomas Rice was the 'Daddy' of minstrel shows in the States in the 1830's, with a Jim Crow routine. Joe Brown can play the banjo, Brucie can do the clog dancing which evolved into tap. Wow, I hear you say. If you really want to be controversial, throw in a religious minstrel. A sort of 'Imammy, how I love you' sort of guy.

Religions don't mind satire, do they? Comedy shows everywhere. Look at that Citizen Khan, a sort of Pakistani Harry Worth, a funny and gentle type of humour. You would have to be pretty extreme to be offended by that. Bet the BBC Trust think about taking it off though. There's always some moron in some pressure group ready with his finger on the button ready to complain. They replayed the old debate about pornography between Malcolm Muggeridge and Bernard Levin on the radio the other day. The one where Muggeridge made a complete arse of himself. Levin pointed out that Muggeridge's committee had spent weeks reading pornography yet wanted to ban it because they thought it would deprave the masses, despite there being no evidence at all that any of them had been in the slightest bit affected or depraved. Typical patronising establishment. Both of them great intellectuals though, no morons on display on that programme. "See the happy moron - he doesn't give a damn. I wish I was a moron - by God! Perhaps I am!" One Morse Cartwright is said to have first brought this little poem to the US public's attention in 1927, but although it is sometimes attributed to Dorothy Parker, I have yet to see a confirmation. Do watch the spelling though, don't want to offend any other religions. Leave that to South Park, Dane Park has enough to contend with.

"I must have women. There is nothing unbends the mind like them".

John Gay – 'The Beggar's Opera'

I was working for the bakery as a summer job in 1965, delivering pies, pastries and cakes. Loved the girls in the shops. Great bakery, Rogers, out at Westwood. I drove a white delivery van for them, a white van man. I had to start out very early every day cycling across the fields past the blacksmith's forge in Garlinge and along to Shottendane. Then I turned up along a narrow footpath which took you past the back of the cemetery out towards the bakery. A couple of hot meat pies straight from the ovens and you would be ready for anything. On a Saturday I could be finished by lunchtime. It was the first summer that I was available for all of the Saturday and Sunday cricket matches, but played mainly in the A team on Sundays, occasionally called up to the firsts. That made the Dane Park business harder to take, when you have the opportunity to play and Mr Plod wants to trawl the park grounds. Mind you, those BBC 'Silent Witness' forensic scientists would have closed it for the summer and by the end of that six others would have died. Some girl had been killed and they were threatening to stop us playing cricket. I didn't care that she was someone's daughter or the fairness of it all. Why would you be in the park anyway at that time of night? I knew what holidaymakers were like, had seen them in action. The previous three summers I was at the council café opposite Pav's at St Mildred's Bay in Westgate. I cleared tables at first before gradually being allowed to work in the soft scoop ice-cream kiosk. I used to give my friends free cornets, carefully choosing a time when the manageress was busy. Damn close run thing.

My last year was the best, being sent to open the tiny hut at the end of the promenade, by the Sunken Gardens. I was allowed to take a transistor with me so could spend all day listening to music from Radio London, thinking all the time about cricket, music and girls. One of the antique DJ'S recently boasted that he had slept with five thousand women. Incredible. They would have done better to sleep with his imaginary dog Arnold. Worf, Worf. Worf was a Klingon. And you tell me that women don't ask for it. My generation. The public were always a problem wanting to be served, with choc ices, wafers and mivvis. I never minded the tall donkey man, probably one of the Browns, who used to take long strides across the sands. He had rugged good looks, but not in a bona way, and in hindsight looked like Clint Eastwood, wearing a cloak thrown back which could have come from a spaghetti western. I think he did well with the lady holidaymakers, presumably those who had seen the saucy postcards about donkeys on the beach. Not sure about his tag line. For a fistful of dollars, you can ride my donkey? Might have turned some of them on, warming the squeezebox in time for the evening action. Bet he wasn't short of a length. Truth to tell, the lads on the pedaloe's and the deckchairs had better joy in pulling. They'd had a few waitresses. Rocking on the sea or resting on the sands. What sort of girl could resist? Just need to be firm. Be strong. Handle them right.

The year before, Whitsun 1964 was the march of the Mods. Dozens of them down from South London, outnumbering the Rockers with their Triumphs and Nortons. Seemed significant at the time, but a bit pathetic when you look back at the television footage. Giles in the Daily Express based a cartoon on the riots. They didn't burn down embassies just because he had drawn a cartoon of them but hey, different culture. The Mods tended to be all testosterone and posturing for their women when the cameras rolled. 'Sawdust Caesars', old George Simpson the JP called them as he jailed four of them for their part in the Whitsun riots. They came from all parts, from Lewisham, from Eltham, from Sydenham, on their Vespas and Lambrettas. Not many came in Morris vans. Down for the day in their Parkas. The Turner Centre in Margate ran a special exhibition last year on the Mods and Rockers in Margate, 'Talking about my generation'. Peter, our Molesworth, had a Parka that he used to wear. Not much use on the beach as they were so bulky. We used to leave him on the railings at school after lunch. Where's Millsted, the teachers would say? Oh he's tied up, sir, we would reply. Made us laugh. He wasn't a great cricketer, Peter, although his fielding could occasionally be sensational. Good hands, when he opted to move in the right direction. Sometimes he would throw himself in completely the opposite direction to the ball and was genuinely surprised to see it hit the boundary boards. Then again, there were no boards. This was Dane Park and the most you could expect was for the ball to lodge in the bushes.

Peter died, too young, on the squash court. Spent a lifetime playing for Cheam hockey club, clowning and drinking in the clubhouse. In his later years George Best used to appear regularly and quietly at the end of the bar there. Strangely the very next grave to George's carries my family name. Never knew any of the extended family reached Ireland, not on that side. On my mother's side though they all came from there, probably occupying half the cemeteries. I have suggested to one or two friends that George's location is just a sign that the great footballing families are always buried in proximity but those who actually played alongside me just think I have early dementia. Peter's father, Harold, was our music master, banging loudly and vigorously away on the piano. A wonderful eccentric of a man, built rather like Grandma

Giles. Kept all his valuables, probably his complete life story, along with his dog ends, in a small tobacco tin. I'm not really too sure about the tradition of school songs, but Harold led the rebellion when a new headmaster banned ours as being old-fashioned. Apparently at the very next assembly he suddenly opened the lid of the piano, hit the two familiar chords and the whole school burst into song. Together they marched in strong battalions on the foe, clearly identified as the new head. He was not amused and Harold retired very shortly afterwards.

The murder in the town had taken everyone by surprise. All open spaces attract trouble and in recent years the web seems to have reported at least one assault or problem every year at Dane Park. In those days though the old place was really quite safe. The week before Julie was murdered, the press reported a five year and a seven year old being assaulted, but they don't count, do they? Priests have been allowed to do that, so it must be in order. What was really troubling were youngsters on bikes who kept riding on to the cricket pitch during games. They were the ones who kept pulling down the bunting and the poles from the marquees. Not murderers though, although judging by the reactions of the cricketers and the committee, they should have been hung. Part of what caused the split. However not really much trouble reported on the ground since Dane Park was first presented to Margate by one John Woodward many years back. I've seen a poster showing it being opened by the Lord Mayor of London, Sir Henry Isaacs. Not sure why they invited him, even though he was an MP and an architect, as his sole contribution to the world of literature was 'A Treatise on Sewerage and Drainage'. Huh, the vagaries of drainage. He would have been better writing about fifty shades of sewerage.

Woodward didn't buy Dane Park from the Danes. They were long gone by then. In real life the monarchy and the aristocracy have of course tended to appropriate everything they thought might be valuable. That is before the Russians and Chinese came along. No-one wanted this bit of land. Mind you, you can imagine the Danes arriving in their longboats, down for the day, sailing up the stream to the Tivoli Pleasure Gardens near the Brook. Would wander off when bored and use the bushes on this piece of land to relieve themselves. They were asked to take their helmets off when they entered the hostelries though, after completing the risk assessments. Then when they were pissed and had had their share of wenches they used to dance round the helmets, a sort of round the horn dance. There is a wonderful old Danish toast we used at college, 'Pyurs', which is said to mean good luck in Anglo Saxon. More rape and pillage, lads? If you can't find it on Wikileaks, try the old Margate alleyways or maybe head for the park. Avoid the children's playground though, you can do yourself an injury on the swings. Health and safety, as my friend Ian will tell you. He first became interested in the subject when he was sat opposite a drunk on a bus going back to St Peter's one night. Not the St Peter who sits by the Pearly Gates, this one's a place. Worried that the drunk might fall off his seat and hurt himself he tried to engage him in conversation. Ian is that sort of caring guy. The drunk without warning knocked Ian's front teeth out. Could have been worse I suppose. Could have been a woman that he punched, not a future health and safety expert. Wouldn't have been so funny then though, which shows our complete lack of compassion as a group. Not cricket that. Dane Park have recently refurbished the playground and installed security lighting. Not where she died though. Those swings are long gone.

"I have no time for sex. It gets in the way of the action".

Alistair Maclean

It was only around 1965 that I started wearing glasses to play sport. Blind as a bat. Could read well when I went to the Infants in Garlinge but struggled as soon as they put us into classes. I was disruptive and would never stay in my seat. I've disliked authority or people giving me orders ever since. Backward, the headmistress said to my mother, he'll have to stay down a year. That's fighting talk and my mother never lacked courage. The area schools doctor was summoned and in my presence he told my mum to accept the ruling. Mentally deficient was what he said. Happens a lot. We didn't know anything about learning difficulties then. As a last resort she returned to my form teacher one last time. She acknowledged that I could read well from books but I couldn't follow the course work on the board. I kept leaving my seat and being disruptive. However, funny thing. There's a funny thing. I wasn't doing the same sums as the others. I seemed to be making my own up - and getting them right. Odd that. Maybe worth having my eyes checked as a last resort. Authority. Tossers. One pair of Milky Bar glasses later I received a book award for my class position in the Primary school. I still have it. 'Biggles Takes The Case'. I had asked for 'Biggles Flies Undone', but out of print. Ginger would have rolled his sleeves up and made a fist of helping Biggles to find it. To borrow other books in the series I used to cycle to the old Margate library close to Dane Park, right next to Addington Road and just fifty yards down from the 'Mad House'. Later in the library I would discover Gimlet by the same author. He was tough and hard, apparently named after one of W E Johns' Commanding Officers. You can imagine Gimlet boring in, like Wes Hall, to demolish a set of stumps. I do sometimes now worry about my choice of a reading companion as I have found that there was also 'Gimlet Lends a Hand'. Hopefully not to Julian or Sandy in the Marines.

We were the last generation to listen exclusively to the radio and not until 1958 could my family afford a black and white television set. However even after that I always enjoyed heading for bed and listening to the transistor for half an hour, with hopefully 'Journey into Space', 'Hancock's Half Hour', or 'Take It From Here' as the highlight and then Barry Alldis and Radio Luxembourg to lull you to sleep. Not much variety though on the radio but you were glad of it on a Sunday. Often it was all you had. Tony Hancock once did a sketch on how boring Sundays were and he was right. Nothing was open. Sundays were church, morning and sometimes evensong, and in between a day for visiting relatives or them coming to you. When the weather was good we might get to play in Dane Park and if we were lucky would make it up to the swings. Maybe sit on the grass under the trees.

During the week our neighbours across the road at home used to let me watch twice a week at tea time on their box, more particularly the Lone Ranger and the Cisco Kid, with Tonto and Pancho respectively close at hand. I never knew that Keemo Sabeh had a strict moral code, the strangest line of which states 'God put the firewood there, but that every man must gather and light it himself'. Thought that was what Tonto and Pancho were there for. To gather the firewood when there weren't any women or coloured men to do the job. Neither of them seemed to knock women about, but they were normally too busy saving the Wild West, galloping at high speed across the country. Maybe on reflection that was Bronco Layne, tearing across the Texas plain? Very little sport seems to have been documented in those days on the frontier, until Oscar Wilde showed up. So that's where Clint got the idea for the cape. Not one mention about games and sport, other than those played with a Colt 45, in my 'Encyclopaedia of Western Gunfighters'. No signs of baseball or American football either on the big or small screen. 'How The West Was Won' was playing that month in Thanet in 1965 at one of the cinemas. Not by sport obviously.

Actually baseball does get a mention in Massachusetts in 1791 so some version must have been about. Bastard authorities banned it then. Bet they were a council of religious elders. There is huge debate about the origins of baseball, as games like rounders and stoolball were clearly played from an early stage, but the first description of a bat and base ball running game played on a diamond was in 1828 in London, repeated a year later in print in Boston. The Illinois Regiment amusingly played something similar with a wooden leg taken from one of Santa Anna's troops. The first published rules were written by Alexander Cartwright in 1845 for a New York team called the Knickerbockers, but it is said that the game first made its quantum leap when Confederate soldiers watched their Union prisoners play the game during the Civil war, a game played together by all ranks. The first National League was definitely formed by 1876 which was the year Custer died. His soldiers had played it during the Black Hills Campaign and later named the club after Benteen. Benteen, who was once disciplined for exposing himself, had played it in Kansas and it was his troop, H company that were keen. Custer and Benteen hated each other and the thought of Benteen's Baseball Club must have really pissed off George Armstrong. At the Little Big Horn Benteen was told to swing his column to the left of the Indian camp. Unpredictable swing that, Custer said. Never there when you need it. The vagaries of swing.

‘Come on, Big village, Be Quick, ps Bring Pacs’, Cooke’s hand-written note to Benteen had said. Packs he meant, not pac-a-macs. The latter only made it to the adjacent hilltop, relieving Reno’s men, the third column, whilst Custer got his. Reno’s clothes had blood on them too, spattered when one of his soldier’s brains were blown out. Reno lost it completely that day. In panic and shock though, not because of anything the Indian girls might have said. You might of course consider it fairly routine for women drawn into a battle to taunt the men about the size of their dicks, more especially if they had read some of the ‘Garryowen’ lyrics. “Through the street like sportsters fight, tearing all before us....we’ll break windows, we’ll break doors.” At least you knew what to expect if you were captured.

When they ran out of ammunition I think they threw baseballs and survived the massacre. They at least lived to play another day, but Benteen’s pitcher, Joseph McCurry, certainly got a bullet to his throwing arm. Can’t remember John Wayne ever swinging a bat, although the farmer in ‘Shane’ and later Clint in ‘Pale Rider’ seem to use clubs with a very similar shape in their fights. Just seen a news clip of Clint speaking at a conference with a chair as his co-star. I preferred it when he was with Sondra Locke or even Clyde, but perhaps all the screen fights have been taking their toll. How does the song go? “A chair is just a chair”. Get a grip. Mind you, I’ve read there is a lot of money in chairs. That aside a 1959 episode of Gunsmoke does touch on a game of baseball outside town so it’s probably just my memory at fault. Although baseball was mainly an Eastern game, there were teams in Texas and San Francisco before the civil war. Some of the soldiers in the New Orleans prison camp were said to have had baseballs in their knapsacks. Said they got the idea from a Time Lord they had met. Didn’t see any of that in Josey Wales, they were Confederates in any case, although Josey did have a telescope in his pocket. Manufactured in Margate, I believe, so was able to see through the modesty hood on the wagon containing the Union machine gun. Gave him an edge. Maybe Hollywood scriptwriters just didn’t want to write about sport in the west. It was the action that mattered first, and then the women and the potential sex angle.

No sex at first of course, but sport must have been in my blood from an early age. I was born in Hartsdown Road, in a small nursing home, almost opposite Margate Football Club. Three years later Almer Hall became manager, down from West Ham, and was there for an eternity. He came to our primary school a few times and would take the coaching. Try not to go to ground; always turn away from your own goal; if in doubt, put it out. The last rule is apparently now discredited in this new world of holding on to the ball although in any case one or two of the more senior players seem to have mistaken the word 'put' for 'pull'. I still remember the Astrakhan coat he wore, just like Tony Hancock, with a matching black homberg to boot. Margate had a series of good cup runs whilst he was there. One year they beat Hancock's Bournemouth, the Division Three league leaders, away; another they drew with Brentford and narrowly lost the replay. If we weren't involved with school or club games we would go and stand behind the goals. There were a small group of regulars, rattles were whirled, tea and bovril consumed. No expense spared in those heady days. Jim Gaze with his thick bottle glasses was one of the regulars, one lense permanently broken. Then if you walked quickly home you could just catch the opening bars of Sports Report at 5.00. Da dum da dum da dum da dum. I believe Keith runs Margate FC, the same guy who played centre half for Hartsdown FC in the Youth League. It was a decent side and I played full back when I could.

Relevant only in this story because Margate Cricket Club now play just down the road from the football club. Sadly no-one surely plays cricket at Dane Park now, judging by the state of the old pitch. George must be turning in his grave. Margate's new ground is sited roughly at the end of the walk that visitors could take when they visited the Tivoli Pleasure Gardens. Following the huge success in London of similar attractions, pleasure gardens sprang up everywhere. In Garlinge, for instance, Dent de Lion was a popular venue until fashions changed and it went into decline. Tivoli was so successful that they built a railway track there. In the Tivoli Gardens just down the road from where the Coffin House would be built, there was a lake, an inn and a coffee house cum restaurant. There was drinking, dancing and carousing. They had been called the Shady Grove Tea Gardens and by the sound of it the shady element had the best of it. By 1870 there is a comment about the 'low resort of the company attending'. They obviously had never been in the Kent Hotel on a Friday night, with our umpire Roy trying to sing 'Ghost Riders in the Sky'. The landlord used to ask him to sing just about closing time. Never failed. Cleared the pub without a fight. Our mechanic had been in the Kent on the Saturday night before he headed up for the Bowling Alley. Had four pints in there plus ten to fifteen brown and white tablets. Seems a lot of tablets to me, but what do I know? Just before the trial the story seems to have changed to just four tablets but maybe that was because it was thought more sensible if he could then argue that he was just an occasional user. Was anyone singing in the Kent that night? Yippee-yi-ay. How does it go? "Their faces gaunt, their eyes were blurred, and shirts all soaked with sweat". Obviously been a hard night for those cowpokes, wrestling steers to the ground. Got to hold them tight around the neck. At least thirty three pounds of pressure.

"Music and women I cannot but give way to, whatever my business is".

Samuel Pepys

If you're business was to be in a rock band, then both music and women would dominate your life. But you could find time for other diversions. In March 1965 Jagger, Jones and Wyman were each fined £5 for urinating on the wall of a garage in South London. Did the mechanics object? Surely there are worse crimes? On that basis my friends and I must owe the exchequer millions. The church hedge near the Hussar used to take a real beating and looking back I had created over time a sort of fluid hedge fund, environmentally friendly. Wild flowers grew there and butterflies flourished. The trick was to empty fully before attempting entry to our house which was just past the pub. We lived near The Rodney, the pub opposite Wright's fish and chip shop and Bruce's dad's shoe repairers. Bruce's dad was a familiar sight locally as he had lost a leg in the war and used to swing along on his crutches. Some of the younger locals probably think the pub was named after Del Boy's brother but Rodney was an admiral famous for crossing the enemy line of sail, well before Nelson perfected it at the Nile.

In the summer, once past the pub, you could in addition take your shoes off at the bottom of the road to reduce the noise. Fortunately only one dog in our street. At the house you would turn the backdoor key silently in the lock and then try acrobatically to get to bed, holding on to the banisters without putting your weight on the stairs. Foot on the window-sill as the stairs turned to the left. Not easy when you were three parts to the wind. Two more steps and you would be there and under the covers. A tired and faint voice would come from the master bedroom. "Is there anybody there?" If it was a burglar, would he answer? You would freeze in silence and hold your breath. Then as you heard the covers go back and the bed creak, you finally had to speak out. What was the worst that could happen? A burst of "what sort of time do you think this is" before sleep overwhelmed my mother and she fell quiet once more. I would fall into bed, silently mouthing expletives. Tynan said, "Fuck" for the first time on television that year. Mary Whitehouse formed her National Viewers Association. Somehow Ken's expletive and Mary was an association which did not spring naturally to mind.

Bob lived in Dane Valley Road, like Julie. She would have passed his house in the mornings. Another working class man who lived for cricket. He worked for the council, on the bins I had always thought. My kids have no idea who

Lonnie Donegan was but they once knew all the words to 'My Old Man's A Dustman'. Lonnie lived along the road in Birchington. Saw him on stage just before he died. Still a terrific distinctive voice, but not sure he was ever a cricketer. Maybe it was his skiffle band in the Cricketers Arms in 'One Man, Two Guvnors'. That'll have to do. Bob was an unsung hero. He was getting on a bit when I knew him but still took a long run-up to bowl. He would come sidling in, relying on the seam or swing to do the job. Batsmen found him difficult to read. He wore glasses most of the time now, sometimes even when he was bowling, so he must have found it difficult to read too. If a wicket fell he would ease towards the boundary and craftily light up. It was a fair walk from the pavilion down to the hollow where the square stood, but if the new batsmen was keen, Bob would have to put out the cigarette. He would then run in to bowl with it stuck behind his left ear, where it stayed until the next wicket fell.

They banned cigarette advertising on television that year. Bob didn't care, as he stood for an eternity with his pint, discussing the day's play. We all played much better and for longer in the pub than we ever did on the pitch. Sadly both Bob and his young son also went off to Broadstairs. Bob then gave up quickly, he was getting on a bit and not really his social scene there. Dustmen. Big hobnail boots. His son though became a real local talent. He was quick. A sad loss to our club. Later we lost another of our promising cricketers, young John Bowley. Not near the children's playground, gasping for breath. He might have tried to gasp, but then John's throat would have filled with water. He at least reached beyond sixteen, slipping through a life belt on the Norfolk Broads. One minute he was there, next minute he had gone. They never found the body. Lovely guy John. I look at him in the old photos, pale blue eyes, talent unfulfilled, a door never opened. Another bloody guardian angel at fault. Used to play against us in the soccer league at Dreamland, in our small hall by the sea.

The real Hall by the Sea, which became the Dreamland amusement park in 1919, had a tenuous connection to the Wild West. Not too many gunfights in our area, just the odd thunderflash. Sanger, who started it all, was never a Lord, but being a showman knew that an honorary title was good for the business. His father James had learnt conjuring tricks in the Royal Navy, handy with a broomstick too, and set out to tour in a caravan. Never, to my knowledge, said which ship he served in at Trafalgar so not sure if that was just 'showman's' licence. He was always dressed smartly so was known as 'his lordship'. The term 'Lord' stuck and then first John and then George Sanger used the title after they split up. I think they mainly did it for the attendance allowance and the expenses. I know a bit about another form of

Attendance Allowance, ten years now filling in the damn booklets. If only I could meet the civil servant who first designed disability forms, I'd ensure he was suitably qualified for his own benefit. Well I might at least have prevented him having children.

Many of those hereditary Lords in Westminster look to me like they might get a high rate award. Are some of them still breathing? Maybe that's why they don't shout at each other like the Commons. Lack of breath, COPD probably, chronic pulmonary obstructive disease. Of course they argue that in reality the debate is much more informed, less of this party politics and yah booing. They at least try and analyse the issues sensibly and many of the Conservative MP's obviously think it's worth preserving as it is. Mind you, most of them seem to have obstructive disease as well. Well, got to keep the job opportunities open, the "rotten boroughs" as Simon Jenkins calls them. What's a political party for if it doesn't guarantee you a job for life. It's a shame they never admitted any of the Sangers to Parliament. Running a circus would seem to have much more merit to being in the un-reconstructed Upper Chamber, than having a descendant who slept with the King's mistress, who helped him rape and pillage in the name of patriotism or who had been a political jobs-worth or a fawning Permanent Secretary. 'Yes Prime Minister' might well have been called 'Are You Being Served?' had the name not already been taken. Shame because I think we would have known the answer to that one. Over the years civil servants at the Treasury, for example, in the way they quietly obstruct and kill off agreed schemes and initiatives and starve projects of promised funds, arguably seem to have inflicted more damage on the country than Jim Hacker and Sir Humphrey could ever have done.

Sanger had a series of court battles with one William Cody, who at the time was touring the UK with his Buffalo Bill's Wild West show. Never actually used the word 'show'. You can see something similar, but much smaller, in Disneyland Paris today. They used to do a scene recreating the battle at Little Big Horn every night. Sitting Bull toured twice in the States with Buffalo Bill and used to sign autographs for money. Being patriotic they show Custer being the last man down, dying heroically, when it seems to have been his brother Tom who was one of the last to die. Don't hear much about Tom Custer but he fought bravely, being killed by an Indian called Yellow Nose. Kenneth Horne or Marty could have surely done something with that? Another Cheyenne, Wooden leg, was on the winning side, which was just as well, or he might have suffered the same fate as the Santa Anna soldier. Rectum was there too, probably a public school Indian. Heaven help him if he'd been captured. Would they still have called the game softball? Lord

Sanger had a very small show featuring 'Scenes from Buffalo Bill's Wild West' and Cody took him to court for 'passing off'. Known as the Crabtree precedent. Cody won, the judge deciding though that there was no claim to exclusivity on the words 'Wild West'. Sanger tried hard to prevaricate as long as he could by conning people that this was part of the original show and was eventually fined £100.

I always feel this is a little hard on Sanger. At one time the Sanger Brothers had one of the largest circuses in England, with a stud of two hundred horses. They had had trouble before when the American circus Howes and Cushing began to tour the UK, so probably were wary of the Yanks. There were many smaller circuses but not really room for two large ones. Eventually Barnum bought much of their equipment and props for use in the States. The Sanger Brothers also put on a series of spectacular shows in London, their pantomime at the Agricultural Hall in London, Aladdin, featuring eleven elephants. The Sanger memorials in Margate cemetery are striking and worth a look, although there is vigorous debate locally about who is actually buried there. Probably the bearded lady was thrown in to accompany them to the after-life. Why they chose to use a horse to figure on top of John's grave, rather than an elephant is a mystery. Perhaps a Jumbo would use too much marble. Victoria, Sanger's great grand-daughter, was known as 'Queen of the Elephants' so it might have been a more fitting tribute.

One final thought. There was a saying amongst the soldiers of the western frontier that, "Indian women rape easy". The Buffalo Bill Wild West show never tried to replicate Custer sleeping with his black cook, which was one allegation about him. It also never showed his relationship with a Cheyenne captive called Monahsetah, one of fifty taken prisoner, and who was said to have visited his tent most nights on the way back after the Washita campaign. Benteen always maintained that Custer had married her and Cheyenne oral history seems to be divided as to whether her second child was his or his brother Tom's. It was said that many of the squaws were similarly used by the officers. If you wonder about vengeance, Kate Bignose said that Custer's body was not violated, unlike all the other Seventh Cavalrymen, because of his relationship with Monahsetah. Yet the General who found the bodies reported that someone had stuck an arrow up Custer's penis. The report was obviously concealed for many years, presumably to protect Custer's wife, Libby, and the identity of the guardian angel responsible. Genesis 28-9. Angels can act as the executors of God's wrath. Even on behalf of native colonial Indians.

"There is only one thing in CRIKET and that is the STRATE bat. Keep yore bat strate boy and all will be all right in life as in criket".

'How to be Topp' - The Compleet Molesworth

Domestic violence has long been with us. Strange how some of our great Englishmen have treated their wives badly. Dickens, Wellington, Nelson, for example. No actual physical violence but definitely abuse and neglect. Yet they were great in their own special ways and all of them arguably compassionate and caring. Just not for the person they had married. True love, but not for their wives, seems to have made an appearance somewhere on their separate journeys. Wellington got very close to some of his ladies, if not true love then a certain devotion. A devotion initially to Kitty although muttering,"By jove, she has grown ugly" to your brother, the vicar, on your wedding day does not bode well. Charles had Catherine, who grew fat after fathering so many of his children. Horatio had Francis or Fanny as she was known. Max Miller would have liked her. Wellington's great opponent, Napoleon, seems to have been a bit of a lad as well, maybe because he was a Corsican. More romantic perhaps. Apparently his French accent was as bad as Edward Heath's so maybe he just laughed the girls into bed. Being called Bonaparte might have slowed him down, certainly at the end. Never went round the horn, St Helena being too distant.

You can imagine though the 95th Rifles calling across the Waterloo battlefield, Bona Parte, Bona Parte, speaking French like Heath. Soldiers who camped together often had a nodding acquaintance with Bona Polari. Napoleon was a master of movement, of swing, a great tactician. In many of his battles he had out-manoeuvred the enemy, often defeating them by swinging both ways. This time it was Wellington in front and Blucher somewhere on the right. Wrong game though this time. The French have never understood cricket. God gave it to the English. The vagaries of swing. Grouchy tried it, completely misunderstanding his orders, but those damn Germans were too quick. They fortunately didn't understand the technicalities of flight either, just lucky. The Prussians came out of the forest, out of the bushes, in long dark coats, penetrating Napoleon's right flank. Damn close run thing. Every time Ney charged, the British infantry would retreat to their squares. They had practiced every week in the summer on village greens throughout the land. Stand fast in your square and the game would be won. Squares, holy places. Strate bat, gentlemen, hard pounding. We will eventually block his passage.

There are examples of true love even from the Waterloo campaign, one which was largely air-brushed for years and one which caught the public imagination. It appears that Wellington had become besotted with Lady Frances Wedderburn Webster, also married. He wrote to her just before he left for Waterloo promising to tell her if there was imminent danger. Half the British had already made a run for the coast so there clearly were serious concerns about the outcome of the battle. Only those who could play a straight bat would remain in Brussels. He also tellingly penned her a swift note after the battle and even before he began his official report. She was heavily pregnant in Paris and Wellington was confronted by the angry husband. His friends rallied round and the husband successfully sued one newspaper for libel, as it had reported the alleged affair. She later took other lovers and Wellington twenty years later had to buy and burn his letters to her. However the match that caught the high admiration of Sir Walter Scott was that of the De Lanceys. Wellington was privately most disturbed about the calibre of his troops. Many of the experienced British regiments were in America and the troops he had were relatively inexperienced. He also had a motley collection of foreign soldiers and was not sure if they would stand. Apart from his initial battle in India, he had never lost a battle when he was there in person and was well supplied. His quartermasters were as skilled as modern supply chains in getting armament, food and soldiers there just in time.

De Lancey had been the Deputy Quartermaster through the Peninsular War and afterwards had been transferred to Edinburgh, where he had fallen in love with Magdalene. On the 4th April 1815 he was married and the couple set off on their honeymoon to one of her father's estates. Napoleon's escapade was unexpected but had to be answered. Wellington needed a professional quartermaster. He needed De Lancey, who rather grumpily accepted, the couple moving out to Brussels. During the battle itself, De Lancey was riding right next to Wellington when a cannon ball knocked him from his horse. He is said to have, 'bounded up like a struck pheasant'. Those of you from the hunting and shooting brigade will be familiar with the term. Those of us from a more humble background would probably do better thinking of an old joke where a man propels a dog high up in the air with the toe of his boot. De Lancey's wife found him the next day in a peasant's cottage and nursed him for the six days he had left to live. She buried him and left three months to the day after they had married. Lady Magdalene kept a journal of these tragic days and of her true love. Dickens said that he dreamt of it every now and then, in its frightful reality.

Of course it is one of the legends surrounding Waterloo that the English played a game of cricket on the eve of the battle in Brussels. Presumably made up from those who chose to stay and take their chance. Bet the Dutch, our allies joined in, just for the tea break. It is said that cricket derives from Middle Dutch words, krick meaning a stick or krickstoel meaning a stool resembling a long low wicket. Can't be right, can it? Cricket was a gift from God to us. Forget Netherland and Joseph Neill. It started in the Weald and then gradually spread across the country. No sense of structure though until Alan Brodick in 1728 found a set of old scrolls buried on his land. There were three of them and he took them to show the Duke of Richmond. Two of the scrolls had ossified so much that they stuck one in each end of the wicket, between the two stumps previously used. The cricketers just laughed at the third stump and it wasn't introduced until around 1774 to stop dormice running across the wickets. The remaining scroll was flexible enough to open and decipher and that was when they drew up the 'Articles of Agreement'. A holy scroll. Sixteen years later enough scholars had consulted the scroll to build up a body of sayings and codes which became the Laws of Cricket. It was ever thus with all religions. You keep re-interpreting the evidence until you get what you want. Kill or banish the people who oppose you. Control, power and conformity.

"Baseball and cricket are beautiful and highly stylized medieval war substitutes, chess made flesh, a mixture of proud chivalry and base - in both senses - greed."

John Fowles

Many regard cricket as some sort of War Game. That was shot in 1965 but banned by the authorities. Heaven knows why. Maybe just deceitful national politicians, trying to spin away the repercussions of a nuclear explosion. Cricket of course has deceit, guile, spin and swing. The symbols and trappings coincidentally too of the great religions. I have omitted local politics. Have you ever sat on a committee? When Lindbergh landed at Le Bourget, the mayor is supposed to have commented that it was wonderful that he flown the Atlantic unaided. He went on to say that it would have been more amazing had Lindbergh succeeded with the aid of a committee. A cricket committee can be a cauldron. It was the resignation of most of the committee, claiming to be fed up with the lack of support during the festival week, that nearly broke the Margate club. You might be surprised that cricket, being one of the great religions, would cause such debate and bitterness. It is not as if they were discussing something trivial like whether to admit women to the 'senior' committee of bishops and cardinals, like the General Synod. Well at least the Synod has debates. Most of the others just say that the Lord has decided that women can't be umpires. Game over.

Bert, our opening batsman, and his father were actually Bishops. Indeed there must have been a Mrs Bishop, although we never saw her. What is the problem with these women in the great religions, if I can use the word 'great' figuratively? Why don't they know their place, at the back making the teas. Might need a back-hander or two. You have this terrific discovery in a field of a new religion, scrolls and tablets buried for years. Men running into the Cricketers Arms, shouting with excitement about their discovery. Three letters, boys. MCC. The custodians of the religion and laws. The scrolls guarded surely by an angel, wearing whites, probably some form of two piece garment. From that the MCC can create a sort of Talmud, a collection of codas and edicts. They will call them the howzats. Formal dress codes. Blazers, panama hats, striped ties are all part of the mystery. Just the dress code alone will deter any women from playing. Take your example from the Churches. Which women would seriously want to become cardinals and bishops when you have to wear ceremonial frocks? And look at the styling, my dear. Marks & Spencer's?

Just as an aside, there was a well-known attempt by supporters of Hambleden Cricket Club, who played at Broad Halfpenny Down near the Bat and Ball pub, to describe the club as 'the cradle of cricket'. The revelation about children playing something similar in the Weald was meant to disprove this theory, placing the game many centuries before that particular era. Sir Horatio Mann, another MP, was briefly a member and is recorded as arranging matches against the Duke of Dorset's side. The latter described Hambleden as "a bleak place to play cricket". One of the grounds before Broad Halfpenny Down, Windmill Down, even sloped away steeply to the right, even more than Dane Park. Mann consequently begun playing matches at Dandelion Paddock near Margate which was said to have been a first class cricket ground, our local park then being unavailable. The Bow Street Runners must have cordoned it off. The pitch was part of the Dent de Lion estate, originally owned by John Daundelyon, a Norman nobleman. There was also at one time a racecourse there. Mann died in Margate.

There is also Henry Tufton, the last Earl of Thanet, who played for Hambleden as a wicketkeeper and batsman. The Tuftons were reasonably important until one of them supported Charles the First and became a Cavalier. They lost much of their property but somehow kept their heads and survived, supplying several MP's over the years but very few children and heirs. The title, Earl of Thanet, died with Henry in 1849. I am surprised that Kenneth Horne in his 1965 promotional film made no mention of Margate or Thanet as one of the ancient seats of cricket. Just as in 'Only Fools and Horses', where the 'Villa Bella' was filmed in Dalby Square, jolly boys outings must have been in fashion for a couple of hundred years. You can imagine the Duke of Dorset on his return to London, stopping the coach halfway up the Thanet Way to urinate against a water trough. Apparently he would stand amongst the peasants there, tool in hand and quietly practice his swing. The peasants on the ends would note with surprise that their boots would be steaming and in those days they would gratefully warm their hands on the boots. If you ever visit the area around Thanet, you may note that God has provided very little firewood.

"For you and I have a guardian angel
On high, with nothing to do"

Cole Porter

So what is it with guardian angels? Arda Fravas, guardian angels of the faithful. Each person has a guardian angel to act as a guide throughout life. They originally patrolled the boundaries, a bit like Colin Bland and later Clive Lloyd and Derek Randall in the covers, but a little further out in the deep. Bet they couldn't hit a birdbath from twenty paces. We all wanted to field like Colin in that summer of 1965, even if we had doubts about the South African tour. In Dane Park, the angels would have been round the boundaries. Of course there are different sorts of angels so, as this was a seaside town, they would probably be part-time. Work in the summer, and then on the dole in the winter. Guardian angels originally patrolled the boundaries of heaven before volunteering to come to earth. Patrolled the boundaries! Definitive proof that cricket is played in heaven. Certainly not football. Football anyway has always been a raucous sport and the Puritans even banned it as an unlawful assembly. Ah, I hear you say. Weren't two men in Sussex prosecuted in 1611 for playing cricket instead of going to church? A close study of the Sussex Chronicle shows that they were not actually indicted for playing cricket, but for an early case of mutual ball tampering. First known instance of bona law in action.

Footballers such as Sir Stanley Matthews might have got in through the Pearly Gates, but they wouldn't have been welcomed with open arms like Wally Hammond or Tich Freeman. They all died in 1965 but Wally and Tich would have had the easier passage. No soul-searching for them. Wally would have gone straight into the celestial First Eleven. Plenty of men who can assess spin and velocity like Galileo or Copernicus but Wally would have his own kit. In the old days you could be buried with important tools beside you for the after-life. A bottle opener, a pack of cards, a cricket bat. What happens now? Does your soul arrive to see St Peter and get assigned to some form of heavenly store-room or pavilion? Or do you just get a white robe, a blackberry and an all-inclusive wrist band? Whatever the scene, be sure that the gatekeepers will have confiscated anything that smacks of ambush marketing. Sorry sir, can't bring a Duke cricket ball into heaven. Kookaburra are our celestial sponsors. Swing is everything up here. We thought you would know. Swing seemed to be such an essential part of the story down there on Earth. One of the guardian angels reported it. Can't explain. But they can see for miles and miles.

The Book of Daniel mentions Michael as one of the chief princes. Jude says he was an archangel. Hey Jude, not the Michael I knew. Nearest he got to being royalty was when we suggested that he dress up at Newmarket to pretend he was an incarnation of Prince Monolulu, the famous tipster. "I gotta horse!" Matthew has Peter being escorted out of a prison by his guardian angel. Is this just for Peter or can anyone have one? Might be a European Court of Justice precedent there. Hebrews 1:14 says, "Are they not all ministering spirits, sent to minister for them, who shall receive the inheritance of salvation?" So in theory you don't need to be religious. And what about Cole Porter? He should know the time of day about guardian angels. True love. For Cole himself that would be gay love? Great deal of debate about true lovers of the same sex being married in church. Deafening silence about whether they are allowed a guardian angel.

Nothing precisely about remand prisoners either so he might have had a guardian angel at the Assizes in Maidstone in November 1965. Maybe that's why eleven years was all he had to serve. Well he only strangled someone. Didn't try to blow up a plane or a bus. I can believe in angels because they've been patrolling the boundaries but what is it with religions and virgins? See, they could learn something from cricket. Wear a cricket box when you detonate a suicide vest. You don't want to arrive in heaven to claim seventy virgins, with all your bits in a carrier bag. All these ladies and you can't consummate the relationships. Sorry, my tool got blown off in the blast and it was last seen on a number 69 bus, heading for Clapham, heading up the junction. No need to be a martyr, wear a cricket box. In any case, if I ever get asked to sacrifice my life for some sacred cause, badgers, rhinos or something significant, I don't want all those virgins. Stuff the virgins. How about three or four experienced women, different sizes and ages, two or three lady cooks, a couple of cleaners, someone to do the ironing and a few to drink with. I'm a modern man. I'm not stuck in the Seventh century.

High wire performers need guardian angels. On high, see. It is well documented that the Beatles took their idea for Mr Kite and Mr Henderson from a poster featuring those two performing for Pablo Fanque. The original Pablo Fanque was a negro rope dancer and at Nottingham he met William Darby who was into horses and rope and wire walking. Almost like that E L James. Bet she or her husband have shares in a rope manufacturer. Darby was the son of an African slave who had been brought back to Norfolk, became a butler and had fathered young Darby. William changed his name shortly after Nottingham to Pablo Fanque. Maybe the original guy had fallen off the wire. Pablo went on to be the first black circus owner in the country and the Grand Lodge in Edinburgh actually documented their outing to see his show, presumably wearing their masonic gear and Klu Klux Klan pointed hats. He was also responsible for launching the career of the great Chinaman, Ki-hi-chin-fon-fee from Wan Kin, who performed with distinction for several years before being unmasked as an Irishman who knew absolutely nothing about China at all. True story. As a student I lived directly opposite someone who had one of the first copies of Sergeant Pepper. At 9.00 one morning the first strains of 'For the benefit of Mr Kite' came sailing through the window. At one o'clock, when I returned at lunchtime, the album was still playing and it continued non-stop for several more hours. The author must have blown his mind out in his room, although by early evening there were plenty of volunteers offering to do the job properly. William Kite coincidentally also played at Sanger's circus. George Sanger was later killed with an axe by an ex-employee. Hope it wasn't an elderly Kite seeking vengeance.

**"Ever this day / night be at my side
To light, to guard, to rule and guide"**

Traditional Catholic prayer to a guardian angel.

So there were these two guys in Palestine, working as Sales and Marketing consultants. The receptionist called up to say that there was some young man up from Medina wanting advice. We've got this idea for a new religion but we're looking for a point of difference. The market is saturated with new and old gods. The Jews and the Christians are pretty unassailable. Islam or something like that we want to call it but looking for ideas. Two focus groups later in the market place and sorted. Why not have two guardian angels? All the others have a single angel. Join us and have one on each side. Brilliant. Made them rich. They were just on the point of moving to Mesopotamia for tax reasons when the great camel sickness struck. Camels were the single currency for a short period and in the crisis all the money lenders pulled in their loans. The boys were ordered to trim their staff, so they cut off all their employee's right hands. Fatal to a marketing company. Never produced any decent artwork again. Went into decline and were found stoned in some park. You would have thought their guardian angels would have protected them, but the success of the new religion put a premium on recruitment. Two angels per person and you get a shortage. In the end they were having to fly them in from the Balkans and of course the standards dropped. Thomas Aquinas agreed with Honorius of Autun that now it was the lowest order of angels acting as guardians and his view was taken as gospel. True story yet again. I think I read it in Holland's Shadow of the Sword in the Stone. The wizards they had in those days.

The only brothers I knew from London came from near Chelsea. Nothing like the Krays. I think it was the Richardsons who ruled South London anyway and there are those who argue that they weren't really gangsters but property developers. You must be kidding. One of the Chelsea boys, Ron, not the 'Chopper' who actually played for the Blues, used to work in A&E as a junior doctor, tending to people whose guardian angels had abandoned them. Slipped off for a quiet fag in the bushes to rest their wings. Patients would regularly come in wearing long raincoats and walking gingerly. Claimed to have been caught short and got stuck urinating into a milk bottle. Really stuck. Didn't follow the protocol. Why not find a friendly garage wall? Bugger the mechanics. Well best not, some of them might be lethal. Or had been reaching up to a cupboard and fallen from the stool onto the handle of a broomstick. I didn't understand. They never ever seemed to be wearing clothes at the time. I had seen 'Bednobs and Broomsticks' and nothing like that happened, unless it was that 'Substitutiary Locomotion', which brings inanimate objects to life. How unlucky some people are. Tons better now we just have plastic milk bottles or tetrapak. You can make a fortune from tetrapak and it buys a whole heap of tablets. And all those broomsticks. Mind you, there must have been a fair few wizards in London in those days. Presumably spells don't work if they're for your personal benefit or they wouldn't have needed a doctor. I think if you have MB after your name you're skilled in handling Broomsticks, Master of Broomsticks, that must be it. Wizards, of course, have been around as long as dinosaurs. There is strong archaeological evidence of dinosaurs with extensive chest damage. Been poked with a stick, see, a broomstick or a staff. Like Gandalf fighting the Balrog. Thoracic Park they call it.

When I mentioned the Hussar, I didn't mean the Hussar who keeps popping up on the television on Sky Sports offering you gambling odds. You're the daddy. Words that send fear through so many men on the Jeremy Kyle show. Ray's your man. Graham Swift's 'Last Orders' was a fine film. Taking Jack's ashes down to Margate to be scattered from the pier. It's not really a pier, that was called the jetty but looked like a pier. What a cricket team that cast would make. Michael Caine a wordly number three or four. I was going to say cultured but he was playing a butcher. Mind you, I put him high in the order because of the resolve he showed at Rorke's Drift. Bob Hoskins would keep wicket. He should have been in Zulu, playing the Colour Sergeant. Right height you see. How on earth the real Frank Bourne managed to peer over the biscuit boxes I'll never know. Like Gimli at Helm's Deep. No wonder he refused a Victoria Cross. Ray, who played Vince, would bat at number six and probably be quite quick. Broad shoulders. Fred Trueman had broad shoulders. Retired from international cricket in 1965. Tom Courtenay would be a wily off-spinner. Not sure about David Hemmings. He used to be a bit of a babe magnet so safer for him to umpire. Helen Mirren could make the teas. You can tell her, I'm a runner not a fighter.

Jack and Amy were going to retire to a small seaside cottage in Margate. Poetic licence, surely. Retiring to a seaside bungalow, I can buy. Bungalow heaven in Thanet, first bungalow ever built was in Westgate. A cottage? In the Victorian era that was slang for a toilet. Something you do in the bushes. I threatened to throw Mike's ashes from the pier with the boys and retire for a wake in the Ruby Lounge, but the pub's gone and the replacement is just not the same. Can still see the wording on the building though. His ashes went to the Ganges. Life, death and purity. Nirvana. Mike loved India. He felt at peace, close to his ancestors who had sailed off to work in the Guyanan sugar industry an eternity ago. Raj and his beautiful family had made him feel special when they took him there on holiday a couple of times, staying at their house. He probably also wanted to be close to Tendulkar when he eventually goes in a last final swirl. The Ganges has its own unique protocol so Raj told me. Dispersing of ashes requires a great deal of ceremony before they are released into the river. Not like 'Last Orders' where it is compulsory to have a fight in a field on the way there. Filmed before the Turner was built otherwise you would have said that they thought the fighting temeraire was a geezer. At the Ganges you have to provide food for the poor. Did Bob, who played Ray just to confuse people, buy a few bags of chips for the local artists around Margate Harbour?

"Footfalls echo in the memory, Down the passage which we did not take Towards the door we never opened, Into the rose garden".

T S Eliot, 'Burnt Norton'

I never promised you a rose garden. Footfalls down Dane Valley Road and Dane Road led to this once elegant park with wide spaces, bushes and well-maintained trees. Perhaps there were rose gardens in the newly built bungalows but this particular area was full of older houses. The estates were further back down the valley, where Julie lived. From the park you could walk on to Cecil Square with its Georgian facades or head uphill to Betjeman's Cliftonville. Light languishing soft down Norfolk and Harold Roads, sea breezes blowing across the dry promenade. The trams by then had gone but the fairy-lights still twinkled. Not quite Blackpool Illuminations but there was an attempt at gaiety and every town and village had its carnival. Margate, whilst there was employment and business to be had from holidaymakers, was a fun place to grow up. There was true love to be had but often relationships were casual and fleeting. Bar and hotel staff had sometimes come to the seaside for anonymity, for escape. Families were down for the week or just for the day thus ensuring a constant turnover of people. Teenagers could get into pubs. Tim Martin of J D Wetherspoon argues that we should let them back in. They learn to drink more responsibly from being around their elders and it keeps them off the streets and out of the parks. Sounds good to me. Better than putting the frigging price up.

By the sea, there was noise and music, dancing and shows. Butlins had several venues which were thriving. Joseph Conrad wrote of his youth and of a feeling that will never come back. A feeling that he could last forever, outlast the sea, the earth and all men. We have all had a belief at some time in our lives that we are immortal. Julie did not need to fear the sea or the earth. Men were a different proposition. Whom the gods love, die young, said Byron both in Don Juan and then the following year in a letter to Sir Walter Scott when his own daughter Allegra had died. What sort of warped gods are these? Mainly men, of course, although the first reference by Herodotus is said to chronicle a visit to a goddess, Hera. Probably two men hoping to give her one in a park. Is this true love or just an another erection that needs satisfying? One of our lady comics, can't remember who, deals with male hecklers by getting them to get up out of their seat. Wherever you are girls, she says, don't you find that some dick just stands up for no good reason? While I give to you and you give to me. What if I don't want to give to you?

When a girl is sixteen, the cheeky chappie had said. They all want it. Just push harder. Squeeze the resistance out. Sixteen is no bloody age to die.

We had a war hero as our MP. Billy had lost his arm in the war, with the Welsh Guards. He was a cricket blue at Cambridge before that, so he must have been alright. I told my mother. Not sure if he could read spin as a batsmen but he sure could deliver it. He became a barrister. Maybe he might consider defending a mechanic up on a murder charge. There were lots of rumours about Rees Davies. Google him now and you will find only reference to his 'louche' chambers. An odd choice of words, 'louche', signifying a questionable choice of morals. Further on you will find reference to a man who was described as garrulous, a maverick, a man about town. He had close contact with the criminal fraternity, too close some said, defending the indefensible. Yet he was a pillar of our establishment, a barrister and our MP. Strange how the establishment and the criminal element in society have always been close. Witness the scandal surrounding Lord Boothby and the Krays. The Krays liked to be men about town. Henry Cooper even opened one of their London clubs. But he was one of the good guys. We used to see him and his brother walk across Dane Park in the tea interval on their way to see their mum, I think. Might have been his in-laws though.

On one occasion after one of his Championship fights we lined up on the pavilion balcony and applauded him. He'd always give you a cheery wave. You can imagine him at Waterloo, probably as one of the Guards at Hougoumont. The French had a giant on their side, a Lieutenant Legros, L'Enforceur. Built like one of the Klitschko brothers, he caused terror for a while and wealding an axe smashed in one of the gates. Might have changed the course of this part of the battlefield. Our Henry would have stepped inside the axe and brought up that left hook, the 'ammer. As it was, one of the Guards had to shoot Legros. Not quite criket that, an axe against a gun, but hey. Our man in the dock though was not one of the establishment. He could not afford the fees for a top brief. Some men about town got by with accepting brown envelopes, or entertainment, from dubious clients, to keep them in the style they were accustomed to. Like most of us, he probably didn't even own a stock of ordinary envelopes.

Billy was our MP for over 21 years. Despite the rumours and his raffish lifestyle, he was popular with the voters. They liked their MP to be a character. Nothing changes does it? He is said to have been the first to alert the Solicitor General to the activities of John Profumo. In any case, Thanet was a safe Conservative seat. Most of our parents read the Daily Express so there was little chance of him being unseated. Better paper than it is now, with some classic characters. Chapman Pincher, John Gordon, the great Peter O'Sullevan, Clive Graham, Roy Ullyett. Not sure who covered cricket as a writer. Did Desmond Hackett cover that? They don't allow brown bowlers at the MCC so maybe not. I always used to read Hackett first, enjoying his elegant column, until they began to show football highlights on the television. I noticed that Jimmy Greaves had headed the ball in, whereas Desmond described how it had been volleyed with the right foot and each week other examples would come to hand. Alcohol is responsible for some of the finest prose ever written about sport. Parky might know about that. The view from the bar must be quite splendid. If you want marvellous social histories, including commentary on sport and culture, then I would refer you to Peter Hennessy, 'Never Again' and 'Having It So Good' being fine examples. I note that he is now Baron of Nympsfield, Nimet meaning holy place, which presumably denotes a field with an early cricket square. Very holy indeed.

However even beyond him, the greatest recorder of our times was surely Carl Giles. Christmas was never the same if the Giles Annual was not under the Christmas Tree, an oasis of peace and side-splitting chuckling amidst the hubbub of the many relatives. Grandma, Vera and the extended family, each cartoon lovingly penned in Ipswich and capturing the great themes of the day. Cricket naturally features from time to time and there is one in 1968 with Dad batting on the beach, amidst the 'Make Love not Peace' banners. The same year cousin Willy is shown standing at silly mid-off. Seems about right. The cartoons for 1965 show a seething blazered father who cannot get out to his cricket because of the rain and also some sort of MCC initiative for brighter and more active cricket. Giles of course takes this to its limits. Simple answer really and that was just to encourage more West Indian sides. The bowling was fast and the batting adventurous. Strate bats were only to hit the ball back over the bowler's head and not to block for half an hour while you played yourself in. Twenty twenty cricket in those days would have been thought at the MCC to be indecent. The cartoon on 29th August 1965 in the Sunday Express, one week after she died, would have been perfect today. Another seaside setting, might have been at Botany Bay for all we know. I think they might have filmed the opening shots of Hunderby in Botany Bay, rather than in Cornwall. Probably saved a bit of dosh. I think I saw a Klingonese interpreter listed on the credits, which rather gives the game away. The rain is slating down, the wind blowing the beach umbrellas across the sands. A rather large wife in sombrero and pac-a-mac is returning to talk to her husband lying soaked on his sun-bed. "Note from the office, Humphrey - the temporary man in your job is doing fine, so you can take another week ". Priceless. Could have been the summer of 2012.

"Do you believe in clubs for women? Only if every other form of persuasion fails".

Max Kaufman

Ken Higgs was recalled for the last test against the South Africans in 1965. Good medium fast bowler, Ken. A fuller length, relying on seam and prodigious swing. Variable and unpredictable. You would not know what to expect. Some of the many scientists at Cern must play cricket in their lunch-break, otherwise how can you account for their breakthrough on the secret of life. Pinter knew that cricket is the greatest thing God created on earth. We all know too, don't we, that particles are made up of bosons and fermions. Self-evident. It is obvious that the God's particle discovery will eventually explain the vagaries of swing. The Higgs boson particle. Named after our Ken, Ken Higgs, who once took 7 for 19 in an innings against Leicestershire, for whom he later played. Not quite in the Jim Laker class, but Jim of course was only a spinner. Photons feel no drag from the field and probably only want to bowl fast. Electrons feel less drag so might get in the second eleven. But the true opening swing bowler will be a Quark. They're not so good in the pub afterwards, to be fair they can drone on and seem to swerve around a bit when it's their time to buy. Only the English can really understand this sort of logic because, as a chosen people, cricket was God's gift to them.

Incidentally the second Large Hadron Collider was actually first successfully employed by Worf in the Klingon Civil War. It was later hi-jacked by the Neutrinos and abandoned in Switzerland, near a urinal. This could though just be a bad translation and maybe they meant laboratory rather than lavatory. The second pilot for Star Trek was screened in 1965. I never knew that Gene Roddenberry marketed the series as a sequel to Wagon Train, which had ended that year, a Wagon Train for the stars. Captain Kirk for Major Seth Adams. Ernest Borgnine once guested in an episode with Ward Bond called 'Around the Horn'. Not sure it compared with the stuff written by Took and Feldman. They had an episode in 1965 called 'Traffic Wardens in Space'. Much more suited to Star Trek. I believe the wardens slapped a parking ticket on the only Small Hadron Collider somewhere near Uranus and when the fine remained unpaid, the space bailiffs moved in and confiscated the vehicle. Was eventually crushed in a Klingon scrap yard. Only the second Large Collider survived, which is the one the Swiss must be using. There was a prototype, of which more later. Thank God! We will soon be able to pull back the large curtains draped across whichever set of heavens you believe in. The curtains will swing back ceremoniously, perhaps like in Oz, where the Wizard lives. Quarks rule.

The Dutch could not have invented cricket, not part of God's plan, but they may well have had a hand in field hockey. God was never too bothered with this, the white ball tending to get lost against the background of the angels' white tunics. We had some fierce games against Dutch sides, some of whom would appear at the Jersey Hockey Festival. I used to play for a wandering side from Cambridge City, the 'Strangers', and we were regular visitors there at Easter. Having played a hard-drinking side called 'The Partners' twice in previous years, we met in the clubhouse bar the night before a third match. It transpired that the one thing the Dutch enjoyed about cricket was our tradition to disappear halfway through the game to have tea. They thought this to be very English. We explained that the earliest versions were based on nipping off from the village green or holy square to the nearest place serving refreshments. Vicars' wives weren't then as skilled at the cucumber sandwiches as they are now, so the boys would have to make do with a few wafers and some communion wine. You can't hit sixes on a few wafers.

Pretty soon they moved on to the alehouses but then the innings of whoever batted second tended to be greatly reduced. Batsmen would swing wildly and often lethally under the influence, and bowlers would collapse in hysterics. The Hambleden Cricket Club song did indeed include the line, "He's best who drinks most". In some despair and desperation, teas were officially declared to be part of the protocol of the game by the MCC in the early 19TH century, although some attributed it to a large donation from a Mr Lipton. The MCC always denied this but the President shortly after moved to a new large house in Marylebone. The Dutch weren't too sure about this interpretation but at half-time during our hockey game the next afternoon, they and their wives brought on to the pitch a wonderful spread of sandwiches, cakes and pastries. We had a choice of teas, tables and chairs. Only the dormouse was missing. The entire occasion was finished off with several rounds of Dutch schnapps. An hour later and extremely worse for wear, we re-engaged battle, the match ending honourably in a draw. Later we returned the favour with a few crates of Grolsch. Sport at its best. No need for all this warming-up or stretching.

Tommy was our PE teacher at school and a fine sportsman, not to be confused with Mad Thom, from a different era. Tommy's predecessor, Mad Harry, had been a Chindit in Burma and believed that games lessons were largely about us running cross-country in bare feet and without shirts or vests in deep midwinter. I had pneumonia for four weeks after one of his sessions and went down to the 'B' stream for the rest of my days at school. He would organise us in boxing sessions and the trick was to find the few other boys who looked as if they wanted to fight but also didn't enjoy being hit. Tommy was a small man but liked to open the bowling at cricket, fiery and surprisingly quick. Could he swing the ball? Of course, he could, and it got better each time with the telling. He was always proud of having bowled Derek Underwood, when guesting for our club during the festival. Later in his seventies he joined the local bowls team and encouraged them to take on anyone and everyone. He feared no-one and could play with the very best in Kent and beyond, but he had a competitive edge which, of course, not everyone is comfortable with as you get older. It was not that he always wanted to win, but he wanted to play with style and he made his feelings known if he thought his colleagues weren't trying. At the age of eighty one though, he was in three club finals. The colostomy bag never once slowed him down.

His metier though was hockey. Sean Kerly once described him as the best hockey coach he had ever worked under. Nice clip on the web of Sean and the old boy sitting on the school lower ground, as part of the series during the Olympics encouraging youngsters to play sport. Thanet has a small catchment area but Tommy churned out year after year schoolboy hockey internationals, three in the team I played in. Not only did he teach us stick work, not me guv I'm afraid, but how to use space on a field. We knew what our position entailed both in attack and in defence and what to do when the opposition had the ball. We had a variety of routines for short corners and knew how to defend them. He loved to encourage men coming from the back so that unmarked you could score on the second phase. We never lost to other schools in full length games and rarely lost to men's sides. Tommy was thirty years ahead of his time and now I look at the number of coaches and support men football and rugby managers employ with some amazement. I might not have been able to play very well technically, but he taught me to read a game. Stayed with you. Until Thatcher damaged the ethos of teachers giving up their time on a Saturday, there was always a steady supply of similar men and women who would coach and umpire all sorts of school games. Great people. The best of times.

Now I read that government cuts have lead to a 60% drop in the amount of time dedicated to organising school sport. This at the very time another report says that lack of exercise is a bigger killer than cigarette smoking. As I write, the Olympics and Paralympics are finishing with the Brits triumphant, yet there are now one hundred and ten fewer School Sport Partnerships than in

2009. And I and my friends still get a winter fuel allowance that most of us don't need. This should not be a party political issue. It is plain common sense. Some of these so-called 'posh' boys and political geeks have very little interest in sport, even if they do all turn up at the medal ceremonies. While most of us were outside in the fresh air, they were becoming political careerists, research assistants and advisors, studying the small print, sat in committees in darkened rooms. Normal folk wouldn't touch it, but might be nice work if you can exploit your contacts, make a buck from your information. Oppose any motion or anything that is not your initiative, no matter whether it will be successful or not and always ask a price.

Another friend of mine worked at a union head office for many years. He still has his integrity and his idealism but he witnessed at first hand that even there not everyone keeps a strate bat. Of course there are good leaders but too often power corrupts. Salaries are bumped up, expenses and perks exploited. The Germans do these things so much better, both with unions and football, even allowing the supporters to be part of their football clubs instead of the amoral absentee landlords we now have in the Premier League. For a few dollars more. Not premier in morals or integrity, that's for sure. Is that why the Germans keep beating us at football? Mind you, Merkel doesn't look much of an athlete, she's a bit 'gove' like if you know what I mean. Mind you, we do seem to be a bit special at this sort of Olympic and Paralympic stuff, but that's the sort of comparison best viewed from the perspective of time.

"A politician will do anything to keep his job - even becoming a patriot"

William Randolph Hearst

Of course, there are limits to democracies like ours. The early days of the Russian revolution were amazingly democratic. They tried to vote on everything. Then the career politicians moved in and became frustrated when they began to lose votes. So they arranged meetings at inappropriate times, packed the committees and finally eliminated their opposition. I observed some of the career politicians at college. We had Maoists around then as well, waving little books and wishing to impose conformity. Little red book men. They tried to stop all competitive sport and games, largely by taking over committees and voting to cut all funding. The sort of people who would threaten to strike just as you were about to stage the Olympics, the biggest event in our generation. The main man has literally spoken today to his people at the conference urging them to embrace the spirit of the Olympics, conveniently forgetting that some of his more lunatic members actually wanted to strike, trying to stop all access to the games.

Politicians from which ever direction are the same the world over, playing politics with our lives, screwing the public. All for a few dollars more. The Maoists managed it too in three cases back in 1968 before they were rumbled, cutting all funding to sporting organisations. Cricket would have been stopped in its tracks and life as we know it could have come to an end. They probably all went on to have careers in the city. The fact that Ed Balls at least plays football, even if with the intent of a hockey goalkeeper, and ran in the marathon gives some small semblance of hope for any sort of sporting legacy. Schools need a much greater emphasis on exercise and fitness. It is not just about more team sports, more balls, as there are clearly always arseholes in proximity. Now there just seems to be a much larger collection. I have twittered in the hope that a guardian angel might appear, with a cart full of broomsticks. I am also advertising for 'a man with no name' to drive them home. Maybe there's a type of wizard that would fit the bill. And fit the broomsticks.

The patriotism we have witnessed over the last four weeks with the Olympics and Paralympics is certainly inspirational but can be a problem when it becomes a question of 'my country right or wrong'. The quotation is first attributed to Stephen Decatur in 1816 who had become the youngest captain in the fledgling US Navy and a war hero. However it is suggested that it was really meant to be a rallying inspirational cry rather than some sort of ethical statement. The theme was later picked up and developed over a number of years by one Carl Schurz, who lived his own version of the song of fate. He was a Senator in Missouri by the time Custer died, but would have known him reasonably well as both had German ancestors and served through the Civil War on the Union side. Custer had been promoted from the rank of captain just before the battle of Gettysburg, when both men were present. Five per cent of Americans at that time were Germans, over one million of them, and nearly all of the eligible men fought for the Union, often in their own regiments. They had a passion to ensure that this new nation would survive in the form that they admired, a passion that could be described as a type of true love. Many of them had learnt their early politics from an unusual source. Our physical education teachers were important to us at school as we grew up, but at the time of Napoleon's occupation of Germany, physical education or gymnastics became a popular movement in Germany for a different reason. The clubs or unions not only gave young people an outlet for physical activity but enabled political resistance to have some sort of structure.

The word for gymnast in German is 'turner' so these enthusiasts became known as Turners and even today there is a society in the States, the American Turners, founded originally by Germans fleeing the suppression of the revolution in 1848 and 1849. Their watchword is "a sound mind in a sound body". Perhaps the female descendants of Germans in the States have inherited the genetic bosom particle that their European cousins still proudly project, but hopefully don't insist on horizontal toilet seats. About four thousand of the Turners and radicals fled to the States and they tended to be free-thinking and articulate intellectuals, often anti-clerical and pro-democracy. Until the mid 1850's most Germans who emigrated had joined the Democrats, who opposed temperance and laws about keeping the Sabbath, but when the Republican party was founded many newer Germans were attracted to them. The vast bulk of German immigrants though continued to reflect the divisions in German society, evenly split between Protestants and Catholics and mainly bitterly still hating one another, with Catholics tending, perhaps surprisingly, to remain Democrats. Most of these immigrants, except those who disliked coloured people, and there were some, were quick to join the Union army. The Confederates always despised these 'Deutsche' who they liked to refer to as the 'Damned Dutch'. This is not surprising as it is always amazing how little geographical sense many Americans have outside of the States. I can recall on August 21st in 1968 being on a coach heading down to Boston when the sad news came over the radio that the Russians had marched into Czechoslovakia. No-one else on the bus had any idea of where Czechoslovakia was or of the implications of the invasion. It could have been on the moon as far as they were concerned. Plus ca change.

When the Prussian troops finally shut down the revolution in Germany in 1849, Carl Schurz had fled, after periods in Paris and London, to Philadelphia. Some of his other close friends were there already and had joined the fledgling Republican party, although I doubt any of them would recognise the party and its values in its current state. The Dutch and the Germans might be attracted by the English custom of taking tea, but they are also aware of the tendency for tea parties to be dominated by a collection of freaks and at least one mad hatter. Schurz quickly became involved and came to fame with his strong support for the anti-slavery movement and to the attention of Lincoln. In Kansas in 1856, well before the Wizard of Oz made his appearance, he made the telling observation, "I am not sure that this fight can be decided without powder". He was also instrumental, as the envoy to Spain, in persuading Lincoln that it was a mistake to hide the anti-slavery aims of the war and just that one factor was sufficient to enable an improvement in the popularity of the North in Europe. In addition he was one of the Turners who formed a ceremonial bodyguard for Lincoln, both at his inauguration as President and at his funeral in 1865. Joining the army as a brigadier general, Schurz was a keen student of war and moved up the ranks through the battles and setbacks at Bull Run, Fredericksburg and Chancellorville. At Gettysburg he was there from day one with the Eleventh Corps facing north and outnumbered by Ewell's troops, on the opposite side to Little Big Top. Easily out-manoeuvred on that side, which was poor defensive ground, by day three they had eventually retreated back through the town, losing almost half their seven thousand men and reorganised behind a stone wall on Cemetery Hill. This was quite ironic as he had been very critical of his superior Hooker's actions at Chancellorville when faced with the original stonewall, Thomas Jackson, whose troops had disastrously out-flanked them. The German troops had largely bolted and had been loudly derided by the Confederate press. Schurz's attempts to expose the cause of this were for a long time suppressed by the authorities.

When the neighbouring Ohio line was in danger of being over-run by the Louisiana Tigers at Gettysburg, Schurz personally led two regiments to a successful counter-attack. Bill Compton, the True Blood vampire, was originally a Lieutenant in the Louisiana infantry but the 28th weren't at Gettysburg so no chance of any unusual supernatural encounters. Not sure if he had been vamped by then in any case. By the way, Bill just seems to have exploded right in front of Sookie and turned into a God at the end of this current True Blood series, if you really want to know. He's probably a bloody sky-god now. Anyway after the war Schurz moved into journalism before continuing his career in politics and gave a number of fine speeches over the next four decades. His experience in Germany weighed heavily and he always stressed a desire for universal suffrage, honest money and integrity in government. Fat chance. Financiers and politicians then were not so very different from our own. He was to be seriously disappointed on several counts and it is always surprising that he didn't die of a broken heart, rather than from natural causes. He also spoke regularly against imperialism and it is in this light that we should judge his comments on patriotism and my country, right or wrong. He believed true patriotism was about ensuring dignity and free institutions and that the nation should be slow to anger and take offence. There's a thought. "If right, to be kept right; and if wrong, to be set right". In 'True Americanism' he had first set out his vision of the America that he hoped the nation would become in a long and emotional speech at Boston in 1859. However you need to forgive the comments that 'Liberty is like a spirited housewife' and that his listeners should not try not to break her pans and dishes if she misbehaves. Heaven knows what sort of kitchen Mrs Schurz ran.

I witnessed the deep patriotic principle at work at a Klingon-type summer camp many years ago. Each morning we would gather on the hillside overlooking the forest, the flag would be raised and the assembly would stand with their clenched right hands over their hearts. It was deemed to be mandatory that every day there would be a religious reading and eventually my turn came. There were a small group of aliens like me present and our main contribution to the life of the camp up to then had been to teach the boys how to play cricket. Best not go there but a man called Doug was the inspiration for this, having somehow managed to obtain two cricket bats. If you ever wish to establish a reputation for being not of this world, then try to explain the game of cricket to men who do not understand the principle that matches can last for five days and still be drawn. The camp members were baffled and largely concerned for our sanity. How on earth did this game of cricket ever become established in so many countries? It can only be because most of them formed part of our empire and actually had little choice other than to obey orders. To make matters worse and to confirm our eccentricity, I managed to persuade them to allow me to read to the Assembly, not from a religious source, but from a book I was reading.

'Vol de Nuit' by Saint-Exupery is a terrific book. Saint-Exupery was one of the first airmail pilots at a time when there were few instruments to aid pilots, so mostly they would fix their position from the stars or look out of the cockpit at the land below. Often cloud covered both the sky above and the ground, thus making flying exhausting and often terrifying. Parachutes were primitive and unreliable. The book describes how battling against nature in this primitive format can be just as valid in the achievement of manhood as many of the other activities proscribed for young men. Specifically Saint-Exupery argues that nature can provide challenges which are the equal of taking up arms and going to war. You do not need to go and fight in order to become a man. He of course had fought in the First World War and witnessed the carnage and futility of much of it. On a hillside in the middle of nowhere surrounded as far as the eye could see by forest, it seemed a wonderful message for young men to embrace. Look around you at the beauty of nature. Here is your challenge.

Wanting to try to modernise the message, I thought that few of those assembled would know much of the World Wars, so threw in what I thought was a soft reference to the war in Vietnam. Big mistake. What people heard was not that you did not need to fight wars to become men, but that you should not go to fight in the Vietnam war. Several of the older veterans were stripping off for action, my country right or wrong, and it was touch and go whether I would be hung from the flagpole. Fortunately these weren't men from the seventh century so tempers were quickly soothed and harmony restored. The celebration of the challenge of nature was accepted. The surrogate Klingons actually turned out to be wonderfully warm and welcoming hosts once they had accepted our eccentricities and I am sure much of that can be attributed to the introduction of the game of cricket to the camp repertoire. Who else but the English could God have chosen to spread the message deep in the forests of Maine. We actually had slightly less success teaching them the words from 'My Old Man's A Dustman', as the cultural divide was never sufficiently narrow to explain 'daisy roots' and 'cor blimey trousers'.

"There are only about twenty murders a year in London and not all are serious - some are just husbands killing their wives".

G H Hatherill

Do swings ever feel remorse? Do they rock back and forth at night in anguish? They at least can still hang for their sins, chains clanking in the wind. Remorse rarely features in dreams, it is best considered when you are awake. If you spend a lifetime with a person or at least know them intimately on a daily basis, are you more likely to repent of your actions than if it was just someone you had met the day before? No appreciation of their needs and wants, of the journey they had made to be here, at this precise spot. No top spot this, face down in the Dane Park grass. Face up actually. Or of the journey they had hoped to take, if they had lived. Family, friends, lovers, true love perhaps. Does familiarity breed contempt, so that a husband wife crime is more easily excused? Ah, I understand the quotation. Men of the establishment are used to power and authority. They expect to be obeyed and take resistance and argument as provocation. Look at the other quotations, Coward, Kaufman, Miller. They imply that women are lightweight, frivolous, provocative. Marriage, as in the old days, can still bring ownership. In many places today, sadly, just the fact of being born a woman implies a second-rate existence. Denial of being educated, of dressing as you wish, of working independently, playing sport, just being free to be whoever you want to be.

God forgive those women who still choose to defend men who deny them these basic freedoms. God forgive women who ever sit in judgement on other women as part of the oppression or who vote to continue it. With the addition of just three letters, laity can easily turn into hilarity, a form of grotesque joke. Does this desire for control, for male dominance, spring from the culture, from the religion? Surely not from God? What if, when the god particle is finally revealed, God turns out to be feminine? Would some of the men who rule and control, whether secular or through religion, be so confident as they approached St Peter or his equivalent? If here there are women who deserve the odd back-hander to keep them in order, then surely that should be put into context as merely the behaviour of a civilised people. My friend eventually told me that this was the case shortly before he died and he was a man who had form. Why was he still my friend? Friendships always contain an inordinate amount of baggage and before he had always denied hitting his women. I had challenged him several times over the years but always there was a valid excuse. Men and women are both creatures capable of deceit and there are two sides to every story. Abusers, whether of adults or children, like alcoholics, are very plausible. They are above all deniers. Remorse therefore is only possible when you accept that your action was wrong. My friend never did but he had become vulnerable, at risk. It was not the time to turn away.

'Murder most foul'. That film, by Agatha Christie, came out the year before in 1964. The indomitable Margaret Rutherford starred in it. Her father, William, actually bludgeoned her grandfather to death in the study with a chamber-pot well before she was born and did time in Broadmoor. Sounds like something out of Cluedo. Then when she was three, her mother hung herself from a tree. Hanging was legal then in any case, unless it was suicide. However you would not have wanted to try striking Miss Marple or Margaret Rutherford with anything, even a pisspot. What exactly is murder most foul? Is it about the method or degree of violence, the circumstances or the setting, the intent or the number killed? The death of a young girl by the seaside would engage the attention of the press, but the trial would quickly be over-shadowed by other darker events. On October 7th 1965 Superintendent Talbot of the Cheshire Police force called to interview a young man, Ian, in connection with a reported act of violence. A body was discovered in an upstairs room and nine days later the first body was found on the moor. Not Ilkley Moor though, Saddleworth Moor. The man was twenty seven, same age as our mechanic. There's a funny thing. And had a girlfriend, Myra. They pleaded guilty to three horrific murders of young people which later stretched to five. No doubt about their eligibility to the Marple club.

So our judgement, our umpiring, must needs be comparative. To take only one life is already better than taking five. If it is also done instinctively, without planning, so much the better. Alcohol or drugs can sometimes shoulder part of the blame and the victim's attitude is of equal import. Hatherill was a Scotland Yard Commander. He was quite clearly not PC George Dixon. He was careless with his words and the quotation is unfortunate. You will see it repeated only in articles about domestic violence and never in context. I hesitate to defend him, merely because I am aware of the extent of the problem, but he might have been a warm family man who would never have contemplated hitting his wife, or his mistress, if he had one. What we do know is that most violence or abuse, whether of adults or children, is related to family or someone close to the family. That can often be explained, if never excused, by the tensions within such groups. Murder by strangers or by someone you do not know well is less frequent, unless for personal gain. Sometimes sadly murder is a way out, an escape.

The answer in life is for men to stop trying to control women, whether for reasons driven culturally or from religious belief. Bullies, cowards and tossers. We know who you are. This is just not cricket. You will not get to heaven, whatever some demented fundamentalist buffoon has whispered in your ear, if you beat up or control women, whatever your status and beliefs. Even if you consistently bowl short of a length and have a dream of a swing, you ain't getting in. I should just say that personally I don't care whether any of you get in. I have thrown away my whites now and my cricket boots. I have already booked an alternative death, my place in infinity and beyond. Buzz Lightyear, you have a companion, a friend, in the next life. I'm heading for the stars and the universe, my hitchhiker's guide in my back pocket, to see the dolphins and the mice. I have faith and it's just as valid as yours. And without all the crap and flummery. See I read that all I needed to do was to listen to Mozart, then perhaps 'A Whiter Shade of Pale' and possibly Bob Dylan and that's what makes a believer. Hey, Mr Tambourine Man. In the jingle jangle morning, I'll come following you.

"W G Grace had one of the dirtiest necks I ever kept wicket behind".

George Cobham

Hockey goalkeepers share with wicketkeepers the reputation for being eccentric, at teatime a sandwich short of a picnic. That may be unfair, although on reflection perhaps not, but there is no doubt that to be fearless, it probably helps to be slightly mad. We used to play at Eltham, I think it was, a good South London side then. The opening bowlers were fast but we were amused to see, as they ran in, that the keeper was standing up to the wicket. When I went out to bat I noticed that he was quite old, a small sharp-featured wizened man crouching behind the stumps, but he had good hands and missed very little. I used to take guard outside the crease in order to hit the ball on the full more often, so keepers who stand up are a problem. My innings was even shorter that day. The bowler slung one down the leg. I left it and the keeper in a pre-arranged fashion removed the bails. It is uncanny how mannerisms are passed on through families, even when the physical resemblance is different. My father, brother and I all shared the same way of using our hands, of half closing our eyes, of posture. In this case the keeper's name was Eric and you could see the identical movements in his son Alan when he later starred for England behind the stumps. In 1965 Alan Knott was 'Young Cricketer of the Year'.

Gladstone and Disraeli both separately visited Margate, staying at the White Hart Inn in the harbour. Gladstone was a prodigious walker so would have strode across the golden sands, scorning the assistance of the donkeys. He was also a prodigious cutter of trees, even in his late seventies, and there was always some sort of ritual with members of his family at home as they produced the Christmas firewood. I thought the Lone Ranger said that God provided that. Must have been the black domino mask obscuring his vision, because the Bible doesn't have any stories of God as a lumberjack. Disraeli had probably just come to take the sea air, although he may have been writing one of his novels at the time. I always thought Vivian Grey was Dorian Gray's estranged brother, which is merely a reflection of the cultural wasteland that I sometimes inhabit. Gladstone was ultimately known as the 'Grand Old Man'. GOM, three letters yet again, of distinction, like DNA. Until that is in Parliament, Disraeli referred to him as 'God's Only Mistake' which must surely have brought the chamber down. Both I think will have turned left out of the Inn and to have been found in the Ruby Lounge next door, cradling their jugs of ale. Sadly Biff would not yet have been there to discuss the day's play in the park. Neither would landlord Les, so they may have been made to feel welcome.

Neither of these politicians had been a cricketer, although they both might have read The Pickwick Papers, with its description of the match between All-Muggleton and Dingley Dell. Capital game, though not in Dane Park. Gladstone was wanting to pilot his Home Rule theories before extending them to the Irish and may have been looking for a suitable test market. Thanet is in theory an island, Thanet supposedly a version of Tenets. This either means brilliant river or a place where a warning beacon is lit. OMG. Brill. Thanet used to be cut off when the Wantsum river was full, right up to the reign of Henry the Eighth. The Thanet Entertainments Committee, in commissioning their 1965 promotional video with Kenneth Horne, briefly considered the unique selling proposition for Margate in those terms. The catch phrase was to be, "Wantsum? Come to Margate". True story. Just look at the minutes held in the mayoral chambers' archive. They decided against, as most Londoners on a day-trip there thought that to be self-evident.

One day at the Folkestone hockey festival in 1970, I had been invited by a good college friend to play for his team of medics, St Tommy's by coincidence. Disappointing. Not a broomstick in sight. The final whistle went and as I passed the main pitch on my way back to the pavilion, I noticed that the game there was still in full throe. My local side was playing the star team that year, coincidentally a Dutch side, studded with internationals and guest players. Amazingly the score was standing at 2-2, but the superior skill and fitness of the Dutch had now told and Cliftonville were penned in their own half. The defence was desperate and everyone had dropped back to help. All except one small figure, hair receding and in long baggy shorts, standing isolated just inside his own half, leaning wearily on his stick. The Ville keeper, Beugg, blocked yet another shot and the ball was thrashed wildly up the pitch. The small figure was Tommy. As the ball flashed past, he shifted slightly and the ball somehow stopped and appeared to have stuck on his stick, on the reverse side, as if glued to it. He was totally on his own and had no choice but to set off slowly, almost in slow motion, towards the opposing goal, running in a crouched crab-like stance. The two full backs opposing him were lined up in single file, as was the fashion, with the keeper behind them.

As Tommy approached the first defender there appeared to be absolutely no danger, but he dropped his right shoulder back in an exaggerated fashion over the ball. His stick then rose in a slow arc over it from right to left, like the single windscreen wiper that veteran sports cars used to have. The arc was full and painfully slow. It could have been a wizard with a large slow motion wand. The fullback, international though he was, was mesmerised, took his eye off the ball and followed the stick through the air. He shifted to the right, over-balanced and Tommy pushed the ball past him with his reverse stick. Surely the man behind would spot that this elaborate performance was a ruse, a dummy. The windscreen wiper kicked ponderously into action once more and the second full back followed exactly the same routine. Just the keeper to beat and Tom was almost down to a walk. Hockey goalkeepers were always considered to be mad and in those days they would have only one intent. They would kick you as high in the sky as they could and if the ball was somewhere in close proximity, so much the better. This keeper was large and came rushing out, arms and legs windmilling. Dutch, see.

Tom stuck out his left arm and pointed dramatically out to the left wing as if it was where he intended to pass the ball. Of course, there was no left winger. John P was a ladies lingerie retailer by trade and had dropped everything to get back to defend. Lingerie can have that effect on you. He was way back down the field but the keeper hesitated anyway and glanced right. He stopped, tried to reset his position, only for the hockey stick to begin its giant arc again. The keeper went to ground to his right, full length, following the stick. Tom never actually touched the ball and it trickled straight ahead slowly past the feet of the prone keeper. He touched it once more to push it into the net, the whistle sounded and the Dutch wondered how on earth they had been beaten. Every schoolboy who left the school could attempt the Thomas dummy, the Telegraph even reporting a dummy being sold by a defender on the goal line in a Varsity match. Tim, another of Tommy's boys. I reminded him of the match one day forty years later when we were viewing the horses in the parade ring at Folkestone. He thought it had been his finest moment playing hockey and was quite overcome.

**"But when on Margate Sands, the British fair,
Safe in the flood the curling surges dare;
When here so many queens of love are seen".**

Edward Thurlow, Lord Chancellor

My aunt and mother would walk through Dane Park most days on their way to school and sometimes to Margate Sands. At the weekend they would go through the town past the Bobby's Department Store and down to Marine Terrace or up to Cliftonville. There were troupes of entertainers on every beach in those days. The black-faced minstrels like Mr Bones were beginning to be replaced by the pierrots, Harry Gold's concert parties, reflecting the desire for vaudeville and variety. There were dance competitions throughout the summer. My mother was always proud of the fact that she had won one of these on the main sands when she was about thirteen. Quite something then. By 1917, when my mother was only four, the bathing machines had already gone. Benjamin Beale, who invented the canvas modesty hood for them, died penniless anyway, his businesses regularly disrupted by the fierce winter storms that swept in. Modesty hoods seriously affected the sale of telescopes. Modesty hoods, eh. There's a funny thing. A lot of cultures like to have those. Men normally invent them and decide what is modest. Not the Klingons though. Mind you, they tend to date only other Klingons, believing non-Klingons to be too frail. You get Klingon enclaves I guess and they send off to the end of the universe to bring in their own, regardless of whether they speak the language at all. Sounds familiar.

Strange some of these religious and cultural traditions. The Clunc Clics are an unusual religion. You've never heard of them? Did most of their courting on the back seats of farm carts and then motor cars, with only a seat belt for protection. Some used caravans. Very democratic as they never minded what age you were. The religious elders were all called Uncles, so there would be an Uncle Ernie, a bit like the one in The Who album, all fiddling about. I believe there was even one called Uncle Jimmy. As it 'appens, the Clunc Clics had a strong break-away movement that sought to ensure a cultural difference by cutting off the left legs of baby Clunc'ers. Then a court in Clone - most Clunc Clics are cloned now, rather like Saruman's fighting Uruk-Hai - declared the practice to be abuse. The clergy were up in arms about the leg amputation ceremony being declared illegal. Made representation about their democratic and cultural rights. Then burned down the court and hung the judges. Sounds vaguely familiar yet again. Daft really because the practice would have had to be abandoned realistically, as so many of the Clunc'ers would have spent the rest of their days on one leg falling over. Would have had a bloody good Paralympic squad though. How important it is for our democratic principles that we allow religious freedoms to continue unchallenged. There should be equality of opportunity for men of all faiths to follow their traditions, whether practicing on boys or girls, whatever the result. Stuff any medical evidence to the contrary. Any doctor in opposition should be shot or euthanised.

Uncanny how events in life sometimes seem to have real meaning. Western Australia on a hockey tour to the UK. Played against the University on the Saturday and then my team at the time, Cambridge City, on the Sunday. We were playing well and I thought we would beat them. Much stronger and fitter than I had expected and we went down 2-1. Afterwards we entertained them regally with real ale and they entertained us with tales of home. Perth, much larger than Margate, but just another seaside place. Sun, sea, golden sands, swimming pools, lager, prawns on the barbie. They'd throw anything on the barbie. All the donkeys had been grilled and eaten. Aussies, just like Texans and Yorkshiremen. Three months later, down in Thanet for a 'do'. Tommy has been offered a job coaching the Western Australia hockey side. Can take the family to live in Perth. Amazing coincidence. I know his wife Shirley's not keen but try to enthral her for ten minutes with the tales I have had from these fine young men. She looked at me when I had finished and smiled. "I love that man dearly", she said. "I've had his children, followed him to hockey games, followed him to cricket games, followed him everywhere in that Dormobile. I'm not following him to bloody Australia".

He sent me a photo of her in the hockey team at Lausanne Girls School. My mother and aunts had all gone there, walking through Dane Park, past the Lodge. Out through the gates into Thanet Road. Then into Addington Road, past number 5, before turning left into Addington Street. You entered through large double gates into a pretty garden. The school was one of the only ones to have stayed open through the war, despite the bombing, and took boys in during that period. The Nissen huts had been greatly improved by the time my sister went there. Nissen huts were pre-fabricated corrugated steel structures, designed by a Major Nissen of the 29th Royal Engineers. They were portable, economical and fast to put up. Apparently the world record for erection was I hour 27 minutes. As I grow older, I sometimes struggle to emulate that. Small school though but tried to keep up a good standard. White blouse, navy skirt, navy and white tie. Julie must have first gone there in September 1960. Would have taken her about twenty minutes to walk to school each morning. You could walk to the right of the Park, along Dane

Road towards King Street, but it was a busy road and I have always found walking outside the park slightly depressing. Most of Dane Park was unfenced but on this side there were railings and thick bushes. Always better to dive left down into the park, taking the path that cut right through the middle, cricket square on your right. You could take the right fork, swing up past the cricket pavilion but then you went into more trees and bushes. Safer to stay in the middle. She would have known it like the back of her hand. Felt the back of his.

Queens of love, Lord Thurlow described. He must have meant the girls down from Wolverhampton for their two week factory or office break. Many people then would have a fixed two week holiday in the summer when everything closed down. We used to get many visitors down from Scotland or the Midlands. There was nothing my friends liked more, of an evening, than to venture on to Margate Sands, looking at the curling surges. There were often four of us, two Mikes, Mitch and I, out unsuccessfully on the pull. Mitch was a very good variable swing bowler, took a hat-trick in August 1965 when we were both playing for the A's. Bit like Flashman in 'Tom Brown's Schooldays'. The Bali Hai briefly and then the Coxswain pub were normally the place of last resort to seek out true love, before you reached the railway station. There, in the Coxswain, we fair folk of Margate paused in the doorway, gazing at the queens of love. Four girls down from Wolverhampton. Normally my tactical sense is acute, but dulled by the ale, I stupidly offered to buy the round for us and the queens. Four pints of best and four halves of lager. An offering fit for royalty.

I waited a while for the cheery bar folk to come to my aid. Ten minutes later I staggered back with a full tray, only to find that three of the girls had vanished, escorted across the road by my friends on to the Sands. Only one remained. A large girl with giant green earrings who seemed to have modelled herself on Beryl Reid's Marlene, in looks at least. Difficult to tell with all the make-up, but she did not seem too impressed with me either. I guess if she had smiled, her make-up would have cracked. Thought of talking to her about the Wolves football team, Billy Wright and Johnny Hancocks, but not sure how the question, "What do you think of our Johnny?" would go down. Thought she might just have thought that we only had one between the four of us. The Wolverhampton accent is not the clearest to interpret and neither of us knew Klingon, so we decided to leave the drinks on the table and follow the others. We had just reached the stairs above the Punch and Judy stall when screams were heard and three figures came running back towards us. Mitch had apparently got caught short and was adding his own curling surge to the flood. The other two had joined him and the queens of love had decided that the premature appearance of appendages, even for the innocent purpose of urinating in the sea, was not part of their protocol. They clutched Marlene as they ran and disappeared towards the Clock Tower. We returned to the pub forlornly and had the lager chasers as consolation. True love is such an elusive concept. I give to you and you give to me. How can a boy tell when a girl is serious? If she willingly walks with you on to the sands at night, you would dream of giving her something. What if you were in a park? Just read the women's magazines. When does no mean no? Or is it just that your presentation is lacking? Request more information? At that time of night, you are doing well to stand up properly.

"That a man should make the most of what equipment he has"

The Lone Ranger

We're all with you there, Clayton. Ex Texas Ranger he was, survived the Indian massacre in the desert until Tonto found him. Mind you, Texas has changed since his days. The men there are even more unreconstructed than Yorkshiremen, hard to believe but true. Just look at the recent legislation there. Men from the 7th century everywhere it seems these days. Clayton never visited Margate. Pointless if he had because he neither drank nor smoked. Would have liked the donkeys, but yelling Hi-Yo Silver on Westgate Beach probably wouldn't cut it. True enough, it was a place where you could always hope to make the best of what equipment you had. On the beach, in an alleyway, in the park. Inappropriate, you may think. Sadly I have no guardian angel. Unlike Saint Gemma Galgani, a Roman Catholic mystic, who said she had spoken to hers and that he had stopped her from speaking out at inappropriate moments. From the old photos I think someone of that name used to have a booth on Margate jetty in the summer, telling horoscopes, before the great storm of 1953. Didn't see that coming. Normally though you could cash in if you had a guardian angel or a time lord close at hand. On the other hand you may well have noticed that although most religions do have guardian angels, they all seem to have different versions of heaven. That will make the travelling to the cricket matches in the afterlife between different planes somewhat tricky. A jolly boys' charabanc would have to be a bit special to make the transition. Sadly that is where the first Large Hadron Collider could have come in handy. Those dodgy stone angels you see on Doctor Who, the ones that keep sneaking up on people, are actually the finest stone masons in the galaxy. They are also a dab hand as mechanics. They were called in to build a machine that could cross timelines and ultimately help solve the meaning of life.

Someone has to test-drive these carts before the time lords get on board, take them for a spin through time and space. Good idea getting the stone angels involved, except that the design briefs should always be posted to them. For goodness sake, don't turn up to a face-to-face meeting. Anyway they built the Large Collider prototype, tweaked the gigabytes, the quarks, the horsepower. You have to put the quarks before the horse. Off went Azariah, got into hyper-drive and hyper-dimensional mode and decided to test the time travel feature. Fatal flaw. The angels had built it with a magnetic field that reacted with stone. Brilliant really and quite unique. Azzie quite liked the

Romans, been watching Spartacus on television, and sets the dial to 121 AD, flying low and fast. Dials begin to glow and then the contact alarm begins to sound. Alarms were made entirely of quarks. What sort of sound do quarks make? Very similar to the noise you hear from a strangled duck.

Only one frontier wall built in the Roman Empire made entirely of stone. Where is it? Just south of Caledonia. Magnetic field overwhelms the Large Collider and it looks to self-destruct against the stone wall. Azzie can't reach the ejector, so pulls a cricket ball from his pocket and throws it at the red button. Shoots out of the machine, pulls the emergency ripcord on his wings and is up and away. Only part of the Collider that remains is the nameplate, broken in half. Hadron. Known ever after, or actually just for twelve months, as Hadron's Wall. Next year Juvenal, the Roman satirist, says to Hadrian if you're going over there Emp, might be quite funny to change the names around. Funnily enough, my stock in trade that, my last poem is all about what the legionnaires get up to overseas which we ordinary buggers wouldn't get away with. Went down a bomb in the Rome comedy store. Hadrian himself does visit the old country and heads north to the wall. Gets the soldiers to put a few more stones on it to make it a bit higher and renames it after himself. They all pissed themselves laughing. One of the good Emperors they always say. Liked women and boys. Famously got cross with his servant and put his eye out. Even in the greatest of empires, you have to dish out a bit of the rough stuff. Satirical really.

Old Bill wasn't around then but he was our regular spinner. He was getting on a bit in years and bowled very slow left arm. We could never work out how he got so many batsmen out, but he did, bowling on a length or just short of one. I think they fell asleep waiting for the ball to arrive. His wife used to follow him everywhere and would sit in a deckchair knitting, rather like Madame Defarge in 'Tale of Two Cities'. Did Bill's wife encode in her knitting the names of those batsmen about to fall to the wily spin of her husband. An association with fate? Certainly not vengeance, as Bill was a gentleman even when being carted over the boundary ropes. Ropes are purely symbolic here as we could not afford them and we are not delving into fifty shades of bondage. Vengeance is always a difficult subject, even when you are called by that name, like the blood-thirsty friend of the good Madame Defarge. Not sure what part it plays in cricket.

'Vengeance is mine, I will repay, says the Lord', Romans 12. What will you repay? A bar bill at the Ruby Lounge? The cost of repairing a window if the ball sails out of the park? Only ever saw anything close to that on the Dane Park pavilion side when the dimunitive Paul Hills, similar in stature and style to Colin Milburn, hooked a shot in that direction during a limited overs game. Vengeance is a term sometimes used by the media, for instance, to describe an India Pakistan game, but it implies extreme emotion and almost a hatred. That does exist between teams in all sports at times but it cannot be compared with the desire for vengeance for the taking of an innocent life. Where is the Lone Ranger when you need him most? Not sure about the silver bullets, though. Useful of course in cases of true blood and vampires. Bill Compton, for example, was in the Civil War but not sure he was ever a cowboy. He's a sweetie vampire anyway. Mind you, not sure about that now if he is going to become some sort of vengeful God. Perhaps just following the normal religious traditions. All you need is definitely not love. Not much call for silver bullets or even silver chains either in cases of murder, particularly where there is no question of true love. So that's why the guardian angel stayed away from our park. Sorry boys, no Cole Porter, no angel.

**"How do you like to go up in a swing,
Up in the air so blue?"**

Robert Louis Stevenson

Recently an Estonian Museum launched a new campaign called 'My Swing'. They wanted stories of self-made garden and indoor swings. Stories of how swings differed, of the vagaries of swings. The project coordinator, Liina Kanemägi, said that swinging plays an important role during Easter. Swinging in late spring was believed to facilitate crop growth, improve the health of cattle and increase fertility among humans. During the summer, young people had gathered around the village swings, the tradition never quite regaining its popularity after the first world war. The village swing is a compulsory part of the contemporary celebration of Midsummer Day in Estonia. For years groups of singers who gathered round tended to be capella vocal groups, as distinct from capello vocal groups which are sporting in nature, but later were renamed in Paris as swingles singers. Has it become a generic term, I wonder? Over here swings are viewed as less beneficial to the environment but are generally seen as gentle, passive things. They entertain us by their comforting rocking and have been known to chant rhythmically in a sort of capella tradition. Only when the velocity of the push becomes more exaggerated,when the velocity of the swing becomes erratic or unpredictable, do they and the occupant breathe more quickly and need to draw breath.

A swing is better with a pusher, a companion. The adrenalin always rises with physical contact. Push too violently and you might be swinging on a star. Pushing though must be done from behind, to the small of the back. It is rarely attempted from the front, by putting pressure on the throat. You are not trying to dismantle a car engine here. You may naturally wish to make the best use of your equipment, increasing fertility amongst any humans you see, but if there is resistance you must back away. The air, the night, is black rather than blue. The swing willed her to run towards it, to perch, to reach sanctuary. The trees will not save you. Trees are uncaring and passive although they like to pretend they give a sense of security and order. Yet in their regimented lines they are cold and impersonal in the dark. After he had left, the rain began to fall lightly, so maybe then they did play some sort of part in trying to give her shelter, dignity. If only she had got to the playground and the swing. What could be the theme Tracey? The last thing I said to you, is don't leave me here. Drag me up the slope along the grass, in a growing sense of realisation of what had been irreversibly done. He said when he could not revive her, he panicked and ran. Did they teach him resuscitation in the army? Too late though now, to press on her chest, however hard he tried. No salvation for either of them. Not even a guardian angel to watch over her till dawn. Just the trees and the swing.

You can see for miles and miles from Arlington House in Margate and can certainly just catch sight of the tops of the trees in Dane Park. Arlington House was the setting for the last of the BBC 'True Love' stories. Built in 1963 on the site of a salt marsh and the old Margate Sands railway station. Eighteen storeys of upmarket residential flats with a small shopping mall beneath. One of the blogs about the building describes it as a form of brutalist architecture. Presumably the sort of block of flats that might take other structures by the throat, leaving them prone and gasping on the ground, so that its view of the sunsets remains unspoilt. Naturally enough it would show no emotion at a trial. It has a fabulous prime site, but could never live up to its billing, the area around it becoming an eyesore, many of the flats, I was told, remaining unsold. I walked past it the other day. It now has some building activity opposite, social housing built in the form of large square huts. Could work because the position is so good, the sands which are Margate's strength a stone throw away. I used the public toilets on the promenade, they're handy as well. Couldn't perform under the Sundeck, it's gone. The Sundeck was actually named in many of the paternity suits. Some girls, three parts to the wind, just thought they had been visited by an angel. Darling, you would have known if it was a stone angel, as they tend to drive large Hadron Colliders with 'go-faster' stripes.

Maybe they should pull most of the Arlington arcade down and try again with some sort of piazza, now that people more regularly troop by to the Turner and with Dreamland hopefully about to be reborn. Someone must still live in Arlington House or they wouldn't have filmed the story. We only came to take notice of it in the winter of its first year. My friend, Brian, and I were walking down to Dreamland one Tuesday evening in the dark and the brutal Arlington was just displaying its first signs of life, like some sort of concrete Frankenstein. Crusaders was conceived one day that term when Brian announced on the way to school that he had entered a team in the new five-a-side adult indoor league. This was due to start on two mid-week evenings in October at the Dreamland Amusement Park on the site of the roller skating rink, which when boarded up was a long narrow walled arena. Chatham House had stopped any soccer after our second year so none of us really played regularly, although one or two of us had joined Hartsdown FC that year. We thought that Brian was mad, particularly as all of the top Thanet teams had declared an interest.

Not only did Brian not have a team, but we also faced the dilemma of asking our parents to let us play as we had homework every night. There were twenty five teams in the league that first year and only two other young sides - another older school team and the Margate Youth Club. Brian persuaded

Barry to go in goal, he went at the back and then Roger was just in front of me in midfield. Jeff, who looked vaguely like Kookie from Sunset Strip, was our marksman. With enormous trepidation we arrived for the first games - heaven knows how our parents let us out - wearing white shirts with a large red cross on the front, an idea nicked from the Daily Express. Thanet Crusaders. On the way to our first game, we looked up at Arlington House to see four lights flickering. That night we scored four goals. Ever after, we would glance up to the giant for an illuminated prediction. An octopus predicting correct scores, fantasy stuff. But a brutalist stone giant, well that's the real McCoy.

Although we were lightweight in build we were fast, agile and fit, and amazingly the narrow pitch played to our strengths. We learnt quickly not to take people on physically but to use the rebounds off the walls to go past them. On any full sized pitch we would have been blown to bits. In the first year we finished 6th out of 25. The highlight came in the third week of the New Year when we played Minnis Bay, the runaway league leaders and previously unbeaten. We went one nil up and were immediately under siege. All of the arena were cheering us on, David against Goliath, and somehow we broke away in the second half and scored again. We also then beat a very strong Garlinge side 1-0 - I hit the ball from halfway and it screamed in, like a gaggle of quarks. In the second year Smithie and Darbs joined and we finished third of 25. 1965 was the start of our final season and at Xmas we were lying second, eighteen then, stronger and very fit, before falling away in the second half. Girls, alcohol and the need to work weakened the format. There were no worst of times. Crusaders have no need of modesty hoods. They used to tear them off in the olden days, but maybe not for the right reasons. At that time of our lives, in this specific setting, we were good. How sweet it was.

"Cricket to us was more than play, it was worship in the summer sun".

Edmund Blunden

After our committee, flat caps and all, decamped to our neighbours, the Margate cricket club struggled. We had one excellent batsman and he became captain. Graham was a modern sportsman. As youngsters we had been influenced not so much by television screens and radio, but by a diet of comics, like the Dandy or the Beano. Then as you began to mature you encountered the Eagle, the Rover, the Lion, the Wizard. More bloody wizards. Characters there did not watch their diet, have toning sessions, consult sports therapists, warm up before games. My friend Andrew, who is now the birdman of Aberdeen, was briefly inspired by something he had read in one of the comics. As prefects at the school, he, I and our friend Ian had found that we had had no alternative but to volunteer for the house cross country event. Each of the eight houses had to field a team of six boys and no other buggers could be cajoled or bludgeoned into taking part to make up the numbers. Andrew had noticed that someone like Dennis the Menace had found a fruit diet which enabled you to reach peak fitness without training. He had researched this and had become supremely convinced it would work. On the day of the race he had done no running at all but had largely eaten just fruit for the last two days. We ran together in 46th, 47th and 48th place for about eight hundred yards of the five miles before he began to double up and retch, his race run. Ian kindly stayed with him until help arrived and also because he was finding it difficult to run whilst doubled up laughing. Andrew the next year went off to study at the LSE but presumably never turned out for their athletics team. His Mick Jagger impressions, on the other hand, were quite amazing.

I hesitated to join in the merriment because, of course, in the comics, athletes like Wilson, another Yorkshireman, would join a race for fun from the crowd in his working clothes. Never trained, yet he once ran the mile in three minutes. Made Coe and Ovett look like amateurs and Mo Farah would have stayed at home! Wilson was naturally supremely fit and could play any sport brilliantly, once even captaining England down under in a test match. Mind you he apparently had learnt to slow his heart down, a trick passed on by some northern hermit, probably gurning in slow motion like Les Dawson. There was also the 'Tough of the Track', Alf Tupper, who would bolt his fish and chips down, catch the bus to the White City and then out-run anyone. Even in his welding boots he would be too good for Johnny Foreigner. Denis Compton in

1955 once arrived for a Test against South Africa and had forgotten his kitbag. He disappeared into the museum and returned with an antique bat, scoring 158 and then 71. Where has that England gone? Not many of them in the comics played cricket though, there tending to be rather too many Roy's of the Rovers. I was also never too sure about Fisty Flynn in the Tiger. Sounds like a Dane Park sport and apparently he always kept something in hand. Graham, to be fair, thought we weren't serious enough and wanted to instil some discipline in the team. He noticed that one or two of the members, Biff and Mike in particular, were sometimes worse for the wear at 2.15 in the afternoon, so he banned all lunch-time alcohol before a match. The next game was at home. Unfortunately rather than deterring the boys, they took this as a challenge and decided to get completely ratted. I was not part of this, only arriving in the pub at 1.30 for a quick pint in sympathy. I'd seen Miriam Karlin in the Rag Trade. One out, everybody out!

Our Sundays at home were very much a ritual, warm and traditional, and practiced by many other families in the land. Cricket had for us boys replaced church on a Sunday although my mother fought tooth and nail to push me through confirmation. I was alright until our vicar decided that we needed a talk on his hobby of bird-watching. Talking to a group of fifteen to sixteen year old males about the tits he had seen lately in the vicarage garden was not conducive to good order. My parents had the radio on continuously on a Sunday, taking us through a mix of the Archers, Have a Go with Wilfred Pickles and Two Way Family Favourites. My vocabulary stretched from 'are yer courting' to 'with a song in my heart'. It was the day though when we all sat down to a good roast with Yorkshire pudding and if I had a cricket match I would be excused drying the dishes.

There is a scene, yet again in Pickwick, where a slim Dingley man is described as trying to catch a ball, only for it to strike him on the nose. The hollow in Dane Park is pronounced on the pavilion side and fielders run down towards the pitch to pick up the ball. The boys were very drunk but Graham, busy with the opposing captain, had not noticed. The boys could hold their liquor well, they were pro's. It would have been fine if we had batted first as they could have slept for a while, but Graham lost the toss and we had to field. First over, Willie bowling. The batsman misjudges the ball and it lobs up in the direction of square leg where Mike is fielding. It is an easy catch. Mike begins to run down the slope, but as he approaches the ball the effects of the alcohol begin to affect his balance. He gains momentum and at the same time is starting to pitch to the right. He still has enough about him to try for the ball as he tumbles and it hits him smack on the middle finger of the right hand. The skipper at first applauds the attempt and rushes to the prone player, whose finger is resting at an odd angle. It is broken and must be exceedingly painful. However Mike feels very little pain, the alcohol numbing any feeling. He is in fact lying on his back gazing at the sky and laughing. Worshipping the summer sun. He went off to hospital to have his finger set and was dropped for the next two games.

In August 1964, a year before our murder, the last man to hang in England, Peter Allen, died at Liverpool prison. Didn't know much about Liverpool until the Beatles broke through. Wonderful now with all of the re-development along the waterside. My dad had manned an anti aircraft gun in defence of the city, second most bombed in the country, but like most of the men in the war he didn't like talking about it. He always felt guilty that he had not been sent abroad, but most of the lads on his course were sent to the Merchant Navy where life expectancy for gunners on the convoys wasn't too good. My brother had taken me to my first real football game at Fulham, Jimmy the beard, Johnny Haynes et al, against Liverpool. Because it was a late decision we had to stand fairly close to the front. The only thing I remember was not the score, it was being told to keep my hands in my pockets in the heaving stand, as some fans had a reputation of urinating in coat pockets in front of them. Couldn't hang them for it. The Homicide Act in 1957 had made a distinction between capital and non-capital homicide and then in 1965 Parliament voted to suspend the Act for five years, substituting mandatory life imprisonment. He wouldn't have hung anyway for anything committed in Margate. Maybe if she had been a prison officer, a police officer, or had a sister with her. And he needed to have done it a bit earlier when he was younger. Tough, eh, trying to work out the fine distinctions in the law when all the street lights are off. Where's George Dixon when you need him?

It is worth just clarifying for the cricketing purists how this celestial cricket is going to work. The MCC have as yet failed to give a lead so it may well fall to the jurisdiction of the International Cricket Council. Until 1965 it was called the Imperial Cricket Council, which I believe truly reflected the gift of this game, this religion, to the English. It was granted us to take out to other countries, to build an Empire, to become a civilising influence across the galaxy and the heavens. In Buddhism there are several heavens, which is a problem unless you create a league system. Heaven is of course temporary, so cricket, with its seasonal nature, is just the job. I have always joked about being reborn as a hedgehog, so that my kids could remind people to drive carefully when they leave the crematorium. Can't set these leagues up on different planes though and find you're sent out to bat with a large hedgehog, even a sonic hedgehog. Need to be some laws on rebirth. Didn't Arthur Dent keep on being reborn and killing Agrajag? How did he manage it?

Christianity is simpler because not so much travelling, just one heaven in the main. Hopefully God just gave the cricket to the English and doesn't want to join in. Firstly who on earth is going to bowl God out? Secondly, if he was batting, Colin Cowdrey would have to move to second slip, as Jesus would be to the right hand of God. He'd be first slip. The wonderful Lionel Blue might know something of Judaic cricket. Their concept of afterlife is said not to be precise, sort of neither here nor there. Mind you I have seen a quote by someone called Rabbi Yaakov. "Prepare yourself in the lobby so that you may enter the banquet hall". Now that's the sort of talking, banquet halls, that would attract my friend Biff. If it was a CAMRA banqueting hall he'd be there already, cradling his pint in one hand, a bowl of chicken soup in the other. Must talk about Islam, despite the threat of fatwas, because they have some fine cricketers. I used to think that a fatwa was only against people who were tending towards the portly, like Biff. Heaven is often apparently viewed in physical terms as somewhere where every wish is fulfilled straightaway. I could learn to swing the ball, score a hundred, hit the birdbath every time. You get very good banquets as well, so there would be some cracking teas. Seven levels so seven leagues. The costly apparel might put a few off. Might become like tennis where only wealthy people can afford to play but at least the rich get saved. Sunni, yesterday my life was filled with pain. Sorted really though, don't you think?

"Reading poetry and watching cricket were the sum of my world, and the two are not so far apart as many aesthetes might believe".

Sir Donald Bradman

Bradman the legend. Crowds flocked to see him. My brother said he had been taken to watch him one day but I was too young. My brother and I rarely played cricket together for Margate because of the age difference. He played when they were a strong side and was a fine batsman. He had scored a century on her last Saturday on earth, against a London side, Alexandra Park. If he had a weakness, it was his inclination to play spin bowling rather like Marshall Ney at Waterloo or General Foch with his spirit of the offensive. He would advance down the pitch full pelt and, when I last viewed old newspaper reports of our games, stumped tends to be the description most used for his dismissal. There was an old boy called George Pope, I think, who used to bowl very slowly from behind the crease and toss the ball high into the air. Sort of absurd donkey drops. My brother knew how to play him in theory, but unfortunately failed to hit the ball on either of the two occasions where he tried to despatch the first ball full on the volley. It never deterred him in the least and in the pub later the strategy would always prevail. He would convince himself that he had been unlucky and that the next time things would be different. I used to watch him play on occasions and always prayed that he would be batting against the quick or medium pace men. Once the slow bowler was summoned, then it was time to head off to the ice cream kiosk or pick up the poetry anthology again.

Lennie and Peter were also brothers, both playing but again mainly not at the same time. Lennie was the extrovert, a ladies' man, tall and handsome. He played football for the town in goal and batted three or four for the club. He always wore his collar up rather flamboyantly, most unusual for the time, but could hit a ball prodigiously. He was not a man who would admit to reading poetry. His brother was quieter, a gentle humorous man, who used to open the innings. Solid player who played for years for the team. He liked to anchor the side. I have always felt guilty about the way he eventually retired, but felt slightly better on reading a piece by Martin Williamson from ESPNcricinfo. In 1978 against New Zealand, Bob Willis sent Ian Botham in when Boycott was batting very slowly with the instruction, "Go and run the bugger out".

Martin opened his article by describing the above as a scenario we had all experienced in club cricket. The problem when you only played at the weekend, before league cricket of course, is that there was a general procedure for club cricket. The protocol was for one side to bat from say 2.15 to close to 5.00. They would then declare, tea would be taken and play would resume at 5.20, giving the team batting last slightly less time to make the runs by 7.30. With a bit of luck, you could be in the pub no later than 8.00. You had waited all week for the religious experience, given up a whole afternoon to play this infernal game, and even if you performed badly you liked to think that you had had an opportunity to contribute. One particular day we batted first and lost two quick wickets. Peter decided to anchor the innings. Unfortunately, against bowling which was not particularly good - we had played this team before - our number four also put his head down. At 4.00 we were 20 odd for 2. We began to urge and encourage both batsmen to advance the score but they continued with straight bats. By 4.30 they were approaching 30 runs. The fielding side were pretty fed up as well.

At this stage the encouragement became more heated and eventually abusive. The rest of us would have no more than 30 minutes to cart the ball around to enable a declaration and of course experience said that you would get out doing so. Our number four batsman got very angry with the shouting and sledging from the pavilion, swiped wildly and was bowled. Our next batsman immediately and quite deliberately ran Peter out first ball. I think he gave up cricket shortly after, which was quite sad. A less sensitive man would have behaved as Boycott is said to have done, draped a towel over his head and sat there muttering. Perhaps he had a poetry book under the towel although I am not sure Geoffrey was ever an aesthete. Even great batsmen have problems with temperament and control and indeed sometimes with their women. Difficult though always to judge, to be an umpire. Who do you believe when the fielders appeal? In life both men and women can be devious, cruel and will brazenly lie. H. L. Mencken said that,"a gentleman is one who never strikes a woman without provocation". How many blows does an act of provocation permit? One, two, several? Do hobnail boots count, as in the case of poor Mary Ann who died in Margate? How about murder? In cricket there are markings to give the game structure. In life, where do you draw the line?

Douglas Adams used to write sheer poetry, but as he claims to have done little work at college perhaps his brain was fresher than most. It is almost impossible to improve on the 'Hitchhiker's Guide to the Galaxy'. Adams was quite splendid. Apparently he had the idea of the Krikkit Wars for Doctor Who, but it was rejected by the BBC so he developed the complex side-plot with a Wikkit Gate and a silver bail for his own story. In short a troop of robots attack Lords cricket ground and Arthur retrieves the Ashes from them by bowling a cricket ball. He takes flight, literally, with the ball and disarms a robot about to detonate a cosmic bomb. Our Krikkit Wars came to a head in December 1965, when the Committee finally resigned, almost en masse. As a very junior member of the committee, I did not resign. Above my pay grade. In the summer we used to turn up weekly at Don's house on the Canterbury Road, near the church.

Don was a very large character. Tall, bespectacled, well built, large hands and very large feet. Had moved down from Grays in Essex and passionate about cricket. Loved the game, almost a true love, and quickly became the Margate Secretary. There has always been controversy in the game about fast bowlers' actions and what constitutes throwing or chucking. Law 24.3 says that for a ball to be legal, the elbow should not be straightened partially or completely. It divided players and even Bradman said that this was a most difficult subject. As difficult as the debate about domestic violence. Our Don was a quick bowler. No subtlety here, swing eluded him. He hurled the ball down fiercely like Zeus with a thunderbolt, but with a straight arm. We had had the Meckiff storm, Geoff Griffin and then Charlie Griffith. Today Muralitharan has stimulated intensive study of his action and some are still not convinced. The aesthetes amongst our boys weren't sure about Don and it spilled over into the politics. The committee, led by Don, did though work ferociously for the club and things came to a head when they asked for help with the Cricket Week.

The Festival involved a whole week of cricket at Dane Park. A lot of people came to sit in the deckchairs and watch, there was a beer marquee, bunting and good invitation sides. Everyone who has ever been on a committee knows the problem. There are those who are prepared to lend a hand and others who just want to take part. The latter are in the great majority. What tipped the Committee over the edge was just a few kids on bicycles showing off. One day they rode on the pitch and were shouted at. They kept doing it so eventually were chased off. Became a game every day and then they pulled the bunting down at night and finally tried to trash the marquee. The police obviously had better things to do. Margate Council were apathetic and basically couldn't care less whether the cricket festival continued. Adding to this was their attitude to staffing the small café in the park that served the team teas on weekdays. Service was slow and the food was a reflection on the current debate between Jamie and Michael Gove. Curious how often very bright men can be a sandwich short of a picnic. The murder at Dane Park was another irritant. The guys were obviously fed up with the Council, the yobs and then their own players. Here were the police closing the park and refusing to give any information on when it could be re-opened. The more we pushed, the more high-handed the replies. I remember the feeling in Don's sitting room. Some stupid girl. Probably deserved it. Park's full of hooligans at night. Police are tossers. We've already lost one match and now we have others to organise. Get your priorities right. These were men to whom cricket was their religion, their life.

On the 1st October, well after the season had closed, Don's fury erupted in a letter to the Isle of Thanet Gazette. It covered two columns and slagged off everyone and everything. The Council had refused to employ a park keeper, to fence off the park, to employ a night security man. The food at the café was poor, the service slow. In hindsight it was not a clever letter, however true and whatever the provocation, as it alienated any of our potential supporters on the council. The council responded with their normal indifference. The Gazette of 17th December carried the headline that four key men had resigned from the Margate Cricket Club en masse. Don, George, Bob and Mike, who had gone with George. Before then, that very summer, two or three other key players had retired, fed up with the atmosphere, or had left the area. The poetry would never be the same again. As the year ended we felt that success in the 1966 season would be elusive. Swing would just have to take its chance.

"Crime belongs exclusively to the lower orders"

Lord Henry in 'Dorian Gray'

How absurd this sounds now in these days when society is afflicted by so much white collar crime. Many of the ruling establishment, once in power, effectively steal from the people, transferring assets to tax free havens. Banks collude and operate on the fringes of legality, giant firms of accountants sign off their audits and those charged with holding them to account, the umpires, have been found to be at fault in both houses. In the old days there seemed to be a connection between crime and the club scene. Now money can be poured into a different form of club, employing over-paid knobheads. There will soon be a new footballing verb, to havelange. Can cricket be regarded as on a different plane? Sadly not, as the recent flurry of activity around illegal gambling in cricket shows. What we need is some sort of avenging angel to smite them all, maybe a man with no name. Clint would fit the bill. Well he would have done in the old days, before he let the furniture get the better of him. In 1965 he was in the middle of the trilogy from Sergio Leone. The following year, in my quest for true love, I believe I encountered the good, the bad and the ugly all in one night in the Cinque Ports pub. Eastwood was playing what is a fairly stock character in Westerns but this was apparently adapted from Kurosawa's 'Yojimbo'. Both involve an unorthodox sense of justice and great proficiency with some sort of weapon. So that's what I was doing wrong.

The Lone Ranger had the right equipment. Cricket or baseballs don't count. It gets more complicated when you are told that all of this had its origin in a 1929 novel called 'Red Harvest'. The author Dashiell Hammett, who also wrote The Maltese Falcon, was in the Pinkerton detective agency and used his experiences as the basis for his writing. Personville is clearly nothing like Margate. No-one either who could kick in doors and carry out an act of vengeance. On the contrary they sent a Detective Sergeant Salter up to the South London suburbs at 9.15 on the Sunday evening. Why on earth didn't our man dump the shirt and the other gear? Even in Dock Green the villains would have tossed them in some nearby dustbin. He had even hung up his grey suit. I guess if you don't have that many clothes, as most of us didn't, they become important, particularly a suit. You look after them and the thought of stuffing them in a dustbin bag would be distressing. Quick response to the police of, "I don't know anything about any murder". Dirty Harry would have smashed him with a point 44 magnum, or a baseball club.

That very morning the Morris van had gone from Addington Street, round the corner from Addington Road, on its way back towards London. However because he had booked into the guest house officially on the Saturday afternoon to have a room for the sex with this Judy - a different Judy to the one I knew hopefully - they knew who he was. They had arrested his mate James anyway, by sheer coincidence, on the Saturday evening at 11.15, presumably on suspicion of possession of drugs. James and the others had headed off that night for the bar at St Mildred's in Westgate but he decided to stay in Margate, as Judy had promised to return. Pretty fateful decision that one. My friends and I would have been in Millie's that night, in the Tudor Bar, as it was always a good venue to drink in, that and the Nottingham Castle being the two principal drinking places in Westgate. The Tudor Bar in St Mildred's appears sadly to have disappeared now although the building is still there. Not normally much trouble there though in the old days.

After holding James for a couple of hours in the station, Detective Inspector Percy Towler went round to his lodgings at the 'Mad House' at 2.30 early on Sunday morning. They parked the police car round the corner in Addington Street in front of a Morris 5 cwt van. By 3.00 am they had finished the search of rooms Six and Eight and departed, although noting with commendable attention to detail that the Morris van had gone and that the rain had stopped. At the time, they did not recognise the significance, but why would they. Not sure if the landlady appreciated being woken up at that time, although she thought it was earlier. Times are important and the police would have been precise. James appears to have stayed at the 'Mad House' a few times before, so he must have known the drill and that his Birmingham friends were of like mind. Obviously had not thought there was any danger of being raided by the police so there would have been no attempt to hide any gear. His suggestion to travel down, I bet. A few beers, tablets, maybe easy money and easy women. At this point though, Sherlock Holmes might have drawn the attention of the police to "the curious incident of the dog in the night-time". Our man initially said he had heard his dog in the van bark. Why did he bring the dog in any case? It was a cross between a labrador and a greyhound, black with a white front and he was probably very fond of it. Dogs, of course, do like the seaside and particularly beaches. Maybe that was the thought.

My brother had a golden labrador called Tamburlane, Tammy for short. His girl friend, Paddy, had given him this puppy when he went off to the Army in Germany, which was probably a big mistake. Far from slowing him down I believe he found that it was like having your own on-line dating agency. Who can resist a golden labrador with a wet nose? Not sure I would have wanted to call out 'Tamburlane' across Garlinge rec, the highlight of our youth being the large desolate recreation ground where we would meet for soccer kick-arounds. If you ever left the side gate open at home, even for an instance, the dog would be gone. Runners not fighters. It would somehow traverse the very busy main road and then head for the beach one mile away. You had no chance of catching it. It just loved the water and would stand in the sea barking, trying to encourage someone to play with it. To get it back we would drive along the cliffs and stop, just listening for the barking.

One particular day when the two of us were down training, playing hockey on the beach at Westbrook with the tide right out, the dog was with us and as usual headed for the water, standing in the shallows. We ignored the barking in the distance, but suddenly noticed that a group of holidaymakers had decided that Tammy was in distress. Now Labradors are phenomenal swimmers so there was no chance of that. However the holidaymakers formed a human chain of at least fifteen people and begun to edge out to save him. Each time they got to him he would move further out in the water. The front six guys were now waist deep in water. And none of them seemed to have bathing costumes. They had rolled their trousers up and got stuck in. Heroic really but we weren't sure what the reaction would be if we tried to explain that the dog was fine and we had just been ignoring it. Cowards to the last, we decided that discretion was the better part of valour. My brother whistled twice, the dog shot out of the water past the human chain and ran back to us. Fortunately we grabbed it first time and were off for the car. As we looked back, the line of very wet holidaymakers was still struggling out of the sea. The vagaries of dogs. We made a hasty exit.

Seaside resorts have also traditionally been places where people can hide away. Transitional populations, a great deal of movement. People whose relationships have failed or are in trouble. In Thanet it is harder to lose your identity now because of the shortage of employment, particularly casual. To survive you need to apply for some form of state benefit and then, of course, you are on the system. They know where you are and in any case without much income you may have to resort to desperate measures. Charles Dickens observed on his visits to the area the presence of boys from the 'Ragged Schools'. It was thought that the sea air and the atmosphere would do them good and instil in them some traditional values. When we grew up, we were never aware of any similar presence. Problems always came from the casual visitor. Somewhere over the last thirty years the Councils have got the balance seriously wrong. The problems are now well documented and when Thanet MP's publicly express concern you realise its extent. One third of care homes in Kent are in Thanet and not one child originates from Kent. They have all been sent away by London boroughs or the like, doing the

Lambeth walk, eh?. Some of the local blogs from people who actually really care about the place, some of the stories about streets where potential predators are now known to live in significant numbers, are quite amazing, sad. The stories about Thanet being over-subscribed with problem children has of course been widely reported and maybe acts as a magnet. Brian and I used to belong to a club on Walpole Bay promenade, a ship-spotting club. We had moved on from train spotting. It was run by an old boy who had a large telescope. No really, he did have a large telescope. If you were a member of the club, you could look out to the sea at the ships free, if a member of the public it cost. You looked for the colours on the funnel and then the name on the stern or the bows. Maybe the club still exists there, just changed its target.

How the hell you recover from such a basic error in allowing people to gather together like this. There is no duty of care for either party, and it would merely accentuate the difficulties for anyone wanting or trying to reform. There are two things that largely set off vigilante behaviour, the sort of reaction that Eastwood or Charles Bronson would take. Men or women who abuse children or abuse animals. Kill a girl in a park, you might live. Kill or abuse a young child, you need to hide. Maybe look to live near others for protection. Form an association, see if there are any hobbies you can share. In his first statement he did talk of hearing his dog bark in the van early that Sunday morning. He said he let it out and walked it around for ten minutes. He certainly had the dog with him in the pub and the bowling alley on the Friday evening but to bring it doesn't seem the wisest course of action. How long did he leave it for? Overnight and all the next day, except for a couple of walks? Holmes would have concluded, "the dog did nothing in the van". No wonder, if your master is mainly concerned with having a good time. I think he loved the dog, so maybe he was really attentive and fed it regularly. Those animal activists are the scariest of them all though. Watch out for them boy, men with masks and no names. They don't mind murder of humans, but possible neglect of a dog! Never let them know where you're living.

"There is a glare in some men's eyes which seems to say, 'Beware, I am dangerous'".

Walter Bagehot

William Munny, Josey Wales, Frank in 'Once Upon A Time In The West', Hannibal Lecter, Anton Chigurh. Men whose eyes give little away and then change in an instant, narrowing, the intent hostile. Yet there are also men like Vito Corleone, who smile and cause you to relax, making an offer you cannot refuse. Which poses the greater threat? On the sporting field the man to heed is rarely the one who mouths off. It is the one who just looks and smiles in a certain way. There is no evidence at all that our mechanic was dangerous from any of the statements from people who were there. They just accepted him into the group. The police years later referred to him as dangerous, but then he had done a runner. He slept on a chair in the guest house the first night before getting into bed with James for a couple of hours. Mates could do that then without any undue sexual associations. Was that just because he was short of cash? No, that can't be, because he was seen to give Julie a ten shilling note. Who remembers ten bob notes, withdrawn in 1970? Had the old Queen's face on them, Elizabeth's not Danny La Rue. He'd seen Julie that first night briefly with that Birmingham lad, Wally. She'd been in bed with him. Wally seemed to have lost interest in her the next day, bloody typical that. Really upset her. Tara said Julie compensated by taking some tablets, green and white ones she thought, with some milk in the toilet. Of all the witnesses, you feel you can quite like Tara, despite being only thirteen years old. Down from Birmingham for the summer and staying in Westgate, she tried to comfort Julie both in the Tahiti and in the Bowl. Had met her the year before and told her straight, go home, both when she was on a real downer and then when she had topped up again. White as a ghost and very agitated. She was sitting with him by now, after having taken the money for more tablets.

Julie was starting a new job in the Department Store as an assistant on Monday. Probably at Thornton Bobby's. My aunt worked there at first before branching out into her lingerie business in Alton and she did really well for herself. Quite exciting, starting a new job, but you won't last long if you continue to knock the pills back. The ten shillings, by the way, wasn't one of those that Miss Milko had been giving away. We do know that Julie gave it to Declan who probably gave it to Joyce. Julie's new friend had already taken tablets himself in the Kent yet his tablets were brown and white whereas in Quadrophenia they were blue. Might have learnt to take them regularly in the

Army when he was driving, to lessen the fatigue. He knew Julie had slept with Wally, but he wouldn't have known the context. Wouldn't have known anything about her, unless Wally had said something when they were all in the Kent together early that Saturday evening. He just had a perception about what her behaviour might be, if he had the chance. Actually asked Joyce if she thought Julie would go with him, because he didn't think so. Later, when they were together and she didn't respond in character, it irritated him, pissed him off. It triggered the anger.

What triggers my anger and sadness is that we really did think in 1965 that the times they were a'changing. All you need is love. Naïve,eh? Mind you, we thought that too when Tony Blair and Labour initially came to power. Barnum could have warned us. Good old Lord Acton too. He was the man who famously said, "Power tends to corrupt and absolute power corrupts absolutely". Funny how all these politicians bang on about family life. Juvenal could have told them. Satire Fourteen, "Avarice is not a family virtue". Enough said. He's thinking of returning to politics. No, not Lord Acton. He's dead. Michael Caine was in "The Man Who Would Be King". Wonder if Kipling ever thought to write about a man who would be President or even perhaps the next Pope. The golden rule? Keep a strate bat. In cricket, not in life. In life, he who owns the gold, makes the rules. Make a fistful of dollars, and then a few dollars more. Standard establishment DNA. Ability to disappear up your own arse, pulling behind you a large wheelbarrow of loot. Now that does require help from a wizard and a very large broomstick. Colonic irrigation might help.

Let us return to Margate, small town but still very establishment. Difficult almost fifty years on to understand the atmosphere. Our generation felt we were immortal and that we knew better than our parents. After all they had let the world war develop, had done nothing to prevent it. We were smarter. We had read 'Lady Chatterley's Lover' to understand the basics of sex and the court case against censorship had been won. Films like 'The Knack', Michael Crawford and young Rita, just back from 'Doctor Zhivago', would teach us how to succeed with females, to pull girls. So it wasn't just half a lager? With the music explosion and pirate radio it was a new dawn, a new day. Yet look at the Isle of Thanet Gazette leader comment on 2nd July 1965. "Regularly the question is asked these days, 'are the pop groups on the way out?' The sooner they disappear, the better". As the Rolling Stones celebrate fifty years together, you do wonder whether the Editor was all there. Maybe he had gone to the fortune teller on the jetty, that Roman Catholic mystic who could commune with her guardian angel.

I have mentioned that Thanet became a terrific source of good hockey players. However as a source of cricket players or murderers, it seems sadly deficient. If you study the long list of wonderful Kent county cricketers, the Cowdreys, Godfrey Evans, Les Ames, Doug Wright, to name but a few, I could find no-one who had started their careers back at the old home town. I did have hopes of the 'Lion of Kent', Alfred Mynn, probably the most famous cricketer before WG Grace. Over six foot, twenty stone and shoulders like an ox. Kept a tankard of ale by his bedside. Had to be a Ruby Lounge regular. Swung the ball both ways and took 12 for 88 playing for Kent against England. Sadly, born in Goudhurst. What was it young Phil Tufnell said, "You can't smoke twenty a day and bowl fast". Listen young Phil, most of our quickies all smoked at least twenty a day and look at them. Mind you, they are all dead now. We've missed out on the murder front as well. Must be something in the air. Thomas a Beckett wasn't too far away when Henry's knights visited him and the Mayor of Faversham was strangled by his wife's lover. Can't really claim any credits or assists for those. 'Mad Thom' sounded promising, perhaps into physical education. Thom was Sir William Courtenay who declared himself to be Christ, glared a lot and shot a constable, but Canterbury again. The Herne Bay 'bride in the bath' killer was actually featured at Tussauds. George Smith killed three of his seven wives in the bath before he was caught. How he got them all in there, I'll never know.

Only Margate murderer of any note was a man called Thomas Fordred. He met his young lover Mary Ann Bridger in the Liverpool Arms in 1867 and murdered her out near Salmestone Farm. Close to where the Coffin House shop would stand. Assaulted her very badly and kicked her to death with his hobnail boots. Quite a lot of blood on his clothes. Mary's guardian angel had stayed in the pub to finish a game of arrows. The Lord had a quick word about vengeance. Fordred's executioner was called Calcroft, who had a bit of a reputation for not getting the knots quite right. Complaints, not from the men Calcroft hanged of course, they struggled to say anything, but from the authorities. The men he executed tended not to die instantly but to hang around choking. Fordred took three minutes to die. The vagaries of swinging. The guardian angel was re-instated. Whatever happened to capital punishment? Such a humane way to go, particularly if you have three extra minutes to wave goodbye to your loved ones. You would have to wave your legs about though as your hands are bound behind you. How does it go? Put your left leg in then shake it all about.

Tommy, six months after his triumph at Folkestone. Taking the lads after school for hockey practice on the basketball court, posts left over from the war, probably surplus stock from Manston. End of session. Decides to showboat. Weaves down the pitch, head down, senses just one defender left. Huge dummy, stick moving slowly in giant arc. Basketball posts, like swings, have a different DNA to the rest of us. Swings will give a little here and there. They will rock back politely and gently, no matter what the provocation. Even murder just leaves them dangling. Basketball posts are stern and unbending. They have their own code, their own protocol. Concrete and clay. They have no concept of deception, of a dummy ploy. They do not take their eye off the ball. Tommy fell like Gandalf, head spinning. When he regained consciousness, the wizard had become a grand wizard, Thomas the White. He gave up hockey shortly after. The post was later feted in the annual basketball awards, the only known thing never to buy a Tommy Thomas dummy.

"Cricket, however, has more in it than mere efficiency. There is something called the spirit of cricket, which cannot be defined".

Lord Tennyson, the cricketer

Lord Tennyson, 3rd Baron, was one of those who was fortunate to have played cricket before and after the First World War. Having played against South Africa in 1913/14, he survived being wounded with the Rifle Brigade in France and went on to captain Hampshire afterwards. He was recalled in 1921 against the Australians. Two of his great aunts, sisters of the poet Alfred Lord Tennyson, godson of Alfred Dickens, are buried in Margate cemetery. Emily and Mary both died before he was born, otherwise he might have come to visit and perhaps played for Kent. As Jingle put it, "Kent sir - everybody knows Kent - apples, cherries, hops and women". No mention sadly of cricket. So if we are to ask what is the spirit of cricket, we may have to search elsewhere. The spirit of Margate is a little easier to define. Just forget the fruit? Much of the local history actually causes a great deal of debate amongst the historians. For example, after Vince had visited the Shell Grotto in Margate, we began what I guess could be described as our Emin period. We covered the prefects' room wall with beer mats, sourced from far and wide, and shaped in the style of a mosaic. The Grotto is an ornate underground passage, two thousand square feet of shells, discovered in 1835 but age unknown. It is quite extraordinary and I thought it would help to shine a definitive light on the origins.

As was often suspected, the Phoenician Goddess, Tanit, did use to come to the island on vacation. The Wantsum was in full flood then and the island of Tanit, named in her honour, represented a haven from the Canaanite paparazzi. Obviously the high zoom camera hadn't been invented yet but you wouldn't have needed one to observe her naked. Some Gauls had once tried to create an impression of her breasts for their etching collection magazine, 'Too Bloody Close', but the Frankish police said they were unable to hold them. The Gauls, that is, not the breasts. The Phoenicians, as you may know, were a maritime trading culture and their small winged galleys had made it this far fairly regularly. There is, however, no evidence that they had found the Murex Snail here, the snail being the source of the purple dye for which they were famous. The snails obtained the dye from feasting on purple beetles, known as people eaters. The original purple people eaters were the Minnesota Vikings, well before the Vikings and the Danes ever evolved. Tanit is the face of Baal, a mother goddess of war but also a nurse, associated with fertility and free at the point of delivery. She is normally virginal but is often the consort of Baal Hamon, chief god of Carthage, a bearded older man with curling ram's horns. You know the type. Definitely not a cricketer but often seen at the seaside.

When Tanit was in occupation, a few of the other Phoenicans based at Reculver Towers used to pop over and light a beacon. Made her feel welcome, they could throw a few shrimps on the beacon barbie and she could see to get home at night. Inevitably a cottage industry rose up when she was there and a flourishing wine bar was opened by a sailor called Rubius. There were loungers set out for the guests, a sort of Rubius Lounge. He started serving food and obviously the island was rich in seafood, particularly shellfish. The Phoenicians used to throw the empty shells over the cliffs until the health and safety elders asked them to stop. We were similarly told to stop throwing the tea leaves out of the school window into Chatham Street in Ramsgate. Our deputy head boy, destined I believe for the clergy, felt compelled to chisel a passage through the massive school wall so that the dregs could be safely rolled unseen into the street. The Phoenicians must have begun to fashion rather larger channels as their shellfish walls grew, very similar to the beer mat wall in the prefects' room. A few years later the Grotto is up to two million shells and winding down through all the caves. Great builders the Phoenicians. Solomon used them for the building of the temple at Jerusalem so a grotto would be a piece of piss and they were renowned for their shell symbolism. Shortly after that there's a fierce winter storm, like the one in 1953, a landslip, and the caves get covered until the discovery in 1835. Tanit left just after the Phoenicians lost to the Persians on penalties and by the time she got to Phoenix the whole team were in decline and in danger of relegation. For many years though, bands of smugglers used the tunnels before the official re-opening, as they were by then large enough for donkeys to traverse, bearing spirits by night. I'm just surprised none of that has been recorded before, because it seems fairly obvious.

Returning to the theme of sport, you may well be aware that one country almost failed to send any women to the Olympic Games. Can't recall which one that was, but they somehow found a runner and a judo competitor. Am also becoming a little concerned about how to organise this celestial cricket with the different concepts of heaven and worried that women might want to join in. Popped down to see my good friend Ant, who took his degree late in life and, as a very wise man, now gets to sit most days in a small information kiosk overlooking Broadstairs harbour. If there is a strong smell of seaweed you might assume it had emanated from the beach, just check that he is not still wearing his purple Games Maker uniform, which of course has been worn continuously now for some weeks. The kiosk is based on the principle of the Delphic Oracle. The Oracle was of course home to the Pythian Games, precursor to the Olympics. This is distinct from the neighbouring Delphic Orifice, which was largely used by politicians. Ant has been known to slay pythons and can answer any questions visitors ask about life, the universe, or if any of the surrounding houses are bleak. Not everyone in Broadstairs is bleak. Ant also spent many years teaching English in the Arab world, funnily enough largely in Saudi Arabia. He'd give me some guidance. Can't see them playing much cricket there, unless all the migrant workers have teams. Can you imagine running up to bowl at Dane Park with all those T E Lawrence robes? Wasn't O'Toole brilliant in that? Tall, pale blue eyes. Not sure why they didn't include him in 'Last Orders'. He took that Jessie to the seaside in 'Venus' so he obviously has a way with young women and knows the type of neighbourhood. Maybe last orders might be a step too far.

Lot of dressing up in very flamboyant gear in 'Lawrence of Arabia'. Wouldn't just be to impress the camels, even if you do spend a lot of time with them. Flamboyancy, ceremony, flummery. Reminds me of 'The Wizard of Oz'. Very impressive from a distance. Oz was a bit of a control freak. Lucky that that dog,Tonto, nipped behind the curtains. Apparently it had been stuck in the Tin Man's van overnight. Who would do that to a dog? Maybe the Scarecrow? The story just seems to stall a bit when they out the 'Wizard'. He was apparently a bit of an international playboy, travelling everywhere in that balloon. Lot of wealth stashed away. Owned racehorses, some of them donkeys. So behind that curtain would be a team of accountants, a tax lawyer and a whole host of scholars, beavering away trying to confirm the wizard's legitimacy and creating laws and rules for the umpires to interpret. Keeps the rabble, the lower orders, in check, you know. Not to mention the women. No mention too of Mrs Oz. Might have been several Mrs Oz's. Oz used to tell them how to dress, what to read, what time they could get up. Reminds me of a prison. Never allowed to drive the balloon, oh no. You can just imagine the headlines one day. Maybe part of a Kansas Spring. Mrs Oz has fled with the children. Wizard of Oz found lying on the floor. Been impaled. Police have located a broomstick but as yet have been unable to retrieve it. If it happened to Gadaffi, it could happen to Oz. The vagaries of broomsticks. The main suspects are a woman athlete and a judo competitor, lately returned from the London games. Pull back the curtains yourself Oz, before it is too late. Throw back the curtains.

“Reputation is what men and women think of us: character is what God and angels know of us”.

Thomas Paine

Paine deserves a mention in the story for two reasons, apart from being a hero of mine, grumpy old git that he was. He is recorded as attending the last but one meeting of the Hambleden Cricket Club in August 1796. This was previously disputed, as he was not well at the time and was living in France. However John Keane in his splendid biography believed that Thomas had played the game in Lewes, was a supporter and did make a clandestine journey. Henry Banham, the Hambleden secretary, was a Radical and the meeting on 29th August had three members and twelve non-members present. As a side-note Henry Tufton, the Earl of Thanet, was arrested on Napoleon’s orders when he was in France seven years later, so this may have been a political hotbed. It is suggested that the last meeting was arranged as an act of defiance against the Sedition Act. As an assembly it should have been broken up and the meeting was composed not only of cricket supporters but deliberately included radicals to test the authorities. Daft. Had it been gymnasts, like the later German example, or football supporters, the authorities may have stepped in. Not for cricket, surely? That aside, he surely got all his inspiration for the ‘Rights of Man’ and his other great compositions from the time he spent in Margate. He had married Mary Lambert in Sandwich and they moved to Margate early in 1760. He was a stay-maker and the women there had the reputation of having some of the loosest stays in the country. The very essence of a seaside resort. Sadly his wife died in childbirth and he stayed in the town for the rest of the year. He would never talk of his experiences there and thereafter had little interest in women. Just like Biff. He gave up the trade in stay-making and moved away to become an excise man. In Margate and Sandwich he would also have learnt much about smugglers and their art. Probably added a few shells to the Grotto too. Common sense really.

‘These are the times that test men’s souls’. You can imagine some weary American soldier reading his pamphlet by a meagre camp fire and feeling a flame begin to burn brightly inside. Paine is undoubtedly an extraordinary character who could write inspirationally. His reputation amongst his peers tended to depend on whether you were part of the establishment or not, as he took an inordinate amount of very nasty criticism. However, if you ever doubt the presence of guardian angels, even for those who are not believers like

Thomas, then it is worth looking at Paine's life. "Are they not all ministering spirits, sent to minister for them, who shall receive the inheritance of salvation". There are a number of occasions in his life where fate seems to intervene, some form of guardian angel looking over his shoulder. From the time when his father stopped him sailing on the 'Terrible', to the time when his cell was chosen for the guillotine the next day. He was saved because the door was open when the men came down the corridor to collect those selected for execution by guillotine and could not consequently see the chalk mark daubed on the external cell wall. Destiny? Well certainly 'Boy's Own' stuff. Interest in cricket, see. Angels can't resist that.

There were many sad songs that year of 1965. It's all over now, baby blue. Is it really over? Oh no, not my baby. Goodbye my love, I'm lost without you. It hurts so much, I'll never get over you. I'll never find another you. Still I'm sad, my child, in thought of you. Crying in the chapel. We were a generation who believed we had discovered music. Julie's mother, Doris, let's call her, emerged from the trial after the verdict of guilty and the sentence of life imprisonment. "It's marvellous, it's marvellous. This is a complete vindication of my daughter. I knew she would never have gone into the park on her own. She had been a lovely girl until two weeks ago". Not sure parents are always best placed to know what their children are doing, but you can feel for Doris. "She was a very well behaved girl until two weeks before she died. I had no idea she was on drugs. Friday night was the first time she had stayed out all night. It was only in the last fortnight when she met the teenagers from Birmingham, that she became any different".

The only consolation, Doris, is that it wasn't really your little girl out there in the park. She was out of character, reckless, animated, immortal, not having eaten, but high on the tablets. Blame the bastards who sold them to her or who enticed her into the group. I'm afraid she had had sex before, the police surgeon confirmed that, but it would have been like most of us, a fumbling short encounter or even several encounters. Seaside towns, particularly if you have been a waitress, encourage holiday couplings and even romances. Not often true love you have to say. Cricketers aren't always that romantic either. The earliest surviving minute book of the Hambleden Cricket Club contained a list of drinking toasts. One of them is to 'the immortal memory' of some lady whose name could be said to have a close association with Doris. I looked at Grose's 'Dictionary of the Vulgar Tongue' published in the eighteenth century and their toast was not one which I could repeat. I think one veteran Australian comedian may well raised a similar toast many years back when starting out. No consolation there. I looked up the Grose definition for my friend Biff. Just said Grose.

I should warn you at this point, before you read any further, that I am under investigation by the galactic police force. They have been asked to caution me by the KPS, the Klingon Prosecution Service. I became involved in an online discussion about this whole leg amputation business with the Clunc Clic'ers. I unfortunately argued that they didn't have a leg to stand on, well at least the younger ones, and that they should desist. It was quite a civilised debate but the KPS received one complaint from one Clunc Clic'er, funnily enough the one who owns the ceremonial saw. According to them, a racist definition is any incident which is perceived to be racist by the victim or any other person. I have tried to argue that definitions like this merely assist men from the seventh century who can portray any attack on their cultural practices as racist, which tends to mean that the only practical challenge can come from within their own communities. Unfortunately when anyone is brave enough to stand up and protest, the men in the community beat the shit out of them or expel them. Some of the women help as well.

However I am not despairing as they assure me, like Dr Pangloss, that this makes for a much greater democratic process and is the best of all possible worlds. Better that I am cautioned and possibly locked up, than the Clunc Clic'ers be asked to stop the barbarism. It makes perfect sense. However on this celestial cricketing lark I do get to talk to St Peter now and then. I'm not really allowed in because they have doubts about my religious convictions and there aren't any birdbaths in heaven, so hitting one with a tennis or cricket ball has little value. Birds don't have souls, so no need for birdbaths. I tried throwing a ball against some building called a tabernacle instead but it just knocked over an oil lamp and disturbed the meeting. They were clearly incensed, so I legged it quickly. Nonetheless as cricket fixture secretary I get access to the immense set of files in the building just to the right of the Pearly Gates. I know it looks like a urinal but it contains a small computer terminal with access to a state of the arc cloud-based filing system. Noah and Alan Turing built it. All souls are filed away here, alphabetically. I've got my own back on the KPS. All of their new recruits to heaven will find their souls listed under the letter 'R'. 'R' souls.

**"Look in my face; my name is Might-have-been;
I am also called No-More, Too-late, Farewell"**

Dante Rossetti

Look in my face. My name is Might-have-been. Strangulation has its own protocol, a process, a flow. The protocol largely consists of men, often alone, exerting pressure on individual women, sometimes on a bench, sometimes against a wall or even on the ground in a park. The victim tends to look down but rarely to the side, an automatic reaction to the pressure. A furtive glance is allowed by the assailant to see if the act is being witnessed. Night time is always a pretty safe option but you can choose to do it at home, which reduces the opportunity for do-gooders to intervene. Note that both of you can be permanently scarred by the occasion. You can strangle with one hand, but never lightly, using your other hand to stop the victim talking, to subdue, to hold one or both arms or to help them undress. Two hands tend to be the recommended method.

It is however impossible, unlike urination, to use no hands at all, that is if manual strangulation is your objective. It is also highly unlikely that you could reach out and simultaneously hold anyone else's throat. You may however suddenly notice steam rising from the victim's shoes, if they have any on. Do not be deceived into believing that they have chosen to join in the process in some way, as any urination is often involuntary. Try and exert eleven pounds of pressure on both carotids for about ten seconds as this will render the victim unconscious. Thirty three pounds of pressure, as in rear car tyres, if you have an interest in Top Gear, will close the airways. It is acceptable, in the absence of any spare female victims, to practice on any available Top Gear presenter. They will doubtless be very sympathetic to your display of male dominance, although they may want you to go faster.

Ten per cent of violent deaths in the USA are due to strangulation so there are many other practitioners with whom you could bond, perhaps begin a social network site. Possibly a Facebook or Friends page to compare techniques and numbers perhaps somewhat similar to the new TV drama series 'The Following'. It is important, to achieve the full effect, to hold your position for at least fifty seconds. Try counting aloud or perhaps singing to yourself. Suitable songs might be, 'If You Gotta Go, Go Now', 'Get Off My Cloud' or perhaps 'Almost There'. Holding on to the victim's neck for more than fifty seconds, think four hundred metres hurdles here, will make the bounce-back reflexes inoperative. This is a most important point. It also avoids any awkward conversation. Do not try manual strangulation unless there is a clear disparity in physical strength. It is just much more successful if men strangle women. In addition, depending on the force used, the victim may bleed from the ears, nose and mouth. Do not worry about this as they will not have felt any pain at this point, but the blood might get on your clothes. Best to avoid any unnecessary dry cleaning bills or any unwanted evidence. Sometimes the whole process can be more assured if you can rest the victim against some form of object. Something mobile like a swing would not deliver the complete effect. Please be aware that this is just a general commentary on strangulation and should not be taken as representative of anything in this story. The object is to enlighten any interested readers who are considering taking up the activity as to its rather tragic consequences. It is normally a savage act of male dominance that does not end well.

In view of the rather unsympathetic response of passers-by or indeed the police, usually in television series or in films the assailant likes to dispose of the body. If you don't have any friends in the East End or in the local mafia who will give assistance or don't carry a spade with you out of doors - I normally strap my cricket ball on to the spade handle when I go out - then you are very much on your own. Sometimes in the dark it can be very confusing and often a safe hiding place is only a few yards away from where you decide to abandon the body. For health and safety reasons, try not to leave your body on a path or a main road. If someone like a council workman, perhaps a road sweeper, is walking or cycling along at dawn, then you can imagine the health and safety guidelines that would be breached if they stumbled over your victim on the path. We have all seen the advertisements for personal injury lawyers, when saying sorry isn't enough. Add trade union involvement and also additional claims for emotional distress and whiplash injuries, you may well wish you were somewhere safe and out of their jurisdiction. In the rare event that women are unavailable or if there are no motor car television presenters to hand, very few people would object if you practiced on personal injury lawyers. Pull the body off the path. About seven feet will do nicely.

"My classmates would copulate with anything that moved, but I never saw any reason to limit myself"

Emo Philips

According to the laws of cricket, the Umpires are the sole judges of fair and unfair play. They are authorised to intervene in cases of time wasting, damaging the pitch, dangerous or unfair bowling and any other actions deemed to be unfair. If life is like cricket, then who are the umpires of fair and unfair play in society? The Judge, Justice Sachs, said about the 'Mad House' that, "There were in this place men of twenty six and twenty seven whom, you may think, had gone there for one real reason - taking advantage of girls of seventeen and eighteen". Lucky bastards, most of us would think, when we were young. It just depends on the context. Dr Ian George of the Metropolitan Police Laboratory told the court that four tablets were found in Julie's handbag, so she presumably took six. These were Drinamyl Spansules containing amphetamine and barbiturate. Marilyn Monroe and Judy Garland both died of barbiturate overdose and the symptoms, when combined with other chemicals, can lead to unusual excitement, irritability and impaired judgement. The highs can give a feeling of relaxed contentment and euphoria. It's really there to counter the side effects of the amphetamine. Drinamyl, also known as Dexamyl, was of course used by Anthony Eden when he was Prime Minister. A few years back, Lord Owen, probably using his Attendance Allowance for his rail travel, gave a lecture in Liverpool about whether Eden's judgement during the Suez crisis was influenced by the stimulants, purple hearts, he was taking. Perhaps Eden was the first Mod. We know he was in Margate in 1953, because his speech to the conference went well. Forget the history books. I bet his dependence started down there by the seaside. Probably bought a few tablets from the Punch and Judy man to settle his nerves the night before.

Amphetamine and Benzedrine were freely available for both Allied and enemy soldiers to combat battle fatigue, seventy two million tablets apparently used by British troops. Not sure what they gave the Russian troops, because as they raced through towards Berlin they put the US cavalry well in the shade in terms of their treatment of women. Classmates, comrades, of Emo Philips obviously. In actual fact, if you read Catherine Merridale's 'Ivan's War', you get a feel for the violence that was common place when the Red Army encountered its enemies. The flow of alcohol numbed the senses and the incidence of rape is thought to have doubled under its influence. Our own boys clearly also had both alcohol and tablets. Smith Kline and French manufactured Dexamyl tablets for years very profitably, initially as diet drugs. Then they were adopted by musicians, some athletes and students. Finally in the sixties, Mods really took to them. The film 'Quadrophenia' is set in 1965, inspired by the Who album. I noticed young Ray even got into that. Is there any film now where he isn't included? Mind you, didn't see him in any of those recent Shakespeare plays on BBC television. Henry could have done with him at Azincourt, while the French were self-destructing and getting their last orders. Once more unto the beach, dear friends, a few thousand urns of French ashes to toss into the wind at Calais. Could have had another fight in a field, Ray.

Amphetamines had been banned the year before 'Quadrophenia', unless on prescription, thus opening the way for pushers and suppliers. Two Who tracks are interesting, to whit 5.15 and Doctor Jimmy. The first tells us how Jimmy gulps down a great many amphetamines on his train journey down to Brighton, whilst the second shows him to be deeply damaged by the combination of drugs and alcohol. Even Jimmy comes to realise that it is destroying him. Apparently much of the story was based on events in Margate in 1964. Peter Laurie found that for those on drugs, the average nightly consumption was four tabs or twenty milligrams. Remember too that the Who came to Margate ten days before Julie died. Maybe that was a trigger for some local kids to try them out. Dexamyl created very intense emotions and mood swings. One regular user has recorded his experiences on the web. You could dance all night in clubs and take long summer walks at night, wide awake and talkative, sometimes agitated and combative. Sounds spot on for this tale. A park would be nice, if you knew the way in. The mood swings were hard to predict, erratic and inexplicable. The vagaries of mood swings. The lows, however, were extreme for people coming down and the effect if you were inexperienced would have initially been pretty fearful. Just keep groaning until some kind person eases the pain. More tablets are not really the answer. Pressure on the carotids even less.

Terrific article in today's paper by Helen Pidd about the treatment of women in India. Included in the story was a footnote on a group of village elders in Baghpat, Uttar Pradesh, who have banned women from carrying mobile phones, choosing their own husbands or leaving the house unaccompanied. Juvenal our famous Roman wrote another poem, his sixth, about guys like these. As he pointed out, quis custodiet ipsos custodes? Who will watch the watchers when you lock the women away? You see, village elders, strong on family and discipline, often have surprising social tendencies. They may already have women on the side plus they might be grooming a boy or two, even a goat. You don't believe me? Well maybe I made up the bit about the goat. There is also currently no special law in India against sexual assault or harassment so nothing to stop ignorant morons who believe women are their's to own and control. But men generally don't like women to know what they are up to. Inhibits their ability to play away. In any case a poll of gender specialists voted India the worst place to be a woman out of all the G20 countries, with Saudi Arabia next.

I am sure that had the researchers only bothered to extend their research to some of India's near neighbours where the attitude to women is medieval, then the results might have been different, but there seem to be men from the seventh century lurking everywhere these days. Research from Unicef in 2012 found that fifty two per cent of adolescent girls think it is justifiable for a man to beat his wife. It quoted Maini Mahanta, editor of an Assamese women's magazine, to illustrate how culture and tradition largely drives these attitudes. Men always determine the culture and the tradition in these countries. Bullies, cowards, goat tossers. Call yourselves men? One of my good lady friends is involved with an international organisation striving to improve women's rights. She's exactly right for this sort of task. Courage, integrity, good brain. Has some status now, jet-setting. Probably got her own balloon. Talking about co-opting some men on to the fringes of the organisation. Probably already meets a fair number of important men now in her present capacity, some in suits, some in tunics, some in long flowing robes. Just a tip, Suzy, let's call her. I abhor violence like the next man. Mind you, I have just looked at the next man, so perhaps not. If you meet these powerful leaders who have the capacity to change society, but do nothing other than pay lip service and patronise you. Take their hand, pull them gently towards you, smile and then kick them in the balls.

"France was a lady, Russia was a bear and performing in the county cricket team was much more important than either of them".

Siegfried Sassoon

Although Sassoon studied history at Cambridge, this may not rank as the finest assessment of France and Russia's respective roles in the First World War, but you do quickly get the gist of where his own priorities lay. Sassoon, like Kenneth Horne and Betjeman at Oxford, left without a degree, presumably cricket getting in the way. I had to include something about Sassoon. I live in a neighbouring village and quite often pass the Matfield cricket square. Not able though to find any trace of the Blue Mantle or Bluehouses team that he played for in Tunbridge Wells, at the Neville. Conan Doyle apparently played occasionally, bowling artful slows. Don't remember any 'blue' teams from the area in the sixties and without success asked my newsagent, who himself lives for cricket and is a more than useful local fast bowler, if he had ever heard of them. James Coldham penned a pretty exhaustive detail of Siegfried's love of and association with cricket. The Matfield village captain was one of their servants. Those were the days, although not really true love if you have to use the tradesman's entrance. Well maybe, in retrospect, it could be. Coldham sadly deems Sassoon's poems about cricket to possess no outstanding merit and Sassoon, of course, was never quite good enough to play for Kent. During the war, where he describes the men playing cricket in their rest period, like the American soldiers playing baseball, his men began to call him 'mad'. 'Mad Jack'. Becoming ever more disturbed by the horror of war in the trenches, he began to respond with a fearless courage. Men at a distance will always be in awe of such a man. Not sure if the soldiers in his troop were quite as appreciative, if you are merely trying to survive from one day to the next. Like Muhammad Ali, Sassoon later threw his medal, the Military Cross, into a river.

I was meant to study a short period in Indian history in my last year, forty per cent of the exam. A couple of our friends were class cricketers and wanted some help with net practice. Two of us went down to the nets for a couple of hours to bowl at them and then we all headed off for study. Phil and I were apparently doing the same special subject and he asked me how I was enjoying the seminars. I had to confess that I had missed both seminars and lectures, but had set aside two weeks for the sources and then four weeks for revision. As I explained, how many sources can there be for an obscure thirty year period in Indian history. No more than a bookcase full. It was one of my more stupid but pleasurable periods, alcohol and sport taking precedence over work, but then I had a job lined up. In the library, Phil pointed out not a bookcase, but a complete wall full of sources. Could have done with some Dexamyl tablets myself, as the realisation of my error hit home and the waves of sheer panic began. What I do remember, however, quite vividly from the sources, was the almost unanimous judgement of the respective authors of some of these sources of the complete disregard for human or animal life in Indian society. That was two hundred years ago. These were not the Clive's or the nabobs, gaily pocketing loot, but were largely administrators and civil servants struggling with local government and managing elementary courts of justice. Often men who lived alone in strange surroundings but who tried, rather like Rory Stewart these days, to identify with local people. Why isn't he in the Cabinet? Too much integrity possibly. Life appeared to have very little value, life was cheap.

Read an article by Pankaj Mishra who wrote 'The Ruins of Empire' and wondered whether I should reconsider even mentioning India. He writes very well and with a passion but couldn't help thinking that some of his argument was just irrelevant. Then looked through the many comments on his article on the web, mainly hostile, and found one from 'something missing', someone claiming to be of Malaysian extraction. This very succinctly highlighted part of my own concerns. "It's all about power and what people do when they have it". It so is. Since time began. And women will never be equal or be treated with dignity, if all you ever do is excuse men in power and let them off the hook. There is always a choice. We've just been making the wrong ones. Stop controlling the women. Stop beating them.

Yet cricket came to India as early as 1721, when sailors from the East India Company are reported to have played a game on the shore. By 1792, right at the heart of the period I was meant to be studying, the Calcutta Cricket and Football Club was in existence. 1864 is said to be when first-class cricket started in India, with Madras against Calcutta. Where did it all go wrong? Hockey may be the national game but cricket is the most popular sport in India. The game there is the most successful in the world in financial terms. So if cricket is like life, why is it that the rules of cricket have not seeped down through Indian society into life and standards in general? They couldn't even get the basics of strangulation right. Instead of using the well established techniques of the British Raj, they had these lunatics called Thuggees. They had evidently got together through some early version of Sanskrit Facebook and travelled across India in large groups. They were first mentioned by Ẓiya-ud-Din Barani, or Barney to his friends, the first Muslim Indian historian, in around 1356.

The assassins or thugs would join other travellers and tourists and then strangle them by tossing a handkerchief or noose around their necks. No manual stuff, just bloody handkerchieves! Don't they ever read the Articles of Strangulation? To be fair, the killings were in honour of the goddess Kali, Kaley in Essex speak, and followed a certain elaborate ritual. Despite all that, they made sure they legged it with the loot as well. Smart, eh? In many sources Kali is praised as the greatest of all deities and sometimes presented as dark and violent. See they even got that wrong. Dark and violent, should be masculine. She has four or ten arms. Imagine Kali in the celestial cricket team, fielding at cover. Colin Bland would have no chance, she'd replace him, except she's a girl. She is described as being black and sometimes blue. Hope her consort, Shiva, wasn't responsible. Suspected early case of domestic violence. She sometimes has eyes "red with intoxication, is in absolute rage, her hair is shown dishevelled, small fangs protruding from her mouth, and her tongue is lolling". A case of the Dexys Midnight Runners, if you ask me. Blame the corporate world. Somewhere in ancient times there will have been an Oriental version of Smith Kline and French. Surprised Barney didn't mention it.

"Why are there twelve jurors?
Because there are twelve tribes of Israel, twelve months in a year, twelve inches in a foot, and twelve apostles".

Quintin Hogg

The good Baron served for over ten years as Lord Chancellor, so he should know a thing or two about juries and trials. No cricketer though, loved mountain climbing. Rees Davies may have been the first to shop John Profumo, but Hogg famously laid into him on television for telling lies to Parliament. It produced the wonderful comment from Profumo's brother-in-law, that "When a man has by self-indulgence acquired the shape of Lord Hailsham, sexual continence requires no more than a sense of the ridiculous". There were twelve jurors in the trial surrounding Julie's death. They took fifty five minutes to agree on their verdict. Little is known of them. We were not then able to bug phones or hack into e-mails. Maybe journalists were intercepting mail, but Ian, Myra and the Moor's revelations would have concentrated their attention.

Time to begin looking at what the twelve jurors might have learnt from the witness statements. Ellen, the landlady, had been short and to the point. Mind you, Billy had wanted the police to close down the guest house and prosecute her. The Gazette later reported that the police had found insufficient evidence to do so. Mind you, he had booked into Room Two whereas they only searched Six and Eight and then only for drugs in connection with James. They might not have known that his suitcase was still there, given to James from Birmingham on the first evening. He never got it back that day, which is why he had needed to borrow a spare shirt when the dog got his cuffs dirty. So he had taken the dog for a walk earlier in the day. Ellen from the very beginning had played the indignant landlady. She kept a strict and correct guest house and locked the doors promptly at midnight. She said his bed that night had not been slept in. There was a young labourer living at the house and he had been celebrating his birthday with about twenty friends in a top floor room. She knew nothing about any drugs. She had eight letting rooms. No-one apparently came in on Friday, although he and James most certainly did. She booked one room out Saturday morning and one in the afternoon.

Margate in the last ten days of Julie's life. Pretty average. The Gazette reports the assault on the two young girls in the park; woman robbed of £300 in Dreamland; letter from George to the Gazette about the vandalism during the cricket festival; four sheep escape from the sheepdog trials at St Lawrence Church Fayre and head for Margate; The Who come for a one night stand; the Broadstairs Donkey Derby is opened by Bill Maynard; the winner of the main race is Trefonia Dream; Sheriff Danny Arnold is playing at the Golden Garter Saloon - I actually met him once and I think he was from Manchester, six gun capital even then; wrestling at the Oval; the weekly Brock's fireworks display; Bunny Baron staging his 'Give Away' party show at the Lido; Eric Sykes on at the Carlton in 'Rotten to the Core'; 'Mary Poppins' on at the Cameo; Elvis Presley in 'Tickle Me' at the Plaza. With such an array of high class entertainment, why on earth were the general public beginning to think of holidaying in Spain in the years to come? Can't explain. In addition there were also always the ice cream and coffee bars like Pelosi's or maybe the Tahiti in Marine Gardens. The Tahiti was a bit wilder. And to round your evening off, how about the Excel Bowl? Only opened in 1964. Plenty of lanes, wide choice of balls. Noel Coward could have written a song about it. Not only can you get a nice pair of shoes at reception, but if you look carefully you might find someone to help you if you're feeling tired and need a lift. If the supplier is in a good humour, you might be able to put it on the tab. Might not understand the Brummie accent though. If only our generation had all been allowed to take Dexamyl freely, with its dieting properties, advertised nationally and probably recommended by the American medical profession, maybe obesity wouldn't be such a big problem now. What would you rather be? Off your head or obese?

There have always been loose houses in Margate. Charles Dickens wrote to his friend, Maclise, inviting him down for the sake of his health. He could get up when he wanted and eat and drink when he liked. In addition, "There are conveniences of all kinds at Margate and I know where they live". This was not about the protocol of urination, but about the protocol of prostitution. Dickens of course knew the area very well from his frequent family visits to Broadstairs. No mention though of him ever playing cricket at Dane Park. There are a couple of references in his diary to matches at Gad's Hill and the cricket on the hearth doesn't really count, so safe to assume he would have diarised anything similar, had it occurred. Not sure he ever brought his mistress Ellen Ternan to Margate. However after his death she married George Robinson and they came to run a boys' school here in the late 1870's. He was the head and she the matron. Might even have been close to Addington Road. Two of Dickens' daughters, Georgina and Mamie, both came down to stay with them. For some years Ellen, or Nelly as she was better known, gave dramatic readings for charity in the town, often of Charles' work. We know she read 'A Christmas Carol' and also selected pieces from 'The Old Curiosity Shop' and 'David Copperfield'. Amusingly her age in the census carried out in Thanet was put at twenty eight whereas she was actually forty two. Not sure if husband George knew, or if he cared. Maybe she was giving him fifty shades of hard times or perhaps he just had great expectations.

"No brilliance is required in the law, just common sense and relatively clean fingernails".

John Mortimer

Mr Edward Sutcliff QC was prosecuting at the Kent Assizes in Maidstone when the trial opened. Of small interest is that the year before, a man with an identical name had been the Chairman of a tribunal investigating the conduct of two officers from the Metropolitan Police. They were dismissed the force after compensation was paid to two of the people they had arrested, but were eventually found innocent of any charges and re-instated. There was a debate in the House of Lords as to whether the tribunal had been conducted impartially. Lord Derwent, the Minister of State at the Home Office had to intervene. You will be relieved to know that the Police Officers were totally blameless. Thank God for that. Who on earth would ever doubt PC Dixon and his gallant comrades. Jack Warner would never have agreed to fabricating evidence anyway, even if someone in the East End had tried to steal the blue lamp off his bicycle. Mind you if some pleb had tried to stop him wheeling it down Brick Lane, who knows. The prosecution was in safe hands.

The statement from Carol, a seventeen year old waitress, was that she had known Julie for just two weeks. About the time Doris said her daughter had fallen into bad company with the teenagers from Birmingham. At 8.30 in the evening Julie was in the Tahiti club and went to speak to Wally, with whom she had spent the previous night. She subsequently ran out, returning an hour later and had clearly been crying. What on earth could he have said? Hopefully not on the lines that our Tracey used in her work, but you would guess something close. The Tahiti closed at 11.00 pm and they all went to the bowling alley. After a while she had joined the new recruit and Carol said they had discussed drugs and that he had offered to get some for Julie from a friend. She was obviously still upset. In an earlier testimony, Glynis, a sixteen year old shop assistant, who had known Julie for about two years and been at school with her, thought she had left the Excel Bowl at around 12.40. The club was actually locked up at 1.45 by the management and at least one witness thought they were in there till shortly before that. That seems more accurate but whatever the time, it's a good fifteen to twenty minutes walk back to the 'Mad House', across Northdown Road, and down then up to the guest house.

At the house you can either believe from the different statements that the landlady interrupted them or that the front door was locked and they turned away. He wouldn't have known Dane Park existed unless he had taken his dog there, as the road to Ramsgate is in a different direction. Judy might have known the back way past the park out to Ramsgate but more likely he would have headed back to Cecil Square, when driving her home on the Saturday afternoon. Even then his knowledge would be rudimentary. It was also obviously dark at two o'clock in the morning. The tablets would be kicking in, changing moods and personalities, so a walk to the park in the morning would sound good. It is also on her way home. For a long time I did wonder if he had offered to walk her home, as you just don't know specifically what effects the drugs were having on them individually. Neither would be tired and they might be much more aware and alive. Well, one of them would be alive. Then I saw where she had been killed and I thought I understood.

If you turn left out of Number 5 Addington Road, it will take you five minutes to walk to the park, two hundred and sixty paces to the gates. The gates are tall so if you knew the park intimately, you would not bother to scale them. Too much trouble really but then you may be feeling immortal. Or the gates might just have been open. I think they were, which is just as well as the railings on either side have fierce spikes. If you choose to head to the right and walk round the outside of the park until the bushes and railings end, you reach the site of the old playground with its swings and roundabout. However that is uphill and relatively hard work and you are heading down on exactly the path where she was killed. In addition the ground in the park on that side is very open and exposed. Much easier, if you wanted to be intimate in a romantic or quiet setting and not be disturbed, to head left. Two hundred more paces will take you to the main road and just there is the first of two unguarded entrances. The second small entrance, further along, took you round past the cricket pavilion, but the first one winds rather charmingly down into the park. It is sheltered and peaceful, a sort of hollow, surrounded by bushes and trees. There was a pond then, although these days that is long gone. There are benches dotted around. She would have known all of this, even in the dark. If they went through the open gates it is just a short walk to the left. Tellingly though, they never began to head in that direction. She took the shortest way home, either through the gates or by scaling them and then straight on past the fountain. Yet parks can be adventurous and maybe the spaces and the drugs encourage you to live dangerously. What's the worst that could happen, only fifteen minutes from home.

The Isle of Thanet Gazette on 23rd July 1965. Mr Rees Davies in the House of Commons had spoken last week to the effect that, "the Bill seeking the abolition of the death penalty was ill-considered and ill-conceived". He remained a bitter opponent to the very end and public opinion tended to side with him, despite the obvious cases of mistaken identity which regularly surfaced. In 1810, interestingly, there had still been two hundred and twenty crimes punishable by death, including "blacking the face or using a disguise whilst committing a crime". Would have probably done for all of the Black and White Minstrels, or at least the Black ones. Certainly some of their singing was criminal and Lenny Henry was once their comedian. Bring back hanging, soon as you like. Maidstone, where the trial would take place, also saw the last known hanging by the civilian courts of a person under eighteen, one Charles Dobel, aged seventeen in 1889. It was the Labour MP, Sydney Silverman, who drove the suspension of the death penalty through in 1965 and it easily passed through both Houses. Beheading though was only finally taken off the statute box in 1973. We had become a civilised society.

"One of the best bowlers Durlston has ever had .... bowls a good length ....and swings in from the leg rather late"

Pat Cox, Headmaster of Durlston Court School.

The comedy writer David Croft was also at Durlston and is said to have loosely based the character of Captain Mainwaring from 'Dad's Army' on Pat Cox. Cox was talking about another of his boys, Anthony Hancock. Hancock suffered from rickets as a child, which gave him his hunched posture, but it never stopped him bowling. His mother described how he would go about the house always swinging his arms and bowling at imaginary objects. In one of the radio episodes, 'The Old School Reunion', he told Bill Kerr that he was known as 'Googly Hancock'. Kerr replies that this is because of the way he walks, but nonetheless Hancock remained a fine medium pace bowler. In 1958 he got the Aussie skipper, Ian Craig, out lbw in a charity match. Craig was apparently plumb, but because of the occasion the umpire gave him not out. Five years later, by 1963, his playing days were greatly reduced and it was in that year that he co-wrote the 'Punch and Judy Man'. He began it shortly after tragically, on a personal and professional level, breaking up with his scriptwriters Galton and Simpson.

I have never been able to resist a Punch and Judy show. There was a fine puppeteer on Margate Sands and I would always wait to watch the shows, standing up on the promenade, well away from the children, of course. Curiously Punch's wife was originally called Joan, which was Hancock's last relationship. His Joan, John Mesurier's ex, lived in Ramsgate and he visited her regularly. It was a film, shot in black and white, which did not enjoy much acclaim at the time by a public who expected something funnier from the lad himself. However he had a great affection for it and it is a gentle and amusing tribute to the genre. Hugh Lloyd, who was starring with Terry Scott at the Margate Winter Gardens in the summer of 1965, played the puppeteer's assistant. You may recall that Lloyd used to appear in some of Hancock's television shows, most notably as the patient in the 'Blood Donor' who walks off with Hancock's fruit gums. By then Hancock was already fighting his demons, a bottle of vodka by his bed every night. Sadly he had a fierce temper when drunk and regularly assaulted both Cicely, his first wife, and then Freddie. Cicely told Joan, "Don't let him go near the brandy. He turns into a killer on the stuff". But then Peter Sellers too had a temper. The temper is never the problem. It is the violence that accompanies it that really destroys and scars.

Despite always wanting to write the film, Hancock is amusingly said to have really disliked puppets and particularly Educating Archie, even though it had brought him fame. Archie though was not combative, merely cheeky. How do we deal with the violence portrayed in a typical 'Punch and Judy' Show? By the way, the swizzle which the puppeteer holds in his mouth does not produce a noise like a quark, but rather a squawk or a cackle. What Punch does have though is a slapstick and he lays about him with abandon. He beats Judy, the baby, the crocodile, the policeman, all who cross his path. Only the string of sausages seems to remain intact. There is great laughter from the audience and yet the beatings are very rigorous and quite violent. The law may appear later in the show, signalling its abhorrence of his behaviour, but Punch then even eludes the hangman. The original concept in the commedia dell' arte must have been set in the future, let's say 1965, if you can elude the noose. Perhaps a Time Lord suggested it? How do children or adults view the show? Dickens thought that it was quite harmless because Punch's behaviour is so outrageous, "one secret source of pleasure .... is the satisfaction the spectator feels in the circumstance that likenesses of men and women can be so knocked about, without any pain or suffering".

Perhaps it is like the sort of violence that children see in comics, with Desperate Dan, or on television with Popeye or Tom and Jerry. We are able then to differentiate. We have a choice of how we apply all the visual data we absorb and we use that in a context based on our own experiences, of what we remember, and of the reaction of the people around us, our culture. Fred Karno put on terrific shows, with slapstick and comedy. Both Charlie Chaplin and Stan Laurel were members of his company. Laurel, of course, died in 1965. Yet Karno beat his wife regularly, scarring her for life. It was thought acceptable. I can remember my father letting the flat above our shop to a couple where the husband beat the wife. The neighbours could hear the shouting and screams. My father courageously tried to stop it by talking to the husband and asked me to accompany him and sit in the car outside the shop just in case. He eventually went to the police. A domestic incident, they said, we don't interfere between husband and wife. There is a 1988 song by Tracy Chapman, 'Behind the Wall', which speaks of just this attitude which endured for so long. The screaming behind the wall, what business is it of ours? The only remedy my father had was to terminate their lease in the hope of bringing the husband to his senses. Just moved the problem on.

Not all entertainers beat their wives, neither will all headmasters, bankers or even personal injury lawyers. It is totally understandable if you beat up a personal injury lawyer but only attempt it anonymously. Saying sorry just won't be enough if they know who you are and where you live. Even if you just kick them in the balls, they will claim for the neck whiplash injuries. It is not in any case about a profession or calling but it is also definitely not just a disease of the lower orders. A poor environment and lack of money won't help, but casual and even studied violence are prevalent through the ranks, from Cleese to Barker to Corbett. In terms of the class consciousness shown in the sketch, of course, and not in the context that any of those three might ever have been violent. It would in any case have served no purpose. John Cleese may well have swung wildly at Ronnie Corbett but it would all have gone over his head.

Joseph Grimaldi was the greatest clown and he appears to have been a gentle type of man, despite his strenuous exertions on stage. You might like to know that he once appeared in a pantomime called 'Harlequin and the Forty Virgins'. His agent probably arranged to screw the other thirty when drawing up the contract. This was based on scenes set in China, Persia, London and amazingly Margate. It was not, by the way, a play about multi-coloured suicide bombers at Xmas. Joey got to sing a new comic song, "Don't I look spruce on my Neddy". The Deadwood brothers, a very strange comedy act from western parts, later entered it for the 1807 Eurovision song contest in Silesia but failed to get a single vote. Joey, definitely not the Joey from Friends, would rush around the stage on a makeshift horse, fashioned from a bench, a donkey skull and a broomstick. Joey from Friends, and now Episodes, might not need the broomstick, if you can believe the rumours. See, even in those days, broomsticks were much in fashion. I can find no trace that Joseph Grimaldi ever visited Margate but we do know that his father, the Signor, on two occasions faked his own death, apparently to find out how much his sons cared for him. On the last occasion he was said to have fallen off a cliff at Margate, presumably somewhere near Joss Bay. He later surfaced at one of the pubs in London, even possibly at the Eagle, very much alive.

**“As the riders loped on by him, he heard one call his name.
If you want to save your soul from Hell a-riding on a range,
Then cowboy change your ways today, or with us you will ride,
A-trying to catch the devil's herd across these endless skies”**

‘Ghost Riders In The Sky’

Doesn’t rhyme either, does it? Song writers are obviously cowboys as well. Sadly too late to change his ways as the damage had been irreparably done. Can’t bring Julie back. Could try and get off the drugs. He had said that he was a self-confessed drug-taker, but at the time no-one really understood what it took for anyone to come down for good. The long-term damage wasn’t really appreciated either. Don’t think the jury had details of his previous but he’d had a series of incidents and involvement with the law, mainly petty crime. Then short stays in detention centres and prison. He said he was really trying but then got into financial difficulties. That at least is a familiar story. A weekend in Margate was an opportunity to escape, to lose yourself. James, his mate, had given evidence but merely confirmed what was already known. Declan from Birmingham, the trainee furnace erector, had also agreed that he and his friends had been in the town for three months. His nineteen year old sister, Joyce, was with him, living as man and wife with Robert, the fruit salesman. Robert sold from a stall or perhaps, more grandly, to the markets in the Midlands. Probably from a stall. Declan had taken the ten shilling note from Julie and had given it to Robert for more tablets. Ten tablets.

Wally’s statement, Wally the student nurse, said only that he had sex with Julie on Friday evening and that she seemed to be sexually experienced. Mind you, if you are giving evidence at a court of law in a murder trial, you are unlikely to admit being part of a group encouraging young girls of sixteen to try drugs and then taking advantage of them when their judgement may be impaired. Of course it might well not have been like that and he was just trying to practice some nursing techniques he had seen on Emergency Ward Ten. That was one of the very first television hospital dramas and was still running on ATV in 1965. Featured the first ever kiss on television anywhere between a black and a white actor. Don’t remember any male nurses then, only male doctors. He might have imagined that he had that Nurse Carole Young in bed. Tracheotomy? No need. I can just put pressure on your trachea to shut everything down. Oh, hang on. That requires six times more pressure than pushing on the carotids. Save that for tomorrow, but find someone else. I’ve lost interest. One of the greatest pop songs came out in

1960, Goffin and King's 'Will You Still Love Me Tomorrow?' Tonight with words unspoken, you say that I'm the only one. But will my heart be broken, when the night meets the morning sun? She went straight back from home to the 'Mad House' that Saturday evening as her first port of call but Wally wasn't there. She stayed for a while talking to the Michael whose birthday they had been celebrating. He thought she looked very ill. When she did find Wally, there was a brief casual exchange and she ran out of the Tahiti club very upset. Came back an hour later and had been crying. No change there then, five years on from 1960.

Was reading an article today on tattoos. Never really been attracted to the culture of tattoos and apparently there is a whole hidden language in the chosen design. People from Margate or the seaside generally might have an anchor or a swallow tattoo, although a swallow apparently also means that you have been in jail. Popeye, I think, had an anchor on his forearm. For the record, Swee'Pea was a baby and certainly not Popeye's urine sample. That would have contained far too much iron from all the spinach. It is no surprise that there is a statue of Popeye in Crystal City, Texas, the home of spinach growing. Probably an anchor sculpted somewhere on the statue. Sounds about right. A teardrop can reflect being in prison but more often indicates death or mourning. It can also apparently indicate that you have murdered someone. A dolphin presumably means that you like the 'Hitchhikers Guide To The Galaxy' and thanks for all the fish. One cat means you acted alone, several reflects a gang bang or maybe a pussy riot. Grimaldi had nothing on his forearms that I am aware of, but a clown tattooed somewhere on your body is quite a sad statement. Live now pay later.

The theme of being in prison additionally seems to emerge in clocks, spider's webs or tombstones. I would have thought a tombstone showed that I liked cowboys and westerns. That I had wanted to be at the OK Coral, firing my foot-long Buntline Special like Wyatt Earp. Save the ink because actually it wasn't that heroic. The Earps, who were the law officers, and the Clantons were both thought to have been involved with cattle rustling and stage robbery. The Earps do have their defenders but you pays your money. Too many crooks, eh. Billy Clanton actually had his hands in the air when Morgan Earp shot him, but did manage to draw his Smith and Wesson to return fire before they got him. Tom McLaury had opened his coat wide, not to flash, but to show he was unarmed before Doc Holliday fired his shotgun at him. Wyatt didn't kill anyone then, although he did get two of the Clantons later. Leave the tombstones alone. Personally if I was ever to have a tattoo, I might opt for a butterfly, or an anchor. But that's just me. I yam what I yam.

In the summer of 1967 I spent six weeks in the Royal Sea-bathing Hospital at Margate with a broken leg. Fell off the back of a motorbike. So much alcohol I felt no pain, until I tried to move. Mike for a couple of weeks used to wheel me through the women's wards just for the fun of it, until the matron banned us. We used to take beer with us, which he had brought in, on the wheelchair to share round. For many years the Hospital was in disrepair, but was then being refurbished as luxury residential apartments until the depression struck. It has a great position but the property around it leaves much to be desired. The Dog and Duck has gone from next door, although the welcome there was rarely great. Margate initially came to fame for its quality of sea-bathing and the partaking of sea water to cure all known ailments. You must be joking. We used to regularly swim from the Westbrook beach but in the sixties you would choose very carefully if you planned to drink the water. The Reeves family made money by selling bottled mineral water from Margate but you wonder if it isn't the type of activity which might attract Del Boy. You may recall the episode where he sets up his own water bottling plant.

Dr Lettsome, who founded the Sea-bathing Infirmary in 1791, is an interesting fellow. Born on the island of Little Jost Van Dyke - didn't he sing 'Walk On By' - in the West Indies to a Quaker family, Lettsome was sent on his own at the age of six, to school in Lancashire. He became apprenticed to an apothecary, studied at St Thomas Hospital, probably playing hockey in his spare time, and qualified as a physician. When he returned home, as an abolitionist he immediately freed all his slaves. Back in the UK he founded the Medical Society of London. So this was no quack with a barmy idea, opening a home in Margate by the sea. He was a friend of Benjamin Franklin and knew Mary Wollstonecraft. Nowhere sadly does he show any interest in sport, let alone cricket. Built a villa in Camberwell and laid out a large park with rare and experimental plants. Shame because it would have allowed for a very fine cricket square. He was the man who introduced the mangelwurzel, principally as an animal fodder. However against that, he condemned card parties and intemperance. Not sure he'd get in our team. The only saving grace is that the mangelwurzel has an association in England with sport, a mangelwurzel hurling championship now being regularly staged in Wiltshire. Teams of three throw mangelwurzels at someone called Norman. Maybe Margaret Thatcher started that, in the Cabinet room. Doubtless very much how cricket started.

“My great aim is to discover whether this splendid game is or is not so connected with some of the beautiful laws of motion as to deserve the appellation of a science”

Nicholas Wanostrocht in ‘Felix on the Bat’.

I am indebted to ‘The Essential John Arlott’ for the knowledge that the Earl of Thanet features in one of the twelve watercolour drawings from the notebook of George Shepheard, currently in the possession of the MCC. Arlott said this is the most historically important item of cricket art. In passing he strongly dismissed Hambleden’s claim to be considered as one of the first cricketing areas, pointing out that the game had been played for longer in counties like Kent, Sussex and Surrey. He also contributed a much larger article, ‘A Cricket Treasury’, which can be viewed on Espncricinfo. Sadly all the original paintings of cricketers in Dane Park appear to have been lost, although I believe that ‘Miss Wicket’ and Miss Trigger’ actually worked for part of the summer in the Margate ‘conveniences’.

The finest lithographs are said to be by G F Watts, a prolific artist, with titles such as ‘The Cut’, ‘The Leg Half-volley’ and ‘The Leg Volley’, modelled by Nicholas Wanostrocht and the Honourable Fred Ponsonby. Fred obviously lived in a house with a garden very similar to my family’s. He may or may not have had a birdbath. My brother and I could play leg shots with abandon, as our neighbours on that side, two old brothers, were quite charming if we had to go into their garden to retrieve the tennis balls. This would happen almost every ten minutes. We tended to be more circumspect at straight drives, although I regarded this as a personal strength, provided the bowler or fielder in the match didn’t catch the ball, as in the garden it would rebound straight back at you off the coal bunker. Nicholas warns, in his 1845 book ‘Felix on the Bat’, of this very hazard, describing how the ball in a Lords match rebounded fiercely and dangerously from the tennis court wall. In my case, health and safety issues emanated from my mother. My father would only get involved if you lifted the ball up through the kitchen or dining room windows.

Off drives and any form of ‘Cut’ were fraught with danger in our garden. The ball would frequently rebound off the lawn and bounce over into the neighbour’s garden on the right-hand side. The husband of this particular couple had a passing resemblance to the scientist in the Rupert annuals and could have been played with ease by Richard Wilson. He was an odd unsociable man who retreated to his shed for probably questionable purposes. My mother had never forgiven him for his refusal to help my brother, who had been home alone and had leapt to head the winning goal at Wembley, missed the balloon and headed the French window. His nose was hanging by a thread but our trusty neighbour merely told him to sit and wait for our parents to return to get him to hospital. He would regularly confiscate any balls he saw lying on the grass. We would therefore have to wait until we thought he was out or make swift darting raids over the fence, often provoking fierce banging on the windows. Miserable old git. And short-sighted too. He would have made a fine umpire, if only he had lived in Birchington.

I tell you this merely to explain why it is that G F Watts was unable to capture the 'Off-drive' or 'The Cut', whether square or late, in Fred Ponsonby's garden. The Honourable Fred evidently also had a very unpleasant neighbour to his right, as you faced the back of the house. Such are the vagaries of both cricket practice and art. Watts twice refused a baronetcy from Queen Victoria, the last one presumably she regarded as the deepest cut. Nicholas had no such reservations. 'Felix on the Bat' remains a standard treatise on cricketing techniques, each section being preceded by a Shakespearean quote. What sort of author would intersperse his writings with quotations? Surely a sign of desperation? It is in addition written in a tongue-in-cheek style. For example, you are advised to arrive at the ground with sweet oil for the bruises you may collect and bacon fat to grease the face of the bat. Good God, that's the sort of advice that provoked the Indian Mutiny. Nicholas did, more seriously, pioneer the use of India rubber batting gloves to protect the hands and he also uses mathematical calculation to describe how the 'Forward' stroke, at a forty five degree angle, can become a drive against slow 'insinuators' with just slightly more pressure. In one strange section he pays glowing tribute to women in general, but then counter-balances that with a statement that, "No figure on earth is so beautiful as a sphere". Unless his women are circular in build, this would seem to be very much a confirmation of the position cricket had in his life, rather than his ability to pay successful compliments. I have lately tried to employ this form of flattery, but women do not appear to enjoy being told they are round and sphere-like.

If you were fans of the 'West Wing' and watched 'Newsroom' because of Aaron Sorkin, the Juvenal of his generation, you will probably know the controversy it has caused in the States. The Los Angeles Times described the strangely vitriolic response to the new show, which seeks to expose the dumbing down of American journalism, which has tended to move to the right. Can America really harbour its own version of men from the seventh century? The nearest thing we had in the Margate cricket club to shock jocks were shock jock straps, which held your balls in place to lessen the shock of the cricket ball. I suspect both smell much the same. In 'Newsroom' Jeff Daniels plays news anchor, Will McAvoy. If you ever saw the three-part television series on Gettysburg, one of the critical battles of the American Civil War, you will have seen Daniels play Joshua Chamberlain. He was the Colonel from Maine, on the opposite side of the Union battlefield to Carl Schurz, who heroically ordered his troops to bayonet charge down the hill at the Confederates when his men had run out of bullets. He also apparently ran out of lead in the film 'Something Wild', when he was handcuffed to the bed and Melanie Griffith took off her top.

Daniels is a strong fan of baseball, marrying his wife Kathleen on Friday the Thirteenth. He had worn the number 13 on his baseball uniform when they met. True love yet again. Detroit Tigers is said to be his team. Whether they played baseball on Little Round Top is never mentioned in Longacre's book on Chamberlain, but of course that is some twenty three years before the Little Big Horn and maybe by then the game was better established. The Daniels family apparently own the Chelsea Lumber Company in Michigan, so obviously in that area they provide all the firewood. God never gets a look in. No wonder the Lone Ranger wasn't ever seen around Michigan. McAvoy in the opening programme gets provoked into a long outburst about American leadership. He says that the USA now leads the world only in three categories. The first two, I understand, are true but satirical - defence spending and the number of incarcerated adults. Mind you, if you count women imprisoned at home in the total, there are several medieval countries which could be said to lead the field in the second category. That apart, he then says that they have the largest number of adults who believe angels are real. Aaaron, how can you write this stuff? How can that be satirical? For you and I have a guardian angel. Who doesn't believe? I know I have a guardian angel somewhere, probably two. Buzz Lightyear told me. One of mine bunks off at Xmas to make toys up in Lapland. There is a baseball or a cricket ball for every child to carry in their pocket. Much healthier than carrying a mace spray.

"Foundlings and fledglings are angels of this earth".

Tracey Emin

So you know about angels, Tracey. Something's wrong though, terebley wrong. Margate, Margate Harbour, The Lido. All illustrations from your memory. The perfect place to grow, but keep me safe. Helter fucking skelter, where was your guardian angel? Did you tell her, you forgot to kiss my soul? As always. What was it Madonna said, "Tracey is intelligent and wounded and not afraid to expose herself". Jesus, that's some heavy shit you've been through. I grew up there as well and I feel really sad reading this stuff. Yeah, we were lots of things when young - coarse, basic, immature. But hell, there was a lot of friendship and laughter too. No-one deserves to have memories like these. The Star Trek Voyager was meant to be fun and in the right place socially, the final frontier. You sure met some falling stars if they wanted you to be destroyed. Fuck you, you left me breathing? Hate and power can be a terrible thing. Have you ever heard Miranda Lambert and 'Gunpowder and Lead'? "His fist is big but my gun's bigger. He'll find out when I pull the trigger". Maybe your art is your trigger, but perhaps you should have considered spending more time on the Dreamland arcade shooting range.

Mind you, not sure if that would have really helped. You might then have graduated to semi-automatic assault rifles. I know you could then have wasted a whole tent-full but in those days we would just have thought that a Bushmaster was some kind of vaginal strimmer. Could have joined one of those rifle associations though. NRA. Three letters yet again. Of distinction? Not quite. More in the line of WMD. Are all of the weapons of mass destruction kept at home in closets and wardrobes, like Saddam's? Maybe we need a "right to arm bears"? However I came across this very nice guy on the web called Wayne Lapierre. Unfortunately they don't have a Burke's American Peerage otherwise I would have looked him up. I was sure he would be included somewhere in one of those Burke's collections. I know that he apparently once said that all federal agents are "jack-booted government thugs... wearing Nazi bucket helmets and black storm trooper uniforms", but he was obviously going through a bad phase so you need to forget that little outburst. Here is a man of peace and reason and concern for the human man, particularly those with mental health issues. I am not quite sure how many of his NRA members are suffering from these sorts of problems but I think there are nearly four million of them so this is a very serious issue. The sooner they all get help the better. At least they left you breathing? Julie, poor love, poor thing. Everyone I have ever slept with 1965-1965. Love is what you want. Then a week of hell, it's not the way I want to die. The last thing I said to you is don't leave me here. In thinking of you, always sorry. No reincarnation. Sometimes I feel so fucking lost.

She was found lying at the foot of the fifth tree. It was apparent from the marks on the ground that the body had been moved, dragged, about seventy five feet. The jaw had been fractured and there were numerous marks of bruising round the throat. Death was due to strangulation, asphyxia. He admitted to slapping her and then he hit her again because he said she seemed to be enjoying it. Remember another Goffin and King song from 1962, "He hit me and it felt like a kiss. He hit me but it didn't hurt me". Written after they had heard how Little Eva's boyfriend kept her permanently in loco-motion with his fists. Substitutiary loco-motion. Yet Eva still kept going back to him, because she said he loved her. Sometimes you just despair. Sometimes we believe what we hear and don't explore the reality behind the words. Surely men don't really believe that a blow can feel like a kiss?

His appeal against the verdict, which he always maintained did not seriously take any provocation into account, was partly because she had grinned at him. The pathologist had explained that breaking the jaw could leave the impression that someone was smiling because of the grimace. The judge directed the jury away from that presumably on the basis that at two o'clock in the morning you might struggle to tell whether someone is smiling or grimacing? He had already had one girl that day, he knew that Julie had been to bed with Wally and he could not see why she should be coy. The resistance and the fooling around just caused him to snap. She may well have teased him to a point where he could think he had been provoked, but the hands round the throat were no casual or brief motion. Prolonged constriction, the forensic pathologist James Cameron, said. Prolonged. Think 400 metres hurdles. Two young people on a trip, the drugs diminishing the sense of responsibility. Two lives wasted.

My kids would have been impressed though when he appeared at the first hearing. He was apparently wearing sandals without socks. Obviously a man who studied fashion, unlike me. We have been on holidays when all my family walk as far behind me as they can, when I have worn my sandals. I always wear socks with them and sometimes odd ones, so there. He had worn a smart grey suit and a red striped tie that fateful weekend. Most of us wouldn't be seen dead in ties at the weekend, but suits were part of the code, if not ours. For him and Julie a week that sadly changed both their lives forever. That was the week that was. I did like that Millicent Martin. Finished in 1962 though and replaced by 'Not so Much a Programme, More a Way of Life'. There's a picture of David Frost in the college football team at the Barton Road pavilion, when Tony Kirby, later a fellow, was captain. Tony's wife was Dutch but not sure she ever made them stop playing football for tea and schnapps. In cricket, on the other hand, dress code, dress sense is such a huge part of the game, even in the supporting cast. There is a noted painting called 'The Scorer' from 1842 by William Henwood. It is of the Lewes Priory scorer, one William Davis, who is shown with glasses, beard, straw hat and pipe. He also is wearing sandals with socks, but you can't quite see them. He would know a few Grose drinking songs.

My college side was particularly short one year, just before exam time, and we were looking for recruits to make up the team. One of our friends volunteered to play, although none of us thought he had ever played the game of cricket before. He appeared the next day at the pavilion in full regalia, including cricket sweater and cap. Wow! None of us owned a cap. He was also the possessor of a large black beard and being rather portly, looked very much like the pictures of W G Grace. Despite it being a warm day he kept his cap and sweater on whilst fielding, which caused a little mirth and was mainly positioned in the slips, because it was not thought wise to ask him to run. When we were asked to bat, he was allotted the number seven slot. He duly came out quite slowly when his turn came, clearly taking stock of the field. He looked around attentively and very professionally, then took guard. He finally adjusted his cap, looked around yet again and prepared for the bowler. We were all gripped by the spectacle and watched intently. He played forward, missed the ball completely and it flew into the keeper's gloves. He then without pause set off down the wicket to prod the place where he thought the ball had pitched. Just short of a length. The keeper took two steps forward, removed the bails and appealed. Up went the umpire's finger and our W G Grace, after a brief protest, was forced to plod slowly back. One of my learned friends in the very far north has just reminded me that the bat arrived back shortly before the batsman, striking the pavilion wall with a loud thud. The place was by then in some disarray, not, I am afraid to say, in sympathy and the two minutes were almost up before the next man could stop laughing enough to run out to the wicket. Sadly our W G never played again so we have no idea what happened to the sweater and cap. Maybe thrown disconsolately into the river. On the last viewing our man is now a notable and much slimmer beardless Chief Executive.

"If you can keep your head when all about you are losing theirs, it's just possible you haven't grasped the situation".

Jean Kerr in 'Don't Eat the Daisies'

To eat the daisies you have really to be face down in the grass. There are literally dozens of Daisy's. From 'Daisy Bell', give me your answer do, to Daisy the Engine in 'Thomas the Tank Engine'. From Daisy a porn star client in 'Californication' to Daisy in 'Toy Story 3'. From Daisy the Dog in 'Blondie' to Daisy the meerkat in 'Meerkat Manor'. Jesus, no more bloody meerkats, please. The 1966 movie 'Daisies' was described as a mad-cap feminist farce. Don't want any of those either. Feminists can be even worse than meerkats, wanting equality for goodness sake. Be different if they played cricket. Reference to the 'Flower Expert' on the web tells us that the daisy can symbolize a new beginning, and part of the meaning is "I will never tell". Pretty impressive stuff, eh. Exactly right in Julie's case. The word also originates from Anglo-Saxon as daisies open at dawn, just as the day starts to begin. That is exactly when the poor council employee, 'Trigger' the road sweeper, found her on his way to work just after five o'clock. Our guy would have been almost back home by then.

Of course, in the film 'Pushing Daisies' the pie-maker had the power to bring people back to life. Of all the many jobs he had had, don't think he had ever been a pie-maker. He did say he had tried desperately to bring Julie back to life. There were bruises, scratches and cuts on the back of the body where she had been dragged. He claimed he had ripped open her clothing to revive her, then dragged her further up the slope and tried again. That will have been how the blood got on to his clothes and shoes. At that stage he would have been beginning to panic and in some disarray, even under the influence of the tablets. You would have had to have known the park well to have hidden the body and I doubt he had noticed the children's playground where the swing was standing. That might have meant at least another four or five hours before they found her, but probably would have made no difference. Must have been a much bigger shock when he got back to the 'Mad House' to find a police car parked in front of his Morris van. He wouldn't have known that they had not come for him, but to search James' room. He could have gone to find them to explain, but was quickly on his way. Or maybe in his anxiety he didn't actually spot the car. Maybe he did walk the dog around for ten minutes towards Cecil Square in order to clear his head.

Reno lost his head at the Little Big Horn, Benteen didn't. Joshua Chamberlain grasped the situation at the Little Big Top. Coincidentally his daughter Grace was nicknamed Daisy and he described her as 'an angel of God'. If they ever do commission a film about the life of the man, it is possibly not a great role to play for an actor. Chamberlain was wounded later at Petersburg, the bullet severing the urethra and clipping the bladder. No more sexual intercourse with Fanny after that, although he survived to witness the final confederate surrender and then lived until 1914. Longacre says Joshua had a textbook in his possession by a Captain Duparcq which described the battle of Caldiero in 1805. The French had been surrounded by the Austrians but a bayonet charge won the day. There was always discussion as to whether Chamberlain had ordered the bayonet charge but they have now found a copy of the original report which seems to exonerate him. On the Rebel side, Oates always insisted quite bitterly that his men had turned Chamberlain's flank before the charge and there is an interesting footnote. In 1889 Oates got permission to put a monument on Vincent's Spur, named after Strong Vincent, killed that day during the action, but this was rescinded when Chamberlain got involved and had it stopped. You tend to believe Oates, as he much later said that even if he had taken the whole top, he was so isolated and his men so exhausted that he couldn't have held it for more than ten minutes. Does it matter? Not really unless you are a descendant of either man. The 20th Maine had reunions of the survivors which Chamberlain always attended but not as many as Wellington's troops. The Waterloo survivors met every year. I can imagine Wellington and Napoleon falling out over their result but not about the actual positions each side took. Mind you, last time I visited the Waterloo battlefield many years ago, you would have thought the French had won.

Of much greater significance for posterity was the appearance on the Cemetery Hill battlefield four months later of Abraham Lincoln. Surprisingly he wasn't even the first choice to attend the opening of the Gettysburg cemetery but his two minute speech there has lasted quite well. "Four score and seven years ago our fathers brought forth on this continent a new nation, conceived in liberty, and dedicated to the proposition that all men are created equal". No mention of women? Well he didn't really have much time to knock up his speech being a late replacement for the President of Harvard. Lincoln was also at the theatre when a certain Charles Wyndham made his professional stage debut as Osric in Hamlet. As Charles Culverwell he had crossed the Atlantic to volunteer his services to the Union as a doctor in the Civil War. He sat for two days at Willard's hotel, being totally ignored, before being rescued by P T Barnum of all people. Later in the war, on a break, he auditioned for Hamlet, the star part being played by a certain John Wilkes Booth. Hope

Lincoln gave Wilkes Booth a standing ovation at the end when he watched him perform.

Wyndham thought Booth was a wonderful actor and his two brothers were also well known on the stage, all three playing together in Julius Caesar. Perhaps that was what gave Booth the idea of assassinating the President. Different theatre, of course, when Booth some two years later did the deed and by then he had discarded the idea of a knife for a gun, killing Lincoln with one shot. Wyndham had returned to the UK by then to become one of the great British actors and worked with the Vanbrugh sisters, Violet and Irene, also stars of the time, and with Irene's husband Bourchier. Both of the Vanbrugh sisters had been enrolled at the Sarah Thorne School of Acting in Margate, so the Thanet area must have been quite highly rated for its drama at the time. Round the Horne would have enjoyed Sarah's last performance on the stage, playing Lady Gay Spanker in London Assurance. That was recently revived by the National Theatre and by the Royal Shakespeare Company in the seventies. Judi Dench was in the latter but sadly not as one of the Spankers. For an old bird, she pulled that Bill quite quickly in the Exotic Marigold Hotel, didn't she? Not sure how the young Indian manager managed to combine running that with his duties in the 'Newsroom'.

**"The Protestants hate the Catholics,
And the Catholics hate the Protestants,
And the Hindus hate the Muslims,
And everybody hates the Jews".**

'National Brotherhood Week', Tom Lehrer

To be honest, I am getting quite a lot of stick about the celestial cricket. To begin with, nobody wants to play in Missouri. It isn't that they dislike Missouri itself and there are very obvious marketing opportunities. 'Meet me in St Louis' for the First Test, with a touch of cricketing heaven, sounds terrific. Judy would have to cut out the barbiturates though, this time round. There are, however, strong doubts about Kansas City as they have all seen the film about the wizard. There is always a lot of confusion outside America about which is the real Kansas City so it's no good trying to explain. They in any case liked The Wizard of Oz's curtain for control and secrecy, but got spooked by the wicked witch of the west. Broomsticks again. Springfield was also black-balled, as Homer is thought to lack moral fibre. The official state animal, the Missouri mule, nearly swung it, but then someone mentioned that on the male side, donkeys are said to have borne 'angels by day and spirits by night'. Missouri was always against prohibition, unlike Kansas, and preferred their mules to do the job twenty four seven.

In any case not all of the religions are into alcohol, except in private between consenting adults. In addition, most of them have misgivings at the thought that heaven is in Missouri at all or that a religion can be founded by a man called Smith. I've told them he was very convincing, but they quoted Oliver Wendell Holmes to his friend Samuel Smith when they were both at Harvard, "Fate tried to conceal him by naming him Smith". Tom Lehrer was a Harvard man. There does seem to always be a great deal of jealousy and hatred about between these religious boys, and we're not just talking about poisoning pigeons in the park. Cole Porter didn't help. Thank goodness he didn't write the Missouri Waltz or we would be talking about dark monasteries, Satan in slacks and having an ace in the hole. Heaven knows, anything goes? How many religious captains are going to come and play in any heaven that purports to be in the USA. I haven't even begun to suggest cricket matches on another planet, up there with all the aliens and the cruising spaceships, so heaven help us.

Some of the more religious souls can't understand why cricketers automatically get to heaven, even if they are atheists. Got an e-mail from some Russian Orthodox guy, Vsevolod Chaplin. Looked up the name Vsevolod in my Burke's Soviet Peerage but just referred me back. For Vsevolod, see Burke, the complete version. He says he wants Russia to do away with the secular state. Got some sort of continuing problem with a pussy riot. Groucho Marx once wrote to one of his brothers about the desperate pussy willow season. He concluded that the willows weren't getting enough pussy. Like the sound of that, Groucho was a riot. I'm on the next plane to Moscow, drynamil spansules, viagra and bus pass in suitcase. Have said to Vsevolod that I liked his great grandfather's films, particularly 'The Gold Rush' and that his proposal won't affect my plans at all. Russians don't really do cricket, so the secular versus religious bit isn't relevant. He did write back. Apparently Pussy Riot are a band and had been locked up for months. If you ever get to read this, you will know they got two years, sentenced by some unusual female lady judge and the remaining pussies have fled. The latest happening saw one of the girls released on appeal, although not sure if any defence witnesses were called and the prosecution case seemed to attract a deal of external mirth. Sad if the law courts ever become an appendage of the state, the truth just seeming to be bulldozed into rubble. Can happen anywhere, of course, according to Tom Lehrer. Why does everyone hate the Jews? After two thousand years ago, isn't it time to forgive. In any case, if God is omnipotent then he willed the whole Crucifixion thing. The world is mad. Anyway I always loved all those Hymie jokes that Michael Winner trotted out. He'll be doubtless causing havoc in some celestial restaurant now. Never any jokes about bulldozers though. Can't explain.

The sentence in Russia will be commuted of course in time, when they consider the girls are broken, and they will all die mysteriously on the stage within two months of release from radio-active poisoning. Their judicial trial was apparently willed by God as well. The band protested against the decision of the Orthodox leader, Kirill Bill, who called the Putin era "a miracle of God". God is obviously pretty busy in Russia but of course in the old days he could even heal men who were possessed and the odd leper. Not sure what he makes of men like Mugabe or Berlusconi or which category they will come under when the Grim Reaper calls, but he's going to have his hands full. However we do know that Putin is basically a gentleman, so any violence against the girls will be purely accidental. Don't think Putin discriminates anyway when he locks people up. Maybe an opportunity for yet another Chaplin to remake 'The Great Dictator'. Maria and Nadezhda are the two girls remaining in prison, although my paper says that some commentators think they're too lightweight to support. Lightweight huh? Probably means you can punch them and they'll travel a bit further. Madonna supported them and got denounced for her sins by the Deputy Prime Minister, Rogozin, who took time off to do so from upgrading the armed forces. You know the sort of upgrade that folk like to work on. We'll first invade the Ukraine, then Georgia, Poland and finally the Rhineland. Maybe even Lincolnshire. Depriving the girls of food and sleep was obviously for their own good, much better than diet pills.

Their mistake was the prayer, "Mother of God, get rid of Putin". Big mistake. Why appeal to God's mother anyway? Although Mary is the Mother of God, and not everyone agrees with that interpretation, she is not his mother in the sense that she is older than him. Rather, she is the Mother of God in the sense that she carried in her womb a divine person, Jesus. So if she is no older than God, he's not going to take much notice, is he? Girls, if you want to know how to deal with Messrs Kirill Bill, Charlie Chaplin and even Putin, then I have a friend in this women's organisation. I've been a volunteer adviser for ten years myself now so any advice is based on good experience, even got a kitemark tattooed on my forearm. I told her. Accept the handshake, pull the boys warmly towards you, smile and then knee them in the groin. So you're worried about Putin's judo skills? He's a pussy cat. Actually he probably has cat-flaps in all of his palaces, twenty eight the papers said. Surely not? Even Stalin wasn't that acquisitive, in fact I seem to remember that he was actually quite modest in his personal life. If you are still worried then wear a balaclava, unless of course you're in Paris when you meet up, as it counts as a face-covering garment on the streets.

"It is difficult, for example, from the perspective of the early twenty-first century to appreciate just how powerful a grip cricket exerted on the collective sporting mentality of the English in the early post-war years"

Peter Hennessy, 'Having It So Good'

John Arlott in 1953. The ball 'moves straight for the first half of its course, then, as if an invisible string were tugging at it, swings away towards the off-side of the wicket'. There had been very few invisible strings tugged during the war in Britain. Other countries had been able to play cricket but we had no first class matches at all. When the war ended, the sheer fact of being able to witness sporting occasions swelled the crowds. The Indian tour in 1946 saw fifty thousand turn up to see them play Glamorgan at Swansea. Arlott always thought of 1947 as the vintage year with the likes of Wally Hammond, Compton, Hutton, Edrich and Bedser, but 1948 saw the visit by Hassett's Australians. Denis Compton and Keith Miller were firm friends by then, having played against each other in their respective armies at Calcutta during the war. They even stayed friends after Miller unleashed a series of bouncers at Peter May at Trent Bridge. The first radio broadcasts, reports, not live ball-by-ball commentaries, began in 1946 although the first test transmission had been as early as 1938. What was important in generating excitement were the newsreels like Movietone and Pathe News. Cinema audiences in the years after the war were ten times what they are today, with nearly 1.4 billion attending in 1950.

Bradman was the great celebrity, the draw, when the Aussies came to visit, with his test match average of 99.94. Men like Denis Compton could also be celebrities, certainly with the ladies. "A little dab'll do ya, the gals will all pursue ya". What Beechams didn't tell you about Brylcreem, whose adverts Dennis fronted, was that it might also give you greasy hair and make your acne worse. At least they didn't market it as an obesity aid. There were plenty of cricket professionals by then but only a few counties, like Yorkshire, paid their men an annual wage. Most cricketers had to work during the winter and moonlight during the summer if they could. These were also still the times of the gentlemen and the players, the amateurs and the professionals. At a local level, cricket was solely amateur but had a very real status. Clubs like Margate could attract strong sides by offering the chance for a family day out. The men could play and then drink. The women and children could head for the beach. When they did begin to drive down by car, the three lanes of the Thanet Way could be a death trap, but often the families would crowd into a coach. The men at the back would get out the cards and the crates of beer would be cracked open. Wielding a bottle opener was the only form of stretching exercise that any of them would attempt. Yet the skill levels were amazingly good. It is just the stamina and fitness now that is so radically different.

As a separate footnote, Peter Hennessy, the good Baron, is recorded as briefly going to St Benedict's school, with its all-embracing Catholic virtues. Did all the Popes called Benedict go there? John Julius Norwich doesn't seem to cover that. The likes of Julian Clary and Chris Patten also appear to have attended, for a longer duration. Never a Pope Julian. There's a funny thing, because some of the cardinals would have appeared to have been eminently qualified. Patten once said of Putin in 2004 that, when talking about Chechen or Islamic fundamentalists, his "eyes turn to those of a killer". Here's a man not afraid of the truth you would say and Patten stated quite clearly, "In a democracy everybody has a right to be represented including the jerks". Part of the cricket heritage very probably, the strate bat mentality. Keep yore bat strate boy and all will be all right in life as in criket. Embedded deeply and consistently in the British establishment, like the stripes in a stick of Margate rock.

We have just had another protest in an English religious institution, briefly occupying the headlines. Just supposing that we had a real Pussy protest here though, this time say by three girls in another band, in a Catholic Cathedral. They are chanting, "Mother of God, get rid of Patten". What nonsense, couldn't happen, could it? That's the difference between those countries that play cricket and those that don't. We have nice honourable men in charge of our Trusts, men who know Pope Benedict personally. Well might come in handy if you need advice on how to handle child abuse issues. Mind you that would be like referring decisions to a third umpire, even when he is not really part of the same game, so probably not. Mother of God, don't get rid of Patten, well not just yet. He put up a good showing at the select committee, batting away the questions with some integrity. Mind you, we do need someone to represent the jerks, people like me. And you probably. Perhaps we are already represented on some of the select committees.

Cameron met Putin at the judo in the Olympics, ostensibly to talk about Syria. Someone suggested on a blog that they were probably comparing notes on how to do away with the secular state here. Mind you, Paxman had just been asked not to talk any more hogwash about those who believe in religion. Would make sense. Silence the presenters first. Promote faith schools and academies. Send them all King James bibles. Promote ministers with strong religious principles, mainly geeks. Not sure what Chas and Dave would make of the new Health Secretary in their cockney rhyming slang. Mind you, I fell off one once under the bridge by the Anchor pub in the summer of 1967. They're definitely not for kissing in. We were recently reminded of the amusing piece of writing by the late Gore Vidal, explaining that Judaism, Christianity and Islam are sky-god religions with God the Omnipotent Father. He thought they were totally responsible for the loathing of women for two thousand years. Those who reject the sky-god must be converted or killed, for their own good. Maybe in a democratic society just silenced. Bet you can't even mention the word 'pussy' on air now. Funnily enough, having written this, I noticed that some American newspapers are already doing exactly that when they talk about our young Russian girls, taking out the 'pussy'. Mrs Slocombe would be appalled.

The evening of the 9th October 1953. A newly-appointed publican is just opening up in the Ruby Lounge at Margate. It is his first year in the industry and already he has seen the tills overflow for the coronation. Trained in hospitality in West Wales, where they only speak Welsh and burn down English holiday homes, Les never smiles save at closing time. You may be served if he likes you but there is absolutely no chance of any food or entertainment. Only men drink here. Through the glass-fronted door come two burly men in grey raincoats, shoulders heavily padded. Excuse me, they say, we have Churchill outside. Not that bloody dog, said Les, I'm well insured already. I'm with the Prudential. No, replied the biggest agent, our governor is on his way to the Conservative party conference. Not quite finished his speech yet and wants a quick one to settle his nerves. Saw the harbour and wanted to paint it, but not enough time. He's sent his private secretary on to organise the hotel. Can he come in for a while?

Bugger me, it really is Winston. Not really seen out much after his stroke in February and of course the public have no idea how severe that was. Les draws halves of beer shandy for each of them and a whisky chaser for the old boy. Rab Butler's niece, who was still taking dictation for his unfinished speech, had to sit out in the Bentley. Les didn't like girls in his pub so one of the security men took her out a Vimto and a bag of Smith's crisps. You know the one's, blue twist of salt inside. Needed a stiff drink, said Winston, could do with a bit of advice, landlord. Been wondering whether I can carry on as Prime Minister. Not been well lately and worried about the big speech to the party tomorrow. They have been trying to persuade me to go to the Lords and although the old Attendance Allowance would come in handy for Chartwell, not too sure whether they mean well. Also not sure how to start the speech. Had thought of we will fight them on the beaches? Doesn't feel quite right now, even though this is Margate, and if I say I can see trouble here in the future between groups of people called Mods and Rockers, they'll just say I am a war-monger. 1933 all over again.

Personally, says Les, I find I have to go the toilet now every fifty minutes, since the old war injury. A piece of shrapnel clipped the bladder, shortly after the bayonet charge at Arnhem when we had run out of bullets. Make it fifty minutes and the old pins should be fine. I'd start with something that the boys would applaud, like no coloureds and bring back beheading and transportation. Wait until the applause subsides and then possibly throw in something on cricket too, for Billy as the local MP. The problem is that Winston is terribly deaf now so only catches the first bit. Gets one of the security men to bellow out of the door that the speech needs to be kept to under one hour. Completely mishears the bit about coloureds so actually decides to start his speech on the progress made in British Guiana. Need more Guyanans in Britain he says. Let's organise a boat and it can pick up others from the Caribbean islands. Do wonders long term for the cricket and for the drinks and gambling industries. You had better believe it. Even if it did take my friend Mike a little longer to get here.

Winston is on his third chaser at this point but manages to call out the key quote, "We have tried hard to make our administration loyal, sober, flexible and thrifty". Les not too keen on the sober bit. Winston has two more chasers and they agree to differ. Next day, 10th October, fifty minute big speech in Margate at the Conservative Party Conference goes down a bomb. Good old Winston. Some of them a bit miffed that he didn't include any reference to no coloureds and seemed to want to encourage them but hey. Enoch threatened to leave, again. Anthony Eden looking very thin so in any case there's not much choice other than to allow Churchill to bugger on. Anthony needs a bit of feeding up, get him off those diet pills, those spansules. The Margate sunshine seemed to do him good, well received speech too. What about a spell in Egypt to top up the old sun-tan. Maybe Smith Kline and French would sponsor him. Wonder if there are still three of them running the company? Maybe the Smith is also the one who makes the crisps, but then some of the Smiths in history have been very odd indeed.

"If the triangles made a God, they would give him three sides".

Charles de Montesquieu

What on earth did Montesquieu mean? Of course, the Triangles have a God, he was just being obtuse. By the way, I am very close to resigning from the celestial cricket committee. One of my friends accused me of rambling in this epic account. Bloody hell, you try and organise celestial cricket. Not only am I rambling, I'm probably barking. The first week has not gone well. Thought we should start with a week-long festival in the Kingdom. First two teams turn up and are locked out. St Peter has only gone and lost the bloody keys to the Kingdom of Heaven pavilion. Had to look around to find a rock to throw through one of the pavilion windows to get them in, but eventually settled for a cricket ball. Got Bert's dad to umpire at one end as I knew he would be unaffected by the occasion but Pope Innocent the First was up the other end. Bert's dad, poor soul, ended up having the most enormous argument. Innocent insisted that, as the Supreme Authority, only he could make the final umpiring decisions. At both ends! Wanted everything referred to him. Bert's dad hit him with a stump.

On Wednesday the twelve apostles insisted their team would only play as a complete entity and refused to drop anyone, so the Buddhists had a walk-over. They were fed up and went down to watch the Punch and Judy show by the shores of Galilee. Punch doesn't hit Judy any more as she and the others have opted for passive resistance. The hangman's been replaced and the devil is just another string of sausages, pork ones I believe. The Rastifarians wouldn't come out of the pavilion at all and of course the whole team tested positive. To cap it all some Copts and Nestorians turned up in small Hadron colliders and kept driving on to the pitch. Pulled the bunting down and trashed the beer and communion wine tent. I asked the religious zealots to intervene, perhaps get the heretics turned into frogs or locusts or have them lashed or stoned, but they couldn't care less. Wrote to the Nicaean Council hoping they might reconvene but they're all landlords now. Apparently the church had become the largest landowner in the west, so they were too busy recruiting social tenants to fill the properties. Since this universal credit was introduced up there all sorts of people are turning up to claim it. By mistake they got Athos, one of the three musketeers to administer it, and as he'd never heard of computers, he just doled it out to anyone who applied.

I reckon I have done over one thousand disability claims since I stopped real work and as most of them take a minimum of two hours with applicants, that's a fair number. For some eight years I was allowed to see confidential medical records so I am very familiar with consultants' letters. That was important on home visits so that you could position your approach and the words you used sympathetically and tactfully. You also had to try to minimise the fatigue and distress people feel when they have to admit, often reluctantly, to the many distinctly personal problems that they have because of their illness. Most consultants try, even when you are dying, to send you out of the door with some form of optimism. That's not a criticism but the positive slant they put in their letters sometimes doesn't help someone trying to claim a disability benefit. You know the sort of thing, apart from the constant pain, the leprosy and the fact that he may be dead within a year, he is remarkably cheerful and self-caring. If you are going to die within six months you can actually cheer up quite a bit as you qualify for special rules, but even then the form will take you thirty to forty minutes. Try not to die before it is completed.

Psychiatrists' letters and medical officers' reports in prison also have an agenda. Their principal function was often principally to ensure that you stood trial and the wording may not have helped your defence. The Brixton prison report said that he was calm, pleasant and co-operative, but concluded that "I consider that he knew what he was doing. He had consumed a quantity of alcohol and stimulant drugs, but I do not believe that they had impaired his responsibility to a substantial degree". This was about a man who may have taken ten to fifteen tablets probably seven hours before the murder, when Peter Laurie suggested that four is the average take in a day. The Canterbury report concluded that, "He was perfectly clear as to what had happened….he was in full control". Not sure about either of those. They seem to be based on his perception of whether he was in control. What surprisingly neither of the quite detailed reports did, was to talk in depth about how he came to react in such a manner. That might have helped him in the longer term, because without a more thorough assessment, people would probably later just look at his actual criminal record and draw their own conclusions.

When I began what I thought would be a collection of local cricketing anecdotes, I had no intention of covering the events in Dane Park in such detail. It seemed so long ago. What I do know though, from experience, is that our knowledge or what we think we know is always subjective. At the heart of any interpretation are the various pieces of information which we possess or are known and our separate and subjective analyses of them. Historians will tell you that even when events seem perfectly simple and sources are straightforward, interpretations by people who were actually present can be wildly different. Often people are adamant that they are perfectly clear as to what had happened, only for the detailed evidence to suggest that their impressions might not have been quite that accurate. If you are also tired or your mind is under some undue influence, whether from drugs or alcohol, then you may be not the best judge of how things panned out.

I am also not sure what sort of help was available to young people who got into trouble with the law in those days. Now, over the last few years, I've seen and hopefully helped in a very small way as a volunteer a number of young people who have had difficulties whilst growing up. My work tends to be with kids who are autistic or bi-polar, or who have adhd, whether severe or mild. Even helped one yesterday. My wife was actually a very good special needs teacher for many years so she saw and lived with the problems every day. She taught kids, for example, with adhd who without warning struck other kids for what they perceived were wrong or threatening responses. They would be adamant that the other person was at fault and nothing would shift that impression. Adhd - attention deficit hyperactive disorder. They had difficulty maintaining focus on one task and became bored with any tasks fairly easily. They are often not at all academic, not because they are less intelligent but because their brain just works slightly differently. They may be pleasant and co-operative yet don't recognise rules or boundaries, so are frequently at odds with authority. Their time-keeping will be poor and they will walk away from jobs for no apparent reason. And that's just adhd. We have moved on majorly with our understanding of kids like this, although that does not excuse their actions. We just don't fail all of them quite as much as in the past, as they hopefully get more time and understanding in the early days.

This probably has no bearing on anything in this story but I wanted to explain my world because it inevitably always now influences my judgement. I am always trying to assess people who come for help because an understanding of their symptoms drives our process. But whatever the reason behind your behaviour socially, if you are ever once labelled and stereotyped, then you will struggle to change the perceptions of your peer group. It is then only too easy to get into a spiral of conflict with authority. I always fought against rules and regulations but then my parents were there to try to set strong boundaries. The kids in my neighbourhood who struggled to pass exams did tend to drift into what they were good at practically. Cars were always an attractive option, whether you repair them or just like a fast set of wheels. Some of my friends looked to institutions like the Army or Navy which can stabilise and turn kids around, teach them a trade. However the services do not have a good record with individuals who do not see the need to respect rules or boundaries or who work to their own agenda.

Marriage and children can also turn people around. I have seen boys at first hand whose behaviour has at least stabilised when they have met a girl who can help them and be a strong partner. Yet there is always the difficulty of trying to support a young family when you struggle with paperwork and detail and few have families who can help financially. In any case many of us are always looking for something to turn up. Perhaps in those days the football pools, now maybe the lottery. So many young people just didn't get much help when they were struggling and I am not sure that very much has changed now once you have left school. Maybe we understand the issues a bit better. We are currently working on a project to help children and young teenagers so trends are important to us, part of the discipline. Without analysis how do you ever reconcile the different perspectives?

"The thrill of hearing a jury return a guilty verdict is the ultimate sexual experience"

Judge Gregory Wallance

This quotation is freely available on various websites but I have yet to track down Judge Wallance. It sounds the sort of thing one of those more eccentric American judges might say. In 1965 the trial at Maidstone Assizes lasted five days and the verdict of murder was delivered on the 16th November. The judgement was imprisonment for life and the prisoner went, I believe, to Dartmoor. The Appeal papers seem to indicate that, copying the prison governor there. Mr Justice Sachs had presided. No relation that I know of to Leonard Sachs. Those were the good old days. Reg Varney, later from 'On the Buses', used to be one of the regulars, both in that show and at the Winter Gardens in Margate. He had some form of slapstick routine with a ladder. No hangman's rope either at the top of it, though. Sachs was also twice in Doctor Who but not the ones where cricket balls saved the day. The verdict at Maidstone was quickly followed by the Appeal, which was unsuccessful. Life imprisonment confirmed for Julie's murder, but then out again in eleven years. How does that work?

Release after just eleven years really causes me some personal difficulty. I would have felt that justice had fallen short. Physical resistance and violence, in my opinion, must always be considered as a last resort against bullies and tyrants, where all other methods have failed or where justice has failed. Bullies and tyrants rarely change, they merely proceed onwards and upwards following their own narrow and personal agendas. That is an easier calculation. What part can violence ever play in retribution against perpetrators of acts where justice is perceived as being deficient? Can it really have any justifiable role in society? I wonder what my response would have been if it were my daughter in Dane Park and I knew that the murderer had been released after just eleven years. What if I had wanted to go after him, to the exclusion of all other considerations, as a matter of personal justice. This must be ethically wrong, I understand. It would not though, I think, have been an act driven by honour but by what I perceived as duty, although I recognise that the boundaries can be blurred. In any case does God still reserve for himself the right to avenge? I know Nahum 1:2 says that the Lord is a jealous and avenging God but he's surely a bit Old Testament.

The more up-to-date coverage seems to indicate turning the other cheek, presumably rather like Lady Gay Spanker in London Assurance. Epictetus, another of those Greek philosophers, always argued that vengeance was best served by living the very best life for yourself that you could, maybe endless days spent drinking with old friends in the Albion bar on Broadstairs seafront. But then he believed that external events are determined by destiny and are thus beyond our control. Just like 'Singin' Sandy', Epictetus probably used to ride around singing a type of cowboy's song of fate. We should accept whatever happens calmly and dispassionately and only then can we hope to achieve happiness and peace of mind. Not sure I could live with all that, too stoical for my liking.

If I condemn violence by other men and particularly to women, what right anyway would I or anyone have had to take life violently? My response to want to seek vengeance is certainly not genetic, part of our family's DNA, and probably not cultural because other members of my family and friends would think any such reaction abhorrent and behave very differently. Some of my friends might sympathise with the sentiment but few would be prepared to follow it through, so where does this type of response come from? I cannot adequately answer. I detest the sort of 'an eye for an eye' response which, say, Israel adopts towards acts of aggression because frequently the response is not about justice but punishment. Yet I also despise mindless terrorist acts by warped individuals or groups that maim the innocent. What if, in addition, someone close to me had been murdered by a woman who was then released early? Would I really have ever considered hunting her down? Is it all just about testosterone and concepts of what chivalrous behaviour represents.

Perhaps I have too many thoughts about knights of old, of crusaders, read too many westerns in my youth. Maybe I should have ignored the Old Testament examples completely in my formative years singing in the church choir. Too much anger and vengeance and veiled threats of burning in hell. However not sure if you will have seen the delayed two part story in a recent 'Silent Witness' episode on the BBC about girls being groomed by groups of ethnic young men. Based on real life, of course, but still pretty horrific. How many of you cheered at the end when the father of one of the girls smashed the chief abuser savagely with a golf club, a nine iron I think. I only cheered silently to be fair as it sliced into his head, a silent witness, but I tend to think I was not alone. How do men like Mandela do it, to put aside thoughts of retribution and vengeance. How we will miss him when he is gone.

When I was younger, I had also never thought deeply about the effect on those of us who had passed our eleven plus and those who had failed. But then I passed. Yet my mother had walked for half an hour to Lausanne School to ensure that my older sister was enrolled there, because it was considered the best at that time of the local secondary schools. The girls at Lausanne though did not take exams and any further qualifications could only be through studying at the local technical college. Your options otherwise would be to look for jobs in retail or in the many hotels and guest houses as a waitress or receptionist. Marriage was always an option, sometimes with success, sometimes from necessity and sometimes just as a way out. For those whom the system has not embraced, your social life, your free time, tends to take on a huge importance, particularly at the weekend. Friday night and everything's right for the weekend, as Eddie Cochrane put it so memorably. As a waitress, Julie would have been familiar with folk from other parts of the country, but the group of young people from Birmingham might have appeared different, casual, more worldly, perhaps exciting. There were no sleep-overs in those days so there was little opportunity for teenagers to have more sustained sexual encounters. It was wham bam, thank you ma'am. In alleyways, shelters, on the beach or in parks.

Thus her decision to stay the night at the 'Mad House' with Wally probably takes on a real significance, at least to her. When she had returned home, struggling desperately with the traumatic effects of coming down and presumably not used to it, she explained her absence by pretending to have stayed with Joyce. She expected to repeat the loving experience, giving Joyce as her excuse again, and headed back to find Wally. The swinging sixties. One big party, anyone was welcome. The music was the thing, in its own way a religion. Stranger in town, day tripper, come on over to my place. Look through any window, yeah. Julie had begun to think, in the way that young people often do, that her experience had real meaning. Now you're mine. Then you find that the carnival is over. You've lost that loving feeling, tell me why. It ain't me babe, it ain't me you're looking for. Try to understand, just the price of love. How can you tell, when these things matter? Now every little bit hurts, thanks a lot! Still I'm sad, on the eve of destruction.

When Wally proved to be indifferent, she became emotionally upset and eventually responded by asking a comparative stranger for money to buy more tablets. Presumably to lessen the pain. He knew nothing of her really but may already have formed an opinion of her type. In addition, this was not a callow nineteen year old boy, but a man of twenty seven who had been in trouble for part of his life, sometimes in quite brutal and de-humanising surroundings, and could handle himself. Even when they sat together, for some of the time Julie sat looking at the lanes in the bowling alley whilst he looked out of the window. He said she was talking of drugs and sex. She was inconsistent, talking in bursts, hyper-active, sometimes to him but also to two other girls who had joined their table. Very probably she still wanted to find Wally again, to hear a retraction of words that were not dismissive and uncaring. He had expected to be with Judy again that evening but she had failed to turn up. He would have been disappointed, mildly irritated, particularly as he had run her home. Typical but what did he expect?.

**"Christians have burnt each other, quite persuaded
That all the Apostles would have done as they did".**

Byron, 'Don Juan'

Bugger me, I only found one of the Christian Evangelical teams round the back of the pavilion stacking the firewood. Apparently God provided it. Yeah, yeah, yeah. They wanted to play for a real 'Ashes' trophy and had locked the Russian Orthodox team in the changing room. They were planning to drug the communion wine and then burn all of them in one large pyre. Thought of how Pussy Riot had been given two years and the complete lack of compassion shown by Mr Kirill Bill, so went out to buy some steak and prawns to throw on the barbie once the fire has died down a bit, when the cinders have turned really white. Will serve the bastards right. There has been a written submission too for some form of sex test to check players' chromosome levels. Have tried to read up about this to advise the rest of the committee and failed to understand any of it. Apparently reduced X chromosome diversity can reflect bottlenecks, I suppose like on the M25, and male-biased dispersal. The nub of this request seemed to be that they wanted to reduce the likelihood of female-biased dispersal, of female cricketers.

Our pro-bono celestial cricket adviser this month is Plato and although he knows nothing about cricket, he did wrestle at the Isthmian Games so he has the correct mind-set. Played sport so must be alright. Now I had read that he never speaks in his own voice in his dialogues. He probably has one of those dummies, not quite like Educating Archie, more like the one that Ken Dodd uses, and speaks through a swizzle in his mouth. Quite ironic, although is that Socrates I am thinking of? Went to see Ken Dodd live on stage one Monday evening about three years ago and didn't get home till the Thursday. Finally stopped laughing on the Friday and yes, next time I will take some sandwiches. Of course, it has turned out, after consulting Plato, that it is not really about chromosomes at all. It's the Australians fault, and yes, they do let them into heaven, occasionally. Since they arrived, the sledging has trebled. One of the Pope's invitation elevens got the hump because the Aussies kept referring to all of the batsman as Joan. I have told them categorically there was no Pope Joan and it was just a bit of fun, but then the Aussies started on about all the Pope's mistresses they had slept with. Consulted John Julius once more, the Articles of Popes. Some of those catholic boys certainly gave their articles an outing. Mind you, the evangelicals seem to be no better. The

National Association of Evangelicals report that evangelical young adults have pre-marital sex at rates similar to the rest of the population. We're going to ban that in heaven. No, not the pre-marital sex, the damn researchers.

When the bowling alley closed, she was torn between going home, with Tara's words ringing in her head, or opting to walk back with him 'for a chat' as he put it. In his very first statement they go into the guest house to find Wally but he is sound asleep. That would make perfect sense. There was a much more direct way to her home from the bowling alley but the chance of catching up with Wally was too great. She is emotionally torn either at the sight of him or because maybe he is not around. Whatever the scenario, she will be greatly disappointed. The landlady or someone is hovering around so they move outside. Julie was now heading home. Maybe outside, the dog in the van round the corner did bark, as he said in his first statement and maybe she did indeed suggest they head towards the park. The new burst of tablets were kicking in big-time and she was wide awake and talkative. She was going in that direction in any case. He seemed nice enough, he would walk her home and maybe the evening would recover. They were both high and as they entered the park they are walking quickly. There are a number of covered and quiet spaces where you would not be disturbed, but they pass through and by all of those.

It is only when they come to the end of the tree-line, that they actually pause, in the very last place in the park that you could conceivably stop. The rest is all open space and far too close to the houses. He describes in his second statement how they begin to indulge in the normal petting couples might have engaged in. By now the drugs are making her carefree, reckless and unfortunately argumentative. It's been a lousy day so best try and recover, maybe have some fun. It should though be meaningful and not too easy, so she begins to tease him, pulling away, upset by his directness. He's polite enough, he's already taken one girl home today, but he assumes the talk of sex indicated a simple response. Men and their dicks, eh? Like many men, he sees no reason to delay, for any courting ritual. Yet she cannot seem to make up her mind. What did Max Miller use to say? "I like the girls who say they will, and then they say they won't". I bet you didn't Max. She is sixteen, not used to being high and is unusually agitated, but he believes that she is deliberately provoking him. Her mind is racing and she thinks that it is a type of game. A game that she can walk away from. To him it was rejection, second time today, and provocation. The blows made her realise that this was very different. He does not realise that he has broken her jaw but said he thought she just enjoyed it that way. Sad if he really thought that. She pulls away again, probably in pain. However I doubt she had time to realise anything further as she would have lost consciousness quickly as his hands tightened. In his mind, the blows and the initial pressure on her throat were always justified by the perceived provocation. Prolonged constriction however is surely something else. That will need a hell of a justification. And this is a sixteen year old kid.

Why does this matter to me? Now, after all these years. At the time, as I have said, her death meant nothing, other than it had cost us a game of cricket. Our annoyance spilled over into wholesale condemnation, further confirmed by the revelation that drugs were involved. Justice Sachs in his summing up described the 'Mad House' as "this shameful place....a disgrace to the town of Margate". This was my home town and hers he was talking about. Julie and I were born two years apart on exactly the same day. Not much fazes me but that took me aback, when I read the statement from her father. This girl I never knew who had died just up from our cricket square had the very same birthday. I later went out briefly at college with a girl with ginger hair, who was horrified to learn that she and I were both Gemini's. Gemini's should never go out together she said and that was an end to it. I thought this was garbage because I quite fancied her but then again he was a Gemini as well. Maybe my lady's reasoning was sound. Don't think she thought I would strangle her though. None of my group of friends ever went out with any girls from Lausanne School to my knowledge and so we existed in a parallel universe. We used to do the bowling alley when we had the money and the coffee bars in Margate and Cliftonville. Dances weren't really our scene, we went to the pubs, but were often around the fringes of the Dreamland amusement park and the cinemas were always popular. I must have seen Julie at some time, somewhere, around the town. Then there is the matter of the park. I played cricket there regularly when older, but from a very young age we would be there every other week on the visits to my grandparents. You would then be dispatched either to play ball in the park or up to the children's playground. I had sat on the swings many times, looking down the slopes to where she would die. She would have done that as well, as a child. She would have known this place intimately. It feels kind of personal.

"She, she is dead; she's dead; when thou know'st this
Thou know'st how dry a cinder this world is"

John Donne

Until fairly recently I had only been personally acquainted with death through the loss of parents, family and occasional friends. Then for about eight years I made calls as a volunteer on people whose care had become palliative. Strangely the many home visits I used to do for folk who knew they were terminally ill were quite inspirational. Most of the patients were naturally kind and polite, just struggling to come to terms with their diagnosis, to make sense of it all. Where we have been, the journey we have made to get here, however imperfect, matters. There was much more humour than ever I could have imagined. When you fill in these bloody disability forms, and because of the advances in cancer treatment special rules exceptions are reducing, you do get to talk about personal histories. Anything to deflect the indignity and ease the embarrassment of admitting to a total stranger that they struggle to use the toilet or are incontinent.

The war generation have almost gone now, although I went through a phase where I came across a number of veterans heading inexorably for their own last battle. Juvenal the satirist is thought to have been born in the small peaceful town of Aquinum, just down the road from Monte Cassino. However if you have read the book by Matthew Parker you will know that the latter was also the scene of some of the toughest fighting in the Second World War. Four battles in all. In the space of four weeks I talked to two men, both dying, who had been there on the Allied side and survived. They saw that in terms of fate, of destiny. I then went out to a small village not far from Sassoon's cricket square, where I talked to another man whom I knew from the records had been a German prisoner of war in a Lincoln camp. He began to talk of Monte Cassino as well. His brother had been fighting in Stalingrad and had been sent south with the reinforcements for Italy and had actually joined him there. They were defending the monastery. His brother had died there but had said when they met for the last time that this was far worse than Stalingrad in its sheer intensity and brutality. There was no hiding place for the attackers. We talked about fate and destiny once more, of how people had chanced to be there and how he had survived. He had ended up in this small beautiful place with its stunning views across the Kent countryside, amongst some of the very people he might have been trying to kill.

The lives of my generation, by comparison, have been so much more mundane, so with younger patients you would search for topics where we could share our own cultural experiences. Talking about my generation. Yes, we would normally always agree, we were lucky. No real wars to fight, just a generation that had the best music. Of course there were always terrible songs and crap singers, but the music and the times seemed special. The music was our story. The Home and the Light programmes were swept away, the establishment and the repressive society seemingly defeated. There had always been the oasis of Radio Luxembourg. Then the pirate radio ship Caroline launched in March 1964 and London later that year. Along with the music came inventions like the miniskirt, six inches below sea level, and the birth control pill. There is an enormous pleasure often in recalling when we were young and immortal. There is at least a journey to remember. The saddest visits though were always to youngsters, for whom sometimes the advance of a terminal disease can be frighteningly rapid and overwhelming. Footfalls echoing down the passage we did not take, towards the door we never opened. No-one deserves to die at sixteen, for whatever reason.

Music has always played its part in story-telling on the stage or on screen, with its ability to subtly or dramatically change moods and context. The vagaries of music, teasing out and enducing mood swings, emotional highs. The songs in any case were always subjective and reflected common themes in our lives. The year of 1965. Yesterday, all my troubles seemed so far away. It's not unusual. We can work it out, that's the way love goes. I'll take you home, I know a place. That'll be the day, he's a must to avoid. Don't fight it, in the middle of nowhere, I'll stop at nothing. This strange effect. Set me free, turn, turn, turn. I can't help myself. Just a little bit too late, we gotta get out of this place. Leaving here, please don't let me be misunderstood. Ride away, king of the road, there but for fortune. The carnival is over, over and over, till the end of the day.

After the break-up Margate Cricket Club continued to put out two sides, but we began to lose some of our stronger fixtures, mainly with the London clubs. The festival was never the same again, although the tradition tottered on for a little longer. We had lost three senior players, but more than that we had lost much of our organisational drive. Don had been ambitious and passionate about improving the club. George used to work to ensure the pitches were good. That began to slip and in addition the net practices stopped. No-one to do the additional work that these boys had done, that others take for granted. There was still a committee but largely we would just turn up to play. New players came across, Biff for one, the Newton brothers as well, young teachers always being a good source of talent, long hair notwithstanding.

Jolly boys' outings remained immensely popular as the whole family could descend on the seaside, but the introduction of the breathalyser in 1967 was slowly to change attitudes.

My friend Willoughby, the Grannies cricketer, was never a role model for the younger generation in his attitude to alcohol and driving, particularly on his way back from cricket matches. He once referred to me as a "breathalyser bore". If he was ever stopped by the police he used to plead, very successfully, that he had a problem with his lung capacity and was unable to blow in the bag. This was actually true. He told me that he was however twice detained in the cells by policemen who didn't like the response. On the first occasion one of the sergeants typically recognised his army tie and released him and latterly, shortly before he died, he was only let off by a sympathetic doctor at Tonbridge police station. He actually had a great regard for the law, apart from the drinking legislation, because as a young Cambridge student he had been returning from a debs' ball down in London in the fifties - and for fun had knocked a policeman's helmet off. They chased and caught him, kept him in a cell all night and then sent him all the way back to Cambridge in a police car. The Master though happened to spot the car outside St John's College and was not amused. Those were the days, eh? Not many debs' balls in Margate,that I can remember.

By the way, this guy Plato is proving a real pain in the arse. He knows sod all about cricket but has some theory about the plurality of souls. I thought at first that logo's was all about branding and of course God has all the merchandise and sponsorship contracts strictly controlled up there. What he really meant was logos, which is something to do with the mind, and then there is thymos and eros. Eros seems to be situated somewhere around the area of the cricket box. Plato wants the person batting, the soul, to have three lives. Three souls per person, three chances. I told him, we're not having that. However the whole thing has now kicked off big time. The Brahmins want to ban bouncers, as they say the 'atmas', the soul, resides in the forehead. The Buddhists are arguing that everything is in a constant state of flux, now you see it, now you don't, which means that you often can't see them running up and then they suddenly appear and bowl. Similarly the Samoans, heaven knows how they got in, have a name for the soul which roughly means, "that which comes and goes". Just about sums up their batting. Showed them all the quotation from St Irenaeus, who is some Greek from Smirnoff, about the soul being a 'corporeal character', but just made things worse. When I left them to thrash it out the Calvinists were arguing that, because the soul is immortal, they could never be given out and then the Lutherans were saying that their team of souls could only play after the resurrection of the dead. Just hope the Triangles are more even-handed, even-sided. I shall have to refer them all to the Catholic Encyclopedia website for the final word, which states clearly 'the origin of the soul is beyond our ken'. Round the Horne was without question beyond our ken. Did Feldman and Took have the answer to everything, including the secret of the universe and the origin of the soul? Almost certainly, although I also quite like the 1961 explanation by Jan and Dean in 'Heart and Soul'. It is slightly catchier.

"The town of Margate is eminent for nothing that I know of"

Daniel Defoe

Defoe actually devotes much effort in his 'Tour through the whole island of Great Britain' to describing North Kent and then the area around Canterbury and Faversham, so his remarks about this golden paradise called Margate are pretty derogatory. He acknowledges that King William used the harbour for his journeys to Holland and that the townsfolk regularly send boatloads of corn to London. No acknowledgement that Moll Flanders might have worked in the Margate conveniences or that Robinson Crusoe could have been shipwrecked first off Tongue Sands. Such is fate. Serves Daniel right that he died hiding from his creditors. I then noticed a short article by one Catherine Pepinster, editor of the Tablet newspaper. I thought it might just be about Dexamyl Spansules, but no, not that sort of tablet. They have some excellent well-connected Trustees, naturally enough, with hot lines to all sorts of places. Some know the Pope personally but nothing sinister there. Sherlock Holmes might though have detected a pattern that set the dogs barking and indeed two of our ex-Prime Ministers have also contributed articles to this long-established high-quality Catholic newspaper. I guess they needed to establish their credentials before any real religious commitment, probably another Granita Pact as to who becomes Pope first. Mind you, no problem at all being asked to wear any form of cassock or even the full regalia, but tutus are off limits at present. Don't you just love our Desmond.

Catherine was talking about the Vatileaks scandal and "the petty intrigues of a medieval court". Still they should surely be able to sort that out quickly because Hans Kung thinks that, "the Vatican is no different from the Kremlin.... A process of 'Putinisation' has taken place there". Just build more prisons and put cat-flaps in all the palazzo. In addition they also have some sort of money laundry in the Vatican where they clean up all the money from the collection plates before it goes in the piggy bank. Huge number of pilgrims come in from all over the place and the money gets very dusty and dirty. I expect some of those nice Magdalene sisters from Ireland run the laundries. The real revelation though is that, just like Margate, they have a 'What the butler saw' machine down in the catacombs. I used to put two pence into machines like this at Dreamland and you would get a series of flickering slides showing briefly clad ladies, finishing every time with a picture of a bottom. Probably the same machine manufacturer supplying the Vatican, but would be a bigger arse. A lady called Miss Marie Corelli in her 'Cameos' once wrote, "There is something not exactly high-class in the town of Margate....a vulgar flavour of shrimps floats in the air". A similar odour seems to pervade Rome at present. Maybe the whole place needs a Dorothy from Oz, pulling back the curtains. Pope Dorothy at least sounds better than Pope Joan. Why not an 'Opusy Riot?' Oh happy dei's.

Margate carried on much as before through the remaining months of 1965 and into 1966. The 'Mad House' was sold to a former Deputy Mayor and ex CID officer from Birmingham. Evidently he wanted to keep the Brummie association going but perhaps not the drug supply. The place was refurbished and renamed 'St Margaret's', although there is no trace of that now. Margaret was a Hungarian lady who came to England some years before the Norman Conquest and fled north to escape from William the Conqueror. She was canonized by Innocent the Fourth, as St Margaret of Scotland, so presumably the new Addington Road owners had a Scottish connection. The Eagle Steamers finally withdrew their pleasure cruises from the jetty which did shake the establishment, as it ended the wonderful tradition of boats bringing folk down to the old place at the weekend or taking them off for the day to France. At Dunkirk the boats had proudly brought quite a few back. Edward Heath once again led the Christmas Carols at our school concert and in Broadstairs. Sadly it was the very first year when there was no pantomime in Margate, the performance of the town council being thought sufficient. Billy Cotton and his band were booked for the main season next year at the Winter Gardens with Kathy Kirby returning every Sunday.

We had all by now given up searching the beach huts for Ronnie Biggs as it turned out he was in the Antipodes, and elsewhere the seventy mile per hour speed limit was introduced. Harold Wilson was pipe smoker of the year yet again. On the music front at Xmas the Beatles launched 'Rubber Soul', The Byrds 'Turn Turn Turn', the Who 'My Generation' and the Supremes their Merry Xmas album. On the television front the brilliant 'Not Only But Also' continued to be controversial with Dud and Pete. They had a sketch about a one-legged man wanting to be Tarzan, but didn't include any one-legged Clunc Clic'ers. Alf still didn't want any coloureds in 'Till Death us do a Part'; you could 'Take your Pick' or 'Double your Money' if opportunity hadn't knocked, folks; Sunday night was always at the London Palladium; 'The Avengers' and 'The Saint' provided the glamour; the 'Likely Lads' though was probably most likely to draw us boys in. Terry and Bob down the pub, chasing the girls, up to all sort of madcap escapades. Not the drugs though. We were lucky like that. Morecambe and Wise were on ITV in those days so it was to be a further three years before they began to drive our Xmas offerings with their festive centrepiece and a couple more before the Two Ronnies would emerge. Had Biggs been recaptured more quickly we might have had three of them on the small screen.

In the cricket in 1965 we had beaten the New Zealanders three nil but lost to the South Africans. They would not tour here again until after apartheid had ended. The England boys then headed for Australia, apparently the weakest MCC Team ever to visit. The bespectacled MJK Smith was the captain on tour and his wife went with him. He startled the Aussie reporters by arriving to talk to them holding the baby because his wife had gone out shopping. Sounds very much ahead of his time and you can imagine the sledging that it triggered. The series was drawn one apiece and so Australia kept the ashes. These were the Aussies of Simpson, Lawry and McKenzie, whilst in the England team, Barrington, Boycott and Cowdrey topped the batting averages. Ken Higgs was the most economical of our bowlers. The vagaries of swing, working its magic. Of the other sporting items that attracted our attention, Arkle had won the Gold Cup and Sea Bird the Derby. Muhammad Ali had beaten Liston again, although the latter appeared to have dived. But then he was in the Premier League of fighters. I knew there was a Premier League connection somewhere, Torres has just been sent off for it. Ali then announced a rematch for 1966 with our Enery, giving us all something to look forward to, although we knew that his eyes were always suspect in these big bouts. Perhaps the smell of Brut got into them. It seems amazing to read that when Henry first floored the Champ in 1963, he only weighed in at 12.12 and that included the lead they put in his boots especially for the weigh-in. Imagine that weight and build now in the heavyweight division.

“So on the ocean of life we pass and speak to one another
Only a look and a voice; then darkness again and a silence”.

‘Ships that Pass in the Night’ by Longfellow

I don’t mind this ocean of life business, but as a grumpy old git I do mind having to talk to other folk when we pass at any time, day or night. I can handle the look but do we really have to speak? You head for the supermarket or the gym and some young person wants to know if you’re having a nice day. What’s it to do with them anyway? Mind your own bloody business. I am sorry but if I am quite upset at the moment, it’s all to do with the cricket. You may have wondered how I have been able to arrange the celestial cricket matches when I am clearly still in the land of the living. I may not be of this world - as Robert Owen famously said, "All the world is queer save thee and me, and even thou art a little queer" - but that’s a different story. It’s just that my organisational skills have always been second to none and I was recruited for that very reason by the Guardians’ Inter-planetary Team, or GIT. Rather like Thomas Paine as an excise man you learn to look for all the secret ways of moving around, so I quickly learnt how to gain access to the Day of Judgement Hall. Some of the clergy have been using back passages for years but there is a more direct route and you don’t have to worry about silencing any uppity guardian angels.

I was up there again because a complaint had come in from the Triangles spokesman that while they were playing in a park, one of them hoiked the ball into the children’s playground. A young girl was minding her brother and sister, pushing them gently on the swings, picked up the ball and threw it back. Apparently the ball, being sphere like, is revered by all triangles as holy. Makes sense, I suppose, because if you have always been three-sided, then you might well worship anything that is more rounded. Felix, Nicholas Wanostrocht, would have understood that perfectly. The girl touching the ball was regarded with outrage as an act of disrespect and a group of their supporters marched on the playground, beat up all the women and children there and hung the young girl from the swings. Perfectly understandable and as a student of Tom Lehrer I realised I had to sort this out quickly. As he very discerningly said, “We will all go together when we go”, and this is not a song about using the urinals.

Some of my very good friends are deeply religious and I know that it is never religious belief in itself which is at fault. It is just when the interpretation is hard-line and intolerant and there is a desire for power and control over other people's lives, that we have this type of reaction. You can believe in the fairies, for all that I care, but do not use your creed to tell me how I should live. I asked the Triangular leader, Tobler they call him, where is the tolerance and love in your faith? You have no right, even if the three-sided scholars, the umpires, told you that your triangular God ordered it, to threaten women and children or to harm them. Whoever you think you are, stop this nonsense, otherwise I will have no option to expel you from the cricket league. Tobler responded by accusing me of not being equilateral and added that the crisis was becoming acute. They all talk like that, some form of mathematical double-speak. Not sure what angle to take with the Triangles, but of course the loss of cricket is a powerful threat, so in the end we agreed on some form of prism sentence for the perpetrators. Cricket is without doubt above all other religions and must take precedence, but it should not cause a young girl to live in fear or lose her life. The Triangles, to be fair, did call a meeting, the third Iscoscelean council, and it has been decreed that it is permissible for non-believers to handle the Kookaburras. This was ridiculous in any case as they only recognised their own religion and would therefore logically have wanted to kill all other teams they played against in the league, as soon as they touched the ball. They have agreed for the sphere to be portrayed pictorially for the publicity photos I am preparing and for my part I have persuaded all other teams to respect that the sphere could be a sacred object. We have decide to posthumously make the young girl a saint, Saint Twentytwenty, in honour of the game being played at that park. In addition, the Triangles are now extremely grateful for the general acceptance that their religion is mainly balls.

Returning to the events of 1965, I do not remember having any interest in the details of the hearings or of the trial at the time, but looking back through the Isle of Thanet Gazette they very clearly devoted a great deal of space to the evidence at the trial. Maybe a look and then I passed on. I never heard her voice that I know of, but it would not have mattered. I think we had made up our minds about both of them. Alcohol we could understand, drugs were something else. A sixteen year old girl who hung around the 'Mad House' men and who was out in a park at two in the morning. Then it transpired that the guy convicted had other convictions. Who would believe much that he said. Yet he had pleaded not guilty and obviously felt almost passionately that an appeal might succeed, because he believed some of the detail had not been understood or properly explained by the judge. The trial transcripts are gone now but a verdict of manslaughter had been open to the jury. The second statement in Margate police station early on 23rd August had been very specific about what was said to have transpired in the park. Yet the description of prolonged constriction of the throat would always have been difficult to explain. Particularly when the supporting medical reports seemed to confirm that they thought he was in full control throughout, the drugs merely inducing a pleasant feeling. The Appeal though was registered on the 22nd November 1965 at the Court of Criminal Appeal and rejected in March the following year. I now know I was wrong about Julie. She was just a kid beginning to explore life and I blame the people who first dragged her into their particular and rather sad world. How many lives have been ruined by drugs. It was not Doris's little girl out there in the park.

"If everything else in this nation of ours were lost but cricket - her Constitution and the laws of England ....it would be possible to reconstruct from the theory and the practice of cricket all the external Englishness which has gone to the Establishment of that Constitution and the laws aforesaid"

Neville Cardus, 'A Game of the English Summer'

A body of just laws and a good constitution, whether written or unwritten, of course are essential in life, but it is the spirit in which it endures which seems to me to be pivotal. Mind you, destiny, fate, does work in a mysterious way. I guess if the American Revolution had only been won on the playing fields of Eton, then their constitution might contain different alternatives on what you can legitimately 'bear'. Probably would have made no difference in the end result as politicians screwing the public seems to be an international sport, even for those who haven't been to public school. Cricket however was always one of those games whose unique appeal was that it should be played within the spirit of the game. Neville Cardus was a romantic with a love of cricket, a true love. However the game is much changed. Umpires' decisions are no longer final and can be appealed and then reviewed. Professionalism and gamesmanship permeates every corner of the sport. Perhaps still on the village green, those hard pounded squares, the spirit of cricket remains, although even there leagues have put a premium on winning. I have played sport both in leagues and in friendly matches and you may well know that some of the latter were the toughest and fiercest I have ever played in. What has changed however is the fitness of the players, maybe the sustained skill levels and the science that surrounds sport nowadays. In addition it seems more difficult to lose a fiercely competitive match and yet applaud both the game and the opposition, if the end result is to lose league points. The losers are failures, the winners take all.

It is a reflection of the X factor in our lives, of an attitude seen daily in the House of Commons, of the constant denigration of each other, unless you wear a blue, red or orange shirt. It is the instinct of the mob, of the black shirts and as AP Herbert once said, "a plague on all your blouses". No wonder we are turning away from politics in our droves. It is an attitude which was briefly touched upon as we saw the Olympics and the Paralympics unravel, when crowds enjoyed the various sports for the quality of the offering and would applaud even the losers. Unlike the matches in the Premier League where crowds are hostile and players are largely mercenaries. They have been trained to appeal for a throw-in or a corner even when they know their opponents did not touch the ball. To get opponents sent off by provocation or by over-reacting, diving holding their face. Role models? Ray Winston's early film about life in prison springs to mind. My hockey coach, Tommy, wanted his teams to win, hated it when they didn't, but he could always still applaud the skill of our opponents. He wanted us to play with style but could also appreciate quality in others. Winning is not everything. Even if you are Usain Bolt, someday someone will run faster, but that does not detract from his greatness. There is always someone faster or stronger.

Captains and umpires do though together set the tone for the conduct of a cricket match. No mention of bowlers specifically in the 'Articles of Cricket' but they tend to be a fairly strong catalyst when tempers fray. For example bowlers sometimes like to set their own fields and it is rarely wise to allow them a free hand. We had a fast bowler at college who argued vociferously with the captain that only he understood field placings. This was not an attitude that surprised us as, although not a bad bowler, he did tend to constantly over-estimate his own abilities. He liked attacking fields in almost all situations, which is fine when the bowler has tight control. If some of the deliveries are loose however, close fielders will be constantly turning and chasing the ball. He had insisted on having a short mid-on and a short mid-off and then proceeded to bowl two overs where each of them had to turn frequently after the ball. The captain should have just dropped the boys back but decided to allow the bowler one more over with this field placing. The two fielders were looking quite fed up by now and had a quick conversation.

Our bowler thunders in and the ball is driven firmly back past him towards the boundary. Neither of the fielders moves or will move and the bowler realises that if he wishes to prevent the ball going for four he must actually turn and retrieve it himself. The Barton Road ground is a fine level pitch and has a long boundary but our man is quite quick, even though the pursuit looks forlorn. Amazingly as the ball slows he is almost upon it and drops his head down to make one last despairing effort to catch up with it. Head down he is at full pelt, knees pumping. The ball trundles slowly over the boundary line and underneath the sidescreen. Sidescreens must be made of the same DNA as basketball posts and it did not budge an inch when our bowler tried to run through it. He bounced backwards and knocked himself out for fully two minutes. Well at least that was how long it took before the rest of us had stopped laughing and our wonderful groundsman Bob had run round to see how he was. Benny Hill could not have orchestrated a finer chase. Eric Sykes' plank could not have delivered a more lethal blow. Not surprisingly our quickie never wanted to play for us ever again.

The year after the Margate club broke up, there was one other particular cricketing memory which still remains quite vividly. It transpired that our game that year against the West Indians, the Caribbean CC, had been arranged for the day of the World Cup Final. Of course, at the time of arranging the fixture, we had no idea that England would be there at the last. As the big day approached players began to drop out, but the fixture was always so enjoyable that enough of us felt sufficiently guilty to opt for the cricket and to give them a game. We always played for a full day against them and the game duly started in Dane Park at 11.00 on the Saturday. On the last three occasions they had scored well over two hundred runs against us so we knew full well their quality. However this time as lunch approached they were reeling at ninety nine for nine and we had visions of finishing in time to see the second half of the final. We sat with their umpire and asked him how long he thought the last two would hold out. He told us the number eleven batsman was completely new to the club and no-one had ever seen him play or knew anything about him. After lunch their number eleven batsman lasted long enough to score a century.

However at about 4.30 when we had begun to reply to their score, as if by fate, the heavens opened. Play was suspended and my friend Peter suggested we jump on his Vespa and watch England complete their triumph over Germany at his home nearby. We had been following the game on the transistor radio. We arrived at his house in full cricket gear, leapt off the bikes and ran into his house, just in time to see the Germans equalise. His father, Harold, was so frustrated that he threw his precious tin of dog-ends to the floor in disgust, his entire life's work scattered over the carpet. Peter and I were both regular German exchange students so the chorus of 'bloody Germans' had a different tone to it though. Fortunately the rain continued just long enough for us to see the extra time before returning to the park. Our game was eventually drawn and we spent the rest of that magical evening, with the rest of the country, singing and cheering loudly and drinking the health of the two Bobby's, Moore and Charlton and the toothless Nobby. It must have been what VE Day was like all those years back. The only moment which threatened the general euphoria was our umpire Roy in the Kent singing 'Ghost Riders in the Sky' and he kept getting up on the stage for one more chorus. We finally had to hold him down. Thirty three pounds of pressure on his carotid arteries. They think it's all over. It is now.

"The portions of a woman that appeals to man's depravity,
Are constructed with considerable care,
And what appears to be a simple cavity,
Is in fact a most elaborate affair".

A P Herbert

How on earth did Herbert, our very own Juvenal, work this all out, over seventy years ago, when Naomi Wolf was not even a twinkle. Apparently, as Naomi has explained, women have very complex and different sexual wiring which can lead off in all sorts of directions. What chance does any man have in understanding what needs to be turned on inside such an elaborate affair? How can he trigger this heaven on earth, with lights flashing, music and bells, unless he has some qualification as a biological electrician. Most of us cannot even change a fuse in an earthly wiring system. Women can now perhaps be rightly categorised as wolf-women, whereas men perhaps tend to be more like meerkats. Meerkats and dicks both work on a very simple premise, popping up frequently to see what is about, although I was unable to find a 'compare the dick' website. Just as well.

Fortunately help is at hand. Another medical specialist, who also happens to be an American politician, recently explained the 'Achin principle'. Forget all the foreplay or attempts at courting. What the 'Achin principle' establishes is that women's bodies respond differently according to the degree of force used. Forget any stupid nonsense about whether no means no or having to ask consent. What you need to do is to forcibly penetrate your women as brutally as you can. The objective is to ensure that all of the body is 'aching' and apparently then women move on to a higher plane. They actually enjoy the experience much more, with any number of clitoral or vaginal orgasms or even both, and the best of it is that they never get pregnant. That was the trouble with the Red Army when they marched into Germany at the end of the war. Like soldiers everywhere when they are victorious and high on drugs or alcohol, they wanted women whether moving or not, but didn't understand the 'Achin concept'. Boys, you have to be even more brutal. Forget about life, liberty, and the pursuit of happiness or holding any of these truths to be self-evident. They even apparently get to sing about it now, forcible rap artists. Vidal's sky-gods have spoken. The loathing of women for two thousand years continues. And there will be conferences and conventions of fawning and applauding women apologising for men whose only concept of equality seems to be that all men are created equal. May their God forgive them. Power, control, repression. Try getting off on that Naomi.

On a much lighter note I got a message left in my Pearly Gate's pigeon hole from Juvenal. How about that? Apparently they have a type of celestial literature, a c book, where they can catch up with the galactic news and he had seen something about the Edinburgh Festival and all the Olympics stuff. Asked whether I could submit some of his new work if he printed off an extra parchment. He had re-written Satire Number Five which includes some stuff about elite women performing in a beast hunt. He'd read about another beast in 'Lord of the Flies' and then seen a reference in the TV series 'Angel'. Thought he could do some form of humorous comparison with the one from the Book of Revelation and set it in Las Vegas. I wrote back to say that his stuff wasn't really suitable. It needed to be more alternative and certainly not funny. That's the last thing they like, although jokes about flies might turn some of them on. I suggested that he might change the dactylic hexameter to dictylic hexameter as that would attract half of the male artistic world, but he didn't understand.

He then asked if I could consider a skit on the Paralympics, maybe satire Seventeen, called The Last Leg But One. He was working on an ode where the Tin Man beats Oscar Pistorius and Adam Hills in the 400 metres final at Rio de Janiero in 2016. Then the Scarecrow would get the gold medal in the halitosis section. Is it OK, he asked? I had to explain that the Tin Man and the Scarecrow were only fictional characters, a bit like George Osborne. Also the classification is athetosis, so Juvenal's sketch would certainly not be acceptable. Bloody Romans, what have they ever done for us? However what did cheer me up was learning from one of the angels what the long white building next to the urinals is. Apparently anyone who has had their throat cut or been beheaded by men from the seventh century gets sent to this unit where ministering angels repair them. They get restored to their previous state. Men from the seventh century actually don't get into heaven and have to spend their lives in limbo, but they are allowed to come up and rest in a large recreational area underneath heaven. Strangely enough it is directly beneath the urinals and when the patients have been restored they are encouraged as a matter of priority to empty their bowels. I suppose this is a case of on your head be it. It's rather similar to the fate of the large and rather cruel bear in Toy Story 3. It must be purgatory.

Talking of which, one of the other traits of our external Englishness to which Neville Cardus referred, is of course our love of animals. I had time to kill whilst waiting for the celestial cricket festival programme to be printed off, so had a quick word with a couple of the English guardian angels who mind the menagerie, just behind the stables to the right of the pearly gates. Apparently it's always a job they opt for on the application form as it gives them a better opportunity to relax between flights. They can use the manure from the menagerie in the rose garden, well they were promised that, and for a few vegetables like mangelwurzels. Animals, as you know, have no souls but they keep a few just for ceremonial purposes. You just wouldn't guess how many concessions there are up there. There's a worshipful company of butchers managed by a husband and wife team. They call the girl Halal Dolly. She wasn't that stunning, but I don't think stunning is allowed. I'll remember that one for Juvenal if he ever submits anything to Edinburgh. Better than jokes about girls with dolphin noses. At least if they ever run a category at the Paralympics for people who are just arseholes then one comedian will certainly qualify.

The loaves and fishes concessions are very profitable, as they like to re-tell the stories about miracles regularly on festival days. The concessions were originally spread amongst all of the souls, but a handful of Russians went round and bought them all up. Sort of 'War and Peace'd' on everyone. Sadly there is always a knobhead somewhere who will applaud this sort of thing. I think the only solution is to get them to listen to hours of this forcible rap, until their bodies are crying enough. I certainly like the sound of this "Achin" fellow. That's a principle which needs much wider penetration amongst the followers. Why on earth didn't "Achin" get elected? There's also an underground pipeline for the communion wine and they use a few donkeys to bring in a few select bottles for the real afficionado's. Now that my friend Willoughby has formed the celestial 'Wine Tasters' Cricket Club, they had to up their game from the cheap crap. The donkeys also bear spirits by night because spirits aren't really part of the mix. Souls are fine provided they understand the rules of authority, power and control. Any soul with an independent spirit gets crushed. Well don't blame me, that's how the sky-gods like it.

Strangely enough one of the angels thought they might have seen Mike and George at one of the race days. The Four Horseman of the Apocalypse compete regularly to keep the horses fit and he thought the boys had a right result when the red horse beat the pale horse. Death tends to be the odds-on favourite each time they race but they are both trained by the same saint, Irenaeus, and apparently the boys worked on the old Dumpton greyhound basis and backed the outsider of the two. War pissed it this time and the angel thought the boys had headed off to the sea of Galilee for a few days amongst the sand and the vestal virgins. The menagerie also has a rather nice pedigree herd of sheep as they often have to supply a lamb for God on festive days for the barbecue and quite a few bullocks and swine. For the entertainment, they liven up the harp playing and the massed choirs with an elephant on a tightrope, an idea they nicked from Sangers Circus, and then they have seven seals. Thought they might have something to do with the Four Horsemen, but in fact they leap around like the old Guinness seals, balancing beach balls on their snouts and tossing them around.

More bad news though. A lynch mob of Triangles had rounded up all the mathematicians and started burning them on a large pyre, on the basis that some of their drawings constituted another pictorial representation of the triangular god. Fortunately although they worship the sphere, they tend to opt for triangular forms in their everyday life so their carts don't move too fast. The triangular wheels tend to bounce and jerk along very slowly so they managed to save half of the mathematicians. Some form of formula was worked out on a blackboard but in the end there was no alternative but to banish them to some degenerate two-dimensional Euclidean plane. The measures of the interior angles of a triangle in Euclidean space always add up to 180 degrees, so to my reckoning at 180 degrees they will hopefully all burn up in their own sad concept of hell. But then I was never a scientist, so I might not have quite understood all of that. My friend Tony teaches maths so I'll ask him next time I'm in the Albion.

"What contemptible scoundrel stole the cork from my lunch"

W C Fields

Four years on from 1965 and Margate Cricket Club is still a strong side locally but we have fewer fixtures with the really top sides. Hastings were then pretty useful and with a full day game with them approaching, my brother is down that weekend and gets drafted in to strengthen the side. His great friends Bruce and Keith are both by now playing regularly for us so the three musketeers will be together for a final campaign. The fatal mistake though was to allow them to travel there together. At 11.00 there are just eight of us ready to play and no sign of the musketeers. Our opponents decide to bat and kindly lend us two youngsters to help us field. It is a hot day, we are one short and are getting thrashed around the park. A message is received from the 'lost boys' after about half an hour to say that they have broken down and will be there shortly. There is huge sympathy all round. It could happen to any of us. Just before lunch we are tired and even hotter but are buoyed by a second call that the AA man has now arrived and they will be shortly on their way. Our opponents are in the region of one hundred and fifty for two. Just after 1.30, some ten minutes before we are to resume, a small blue Citroen Dyane, struggles into the car park. Our skipper is delighted with their arrival and welcomes them profusely. As they change into their cricket whites however I begin to smell some sort of a rat. I suspect they have been drinking and quite liberally. Professional to the last though they front it out and no-one else seems to have any idea that anything is wrong. Both my brother and I were useful in the outfield and they put him in the covers. First over after lunch, Willie drops the ball short and the in-form batsman cuts the ball majestically. There is a crack as it leaves the bat. As if to the sound of a starting pistol, my brother is off sprinting to his right and after twenty yards collapses in a desperate attempt to stop the ball. Unfortunately the batsman had smashed the ball to his left, in the opposite direction to which he was running whence it thudded against the boards. Posh ground, see, they did have boards. Our skipper is not amused and accuses them of being drunk. Of course, they all say in unison, we did have one beer whilst we were waiting but only one.

Suffice it to say that our opponents scored over three hundred and I doubt we got over the hundred mark in reply. The musketeers continued to put up a fierce defence, at least to our skipper, all for one and one for all. Indeed as they were slightly fresher than the rest of us they might well have lasted longer at the crease. I learnt the full story later that evening. On the Saturday night they had quite a session and it took them a while to get out of bed and organised on the Sunday. They were late away heading for Sussex and although they got to within thirty minutes of the ground realised they would be late. The traffic was heavy, the sun was beating down and one of them noticed a pub which opened at 11.00. They told themselves that they would stop just for one drink and used the occasion to ring through to warn us of their 'breakdown'. The ale was good, the landlord friendly and one beer just didn't seem to be enough. I guess we have all been there. Working on the principle that they would now miss the pre-lunch session there seemed no rush. The world was becoming more mellow by the minute. Lunch a la W C Fields. It was a story that got funnier with the telling and with time and it was the last occasion my brother ever played for the club. Strangely we never got to play Hastings again. The key point though is that maybe Pinter didn't quite get it right. Maybe friends are the greatest thing that God created on earth, next to real ale of course. Certainly greater than sex, although sex isn't too bad either. Just don't try sex with your close friends - if you want to keep them - or when you are smashed out of your head. So where does cricket figure in all of this? A passion for cricket is in many ways still a manifestation of love, for many men it was and is their life. It takes centre stage. I have known a number of men for whom that was true. It is also not possible to discuss cricket, with its broad themes, its trials and tribulations, without reflecting on life itself.

What has changed for many sports like cricket is the disappearance of the social side of the sport, where you could meet with the opposition after a game and build strong relationships, despite any out and out hostility on the pitch. In the old days that side of sport was never really present with the soccer that you played on recreation grounds, although our sides used to have a beer after a match. It was much more important in hockey and rugby and of course hockey is now largely played on all-weather pitches at different times of the day, so very few of the teams meet together in the clubhouse. The social side of sport and in particular cricket were hugely important and maybe, in the wandering sides that meet on festivals and tours, this conviviality continues. There is no doubt that sports science and its emphasis on good dieting and the absence of alcohol before and after a game, has considerably raised stamina, fitness and performance levels, but part of the social pleasure has disappeared. Cricketers are much more professional at every level. More skilful, maybe not?

We also have a much greater choice of sports nowadays and companies like Sky have revolutionised the way we watch. Is there really still a spirit of cricket that ensures that in the game, as in life, that players do the right thing? Walking when they have touched the ball before a decision is given, admitting that a catch was not taken or that a player was safely in when given out. Sledging or distracting an opponent seems to be routine now. I fear that cricket is now just a reflection of life. We are in the age of celebrity. We follow their tweets and their blogs, forgiving them quickly for a lack of common courtesy, taste and decency, for they are famous. Yet despite this apparent worship of celebrity, of their power and their sometimes amazing wealth, the man in the street, the common man, tends to know who the tossers are. Whether in the next house, the next street or indeed in the next store. Elite cricketers now earn serious money. It is true that it is relatively frugal when you contemplate premier league soccer players, but they are beginning to distance themselves from their audience. There are many people on a weekend who still embrace a true love of cricket and its spirit, but the game is divided, almost as it was in the fifties between the gentlemen and the players. History repeating itself?

The summer has seen a quite amazing upsurge in sporting interest and many commentators have drawn comparisons with the vibrant and refreshing spirit of the Olympic and Paralympics and sports like soccer. What they may be forgetting is that in some of the giant sporting organisations, there was for many years, and still is, an unpleasant odour. Administrators who regard themselves as sky-gods, untouchable, rewarding themselves and their friends with favours and wealth. I refer you back to the quotation from 'something missing' of Malaysian extraction. "It's all about power and what people do when they have it". It so is. Since time began. When people have the chance to live in freedom all too often their rulers seek only to build types of 'morsi-leums' where individual spirit dies, crushed by the regime, whether secular or spiritual. If only the spirit of the Olympic and Paralympic games that we have just witnessed would flow down into the spirit of life itself. Fat chance. The gap between the establishment, the powerful and the wealthy has merely got larger and the world more iniquitous. In 1965 we really did believe that the world would get better with enlightenment. Just embrace the music and the spirit. There was something in the air. Yet beware those who only seek power for its own sake or those who oppress in the name of some supreme authority. My newspaper devoted two whole pages to some latter day apologist seeking to sell more copies of his latest book, largely basing his religious justification not on what he knows to be true but of what he feels to be true. A feeling inspired by music. The vagaries of music, teasing out and enducing mood swings, emotional highs. Well I also get incredibly emotional listening to "A Whiter Shade Of Pale" or even "God Only Knows", but I don't piss off and found a religion. I don't care whether he believes in little elven people, can sense them in the fields and the ether, hear them playing their fairy bells in some great concerto. Good luck to him.

“The universe is sustained by a continual and infinitely patient act of love”. Whatever this man is on, they should market it and inject it into the people who stand outside abortion clinics and shoot doctors; who seek to have evolutionist teachers prosecuted; who seek to murder school teachers in girls schools; who beat up men without beards or women in modern dress; who destroy men who have the courage to challenge ridiculous blasphemy laws; the cowards who shoot schoolgirls like Malala. Religion, what’s love got to do with it? The Star Trek creator, Gene Roddenberry once said, “For most people, religion is nothing more than a substitute for a malfunctioning brain”. A little extreme, I hear you say, boldly going where no man has gone before. So when we read that the Pew Research Centre recently reported a worrying rise in religious intolerance, should we be concerned? Then you look at what actually concerns people are cultural issues like the spread of sharia courts, genital mutilation, forced marriage and honour killings. What on earth have objections like those to do with religious intolerance? Why should we accept any judicial court where a woman’s evidence is worth less than a man’s? What I object to is the whole apparatus that accompanies the beliefs, the hierarchies and sense of values that cults have sought to impose on me. Tolerance and freedom of thought are surely the only basis for a society such as ours. Your brain would have to be malfunctioning not to agree with that. Anything else would surely not be cricket. Religions have never played with a strate bat.

"What we want to do is to give women even more liberty than they have.... Let them do any kind of work they see fit and if they do it as well as the men, give them the same pay"

William Cody, 'Buffalo Bill'

Well who would have thought it. Must be all that time spent as a Pony Express rider or as a buffalo hunter on the vast and lonely plains dulling his brain. To think we even let him meet Queen Victoria when he came over here. Much like Barnum wanting all souls to be equal. Give me a break. Western bloody heroes. Call yourself men? It just encourages all those odd groups like Women's Aid. "Domestic violence against women is caused by the misuse of power and control within a context of male privilege....rooted in patriarchal traditions". Who writes this stuff? This sort of provocation deserves a back-hander or two. If you think you girls are going to get to play any cricket up in our celestial league, even if you can get in through the gates in the first place, you've got another think coming. Not in a million years. And women will never be equal or be treated with dignity, whilst some of you actually support the men in power and let them off the hook. There is always a choice. Some of you have just been making the wrong ones. Stop men controlling women. Stop men beating them.

"He slapped my face and shook me like a rag doll. Don't that sound like a real man?" None of the real men I know believe that if they knock you into the gutter, it's because you like looking at the stars. Real men have to stop the violence. Because your fist is big, that gives you the right to use it? Might is right? Dream on. Girls, if it felt like a kiss, you're singing off the wrong songbook. So how do any of us make a difference? Juvenal in his third satire wrote, "As you love your hoe, live as the steward of your garden". Those of you who were forced to read French literature at school may well have come across a very similar sentiment in Voltaire's Candide. At the end of a great series of adventures and encounters, where death and disaster were never far away, and wealth, power and authority were put into their proper perspectives, Voltaire suggests through the hero Candide and his mentor Dr Pangloss that life tends to come down to simple philosophies. "Il faut cultiver votre jardin". To survive and be happy then maybe 'notre jardin' is where it's at, and that doesn't mean beating your partner around the head with the hoe. Like our Tracey my formative years were spent on Margate beach, so gardens don't do much for me. All you can do is to try to influence what you can see on your own small patch of earth. Try to stop the cowards, the bullies, the tossers. Never easy, but if you can't do it where you live, then where can you? If it was alright for Buffalo Bill, why are you hesitating?

One of the tabernacle angels pulled me aside, partly to give me my ball back but also to tell me that Bert wanted a word. At least I thought he said Bert, so I had visions of our old Margate opening batsman. Bugger me, it was actually a tall geek wearing a crown and it turned out he was called Ethelbert, the old King of Kent. You know, the one who married that 'Big Bertha'. German girl probably. "Listen", he said, "what's all this stuff about men from the seventh century? I'm partly from the seventh century and I always made sure I looked after all the boys in Thanet and East Kent. I was the one who set out the 'justa exempla Romanorum' which only fined you fifty shillings if you were to lie with a maiden and three leud-gelds if you had your organ of generation cut off. If it hadn't been for me your mate Mike would probably have been in big trouble in your century, bankrupt probably. You ask Albinus. I also kept the donkeys in full work toiling up through the caves with the trade between us and the Franks with all the wine and spirits. Plus I made enough to found the abbey at St Augustine's and buy some land up in Londinium, somewhere called St Paul's. We were quite a civilised bunch I'd have you know"

"Blame some of these new-fangled manuscript writers", I replied, "I'm just plagiarising what I read and anyway some of the angels think the Guardian is their newspaper anyway. They all try and read the obituaries every day to know who's coming up next. Anyway you started it by letting in that travelling band of monks, the ones sent by Gregory the Great, the beautiful blonde angelic ones. Well they were angelic before the barbers in Rome gave them all tonsures". "Yeah", replied Ethelbert, "Bede tells me I was the first English king to convert to Christianity and look what good it did me. All there is to remember me in Thanet is one poxy school, even if our Tracey went there. Jesus, she's some sparky babe. All those vagina epilogues. Maybe she had a 'road to Damascus' episode or saw a 'burning bush'. Must be some new form of triangular worship. And what's this obsession with camping and tents? Listen, Blair isn't even up here yet but he already has a Faith Foundation and his own tweet and twitter agency. All of the Popes up here are really worried, praying that nothing happens to him, in case one of them has to give up their place at the banqueting table. Actually most of them are waiters, atoning for their sins, but don't tell anyone".

Funnily enough whilst Brian and I had been ship-spotting in Walpole Bay as kids, we had spotted what we thought were some coins on the beach. When we went down on the sand to investigate we realised that the coins were right under a slot weighing machine on the small wooden platform above. When the machine was being emptied, there must have been an accident when the tide was in, so that the hoard of penny coins had fallen into the water and obviously been abandoned. Over three days we recovered a couple of pounds worth of penny coins which we thought was absolutely wonderful. Yet along with that we also found a piece of faded old papyrus, which Brian thought might be Egyptian or Coptic, as our Encyclopedia Britannica seemed to suggest. The words were rather indistinct but we thought we could just make out something about a wife and a mother. Brian still has it up in his loft along with his complete set of Margate Football Club programmes and his Roy Orbison collection.

We had wondered if the parchment was maybe just part of an old Egyptian joke book which someone like Ken Dodd had thrown away after one of his Winter Gardens shows. I asked Ethelbert if he had ever mislaid anything like that when he was visiting Thanet. He was staggered. "Do you know", he said, "all those years ago I was weighing myself on the new Romanus scales down by the beach café and slipped. That piece of papyrus fell into the sea, I thought it was lost for ever. Pope Gregory sent it over with Augustine as one of their earliest relics, a personal gift for me. For a long time they had thought that the reference to a wife and a mother were to do with Jesus, maybe proving he was married. In fact it transpired that it had been written by some Coptic Christian who was visiting Rome and suspected that some satirist called Juvenal had slept with his wife. The letter just said that, 'if you lay with my wife again I'll have you fined fifty shillings" - which gave me the idea for my own set of Ethelbert laws or dooms – "so stay away from her Juvenal, you mother fucker! Try and find something funny in that'". That solved a religious puzzle that Brian and I had agonised over for years and Ethelbert and I parted on good terms. He went off whistling a familiar tune which he said was called 'a cowboy's song of destiny', which he had learned from some large swaggering American guy called Marion. Funny name for a bloke.

"An Act of God was defined as something which no reasonable man could have expected."

A P Herbert

Tracey, the Turner and many unsung individuals are striving to restore the town of Margate from out of the wasteland. It is high time that it was recognised for its rightful place in the universe. Rough Guide Travel have actually just placed it in their hotlist of the top ten must-see destinations in the world. Not sure where to file this article so have placed it on the bookshelf amongst the 'pure fantasy' section. Someone else obviously on the tablets. Mind you, there has always been a strong oral tradition in Thanet and not only in Dreamland and under the Sundeck. It would little surprise me if the very first big bang that Stephen Hawking describes was actually in my home town, probably one of the sky-gods letting off a giant thunderflash in the square, which he had been keeping under the white tunics in the closet for a rainy day. They probably didn't have rain before the big bang, so he must have just got bored. The shell grotto and the whole network of caves along the beach were certainly caused by some huge earthly disturbance. Why would the sky-gods be in Thanet, I hear you ask? The very same reason that drove the Phoenicians here and the Danes many years later. Shellfish, the food of the gods. Shellfish contain large amounts of an amino acid called tyrosine which makes the mental energisers dopamine and norepinephrine. Stimulants. They are a food rich in copper. There's a funny thing.

The gods came to Margate for the tablets, the spansules, washed down with the life-giving seawater. They processed the tablets from the shellfish, discarding the shells in huge quantities and once high would celebrate by sticking the empty shells on the cave walls. The grotto is a divine art centre. The gods could then hallucinate, chant rhythmically and bathe in the sea at their leisure. Anthony Eden was just continuing a long tradition of folk who came to Margate to get high. Don's Oyster Bar might just have been one of those special sites, like Stonehenge, which have a special religious significance and the Ruby Lounge was very possibly sacred. Maybe we were all worshippers in those heady days in 1965. Biff would have been thrilled to learn that he had spent so much time on holy ground had he still been alive, but the pneumonia took him some years back. Peter Willie succumbed shortly afterwards to a rather nasty disease which had first cost him both his legs and my friend Mike died last year. The alcohol and the diabetes finally caught up with him. Sadly there is no-one with whom I can share this knowledge, this exciting revelation, which is why I wanted to set it in tablets of stone before I too passed on. As Sean Bean recently said, "Eat, drink and be Mary, for tomorrow I die".

Two lives were needlessly wasted in Dane Park in August 1965. I'm sorry I didn't care more at the time. I thought I knew what sort of girl Julie was and paid very little attention to the circumstances. At the weekends in the summer I lived for the cricket, then the beer, the music and sometimes the girls. Talking about my generation. The bastards who sucked her into their world are to blame. At sixteen you think you know everything, that you have all the answers, that you are immortal. Already on an emotional roller coaster and with adrelanin pumping from the fresh intake of drugs, she hugely misjudged her new friend and companion. He had no right, no justification to kill her. I can understand the lashing out, the blows, if he really believed he was being provoked because that is at the heart of the problem which we men seem to have. Which we have to confront and somehow overcome. So many men seem to believe or have believed that you can strike a woman, with or without provocation. That is the circle that we have to break. Even then he could have left her lying on the ground. What red mist possessed him to grip her throat, not as he perceived it briefly, but what was described as prolonged constriction. Strumming her life with his fingers, a song that destroyed him as well.

I have to break off for one final time. I'm writing this whilst mending my smart phone. Got this special type of sonic screwdriver which can screw almost anything. Thought I had lost it when one of the angels was flying me home, somewhere over Ecuador, but it flashes at every possible opportunity so we were soon reunited. Didn't tell you about the final confrontation with all of the sky-gods did I? This deputation of the really heavy mob appeared. Some scary angels, all armed, trying to block my passage. I thought briefly of the Max Miller blue book and then of the Tommy Thomas dummy. I dropped my right shoulder back in an exaggerated fashion and then brought my arms up in a slow arc from right to left, like the single windscreen wiper that veteran sports cars used to have. The arc was full and painfully slow. The angels followed the movement of my arms, stepped to the right and I was through. First time I had ever done the dummy properly, only one in the school hockey team who couldn't. I normally had to compensate by taking man and ball, mostly in close proximity to one another. "Ils ne passeront pas", the order of the day at the battle of Verdun, was our defensive watchword. Purely professional violence for the team, not for its own sake or because I enjoyed it, I hasten to say. Well occasionally I did, but only to restore justice.

I had managed to get to the right side of the Pearly Gates, out of reach, but it frightened the shit out of me. Apparently all the discussion about which souls can play cricket is causing all sorts of heavenly unrest and dissension. They hate anyone challenging the supreme authorities and it has encouraged free thinking amongst the plebs. Now I was feeling quite provocative myself as I had only just watched the opening ceremony of the Paralympics. I found that very moving, all about love and inclusion and the development of ideas. It's that Stephen Hawking guy. I think I remember seeing him as a young research Fellow struggling round the college courtyard on his crutches, at a time when we had no idea how to try to communicate with people with disabilities. If you had a really visible disability you would be encouraged not to appear in the public gaze if at all possible. To my shame we might even have made jokes about his plight and condition. My father had an older brother with mental difficulties and his family put him in a home, hiding him away. We would never have guessed in those days that Hawking would either survive for long or that he could have anything meaningful to say. If you had told us that he would himself become a type of god, his picture displayed prominently in the college dining hall, and dazzling us with his knowledge, we would have been incredulous. You're having a laugh?

I know so much more about disability now, in my own small way some sort of specialist and yet they say hate crime is increasing. I don't see that at all. Maybe we just challenge more these days and insist on it being reported. The Paralympics have been so enlightening, humbling. Don't mind you taking the credit, you bastard politicians, but deliver a legacy and don't let the Treasury kill the bloody thing. Already stuffed my cricket though. Stephen Hawking's words at the ceremony have completely scuppered the celestial cricket league. What did he say? "There should be no boundaries". How the hell do you play cricket in heaven if there are no boundaries, batsmen will just strike the ball and run for ever. This is just one black hole. I'm out of it. I was just beginning to understand quarks and now there's some guy called Wang. Put him in one of the Hadron Colliders and fire him at the Sun.

The entire mob of sky-gods had assembled. Vidal was wrong, there are dozens of them. They surrounded St Peter, gesticulating at me through the gate. Many of them had eyes "red with intoxication, in absolute rage, hair dishevelled, small fangs protruding from their mouths, and tongues lolling". The bastards, most of them had been on the Dexamyl Spansules all night, one even singing 'Ghost riders in the sky'. I should have guessed it, as I had seen the procession of donkeys toiling up to the Gates at night and just assumed it was wine they were carrying. I said to one of the angels, "Bloody hell, most of this lot are off their heads". "What did you expect", he replied.

"How the hell do you think they thought up most of these religions in the first place?" Real scary though and they seemed to wheel round together as I spoke and said almost in unison, "All this soul-searching with the spirit of cricket that you have tried to organise up here. Life is nothing like cricket and heaven even less so. We need to regain absolute power and authority, keep the masses under control. If you do that again, triggering all the stupid debates about the plurality of souls and whether they have legs, we'll effing have you replaced". Fortunately I've been slipping St Peter the odd Katherine Jenkins' dvd, no the ones where she sings, so he played the white man and assured them that all was OK, that they were missing the point. True love, you see. She sings so divinely. Mind you he preferred the Angela & Hannah dvd's. Bit raunchier when Fanny is the guest artist. I felt I needed to establish my knowledge of the laws of cricket and heaven, explained that I was from Kent, a strong cricketing and religious county, had even umpired a league match up in Yorkshire and that they could replace me at any time.

Saw one of the friendly angels later who asked me what had happened. After I had left, the sky-gods had begun to argue and then fight amongst themselves, each of them shouting that they were the true sky-god. Three of them though had donned long white tunics and were heading off separately, walking very gingerly. The angel asked them what the problem was but apparently they had all been reaching up to cupboards and fallen quite separately from stools on to stumps from the celestial cricket pitch. Now all the matches had been halted in any case as they only had the one set of stumps left and no-one knew how to play French cricket. The three sky-gods on their own were desperately heading for the celestial A&E, where they had been told to ask for a Master of Broomsticks, a man called Ron. If you can extract a broomstick, a stump from a sky-god should be 'holy' possible. Apparently you have to ensnare the stump with the suture and gently swing it to and fro. Don't use a full length suture, just short of a length will do. Sadly you can never be sure quite when the stump will re-emerge and the operation, the swinging, could take weeks. Huh, the vagaries of swing.

I at least was safe. For you and I have a guardian angel, on high. That's true love, Cole Porter, and oh how lucky we are. Harold Pinter was apparently mortified at the loss of the celestial cricket. I was told that he felt the betrayal the deepest and had asked if I could once again be some sort of go-between. As a substitute they've just successfully staged the first ever celestial three legged race, although they seemed not to understand why the rules included a tin bath full of Pimms. Naturally enough Plato was so pre-occupied talking to himself, another of his bloody dialogues, that he fell in. Then they only managed to get forty two of the fifty grey handkerchiefs I suggested, as some of the monks preferred to wait for the later bondage events. The race itself was very exciting. The only difficult moment was at the beginning. They had received an entry from that Lieutenant Cooke of the Seventh Cavalry who claimed to be partnering his new Indian friend Rectum. You'll never believe this but he turned up clutching his own rectum, tied to his right leg with one of the scarves. He had to be disqualified for being one leg short. His friends said he'd never been the same since the Little Big Horn massacre. When he was around, you always had to mind your shoes now, nothing though to do with urination.

The three legged race was eventually won by a Chinese Paralympian who actually had three legs. Had been in PT Barnum's circus. Is it OK, he asked in Mandarin and in our brave new world, of course it is. So are we any closer to the meaning of life? Is cricket like life? That answer seems easier. In 1985 John Arlott wrote that, "cricket truly reflects the society in which it is played". It develops to accommodate trends like reduced attention spans, the modern need for theatre and for there always to be a winner. So is life like cricket? Myriads of teams playing and competing within the context of one set of Laws, with an onus on the captains and umpires to ensure that the spirit of cricket is upheld. However in life there are very clearly acts of violence on the field of play, many of them directed at women and intended for the purposes of controlling them. In most of the settings, the captains and umpires do not appear to be at all interested in the concept of fair play. Maybe the answer is that life really should be more like cricket, but just how do we get there? I think Bob Dylan best sums up my dilemma. "So now as I'm leavin', I'm weary as Hell. The confusion I'm feelin', ain't no tongue can tell. The words fill my head and fall to the floor". The vagaries of deep thought, of life. At times during the American presidential election you could have argued that the two most popular personalities on offer were those of the two wives. Yet after the election, to borrow from The Who, the world looks just the same and history ain't changed. Just look at the composition of the various representative assemblies here, in the States and in nearly all other countries. Why do so many women acquiesce in this continued domination of women by men? Why does no-one have the guts to leave the temple? Who are you? Don't get fooled again.

"Woman was God's second mistake".

Frederick Nietzsche

Men or women who play with strate bats rarely seem to win, beaten down by the extremists and fundamentalists on all sides. There's always someone somewhere with their own agenda, prepared to screw the rest of the people, for power, control, ideology or to make a few extra bucks. Anyway, anyhow, anywhere. However if woman was God's second mistake, what on earth was his first? Surely not the creation of man because we are without doubt a supreme race. Mind you, if you were putting man together, any decent creator would have experimented with a few prototypes at first. There must have been a test market somewhere and a few focus groups of gods for feedback. Initially, naturally enough, they would probably have voted for men to have giant dicks but then of course no one would have been able to see where they were going. I wondered if Nietzsche was thinking about the bounce-back reflexes. Perhaps there was a serious discrepancy there. With strangulation the bounce-back reflexes are inoperative after fifty seconds whereas with dicks they seem to bounce back much faster and are rarely inoperative. Only old age and excess alcohol seem to make much of a difference. It could of course be the testosterone levels that are at fault, the old fight or flight mechanism. Too much like animals I suppose, maybe Darwin could have explained the reasoning? I'll remember to ask him if I ever get up there again, although looking through the pearly gates I thought it looked much more a case of the "survival of the fattest". Sadly heaven has become just a reflection of our modern society.

The first mistake was actually not man at all but a belief that we should look to the skies to understand the universe and to believe that a just, tolerant and fair society needed the existence of a Supreme Being whom we should worship. In the beginning we imagined the Gods above the clouds and then began to fashion sky-gods in our own image. Dylan finished his song with the words, "If God's on our side, he'll stop the next war". Dream on. As in every war and conflict, both sides will claim that he is on their side and hatred and intolerance will be the only winner. Tom Lehrer was the true prophet. "The Protestants hate the Catholics, And the Catholics hate the Protestants, And the Hindus hate the Muslims". And the Muslims hate the Christians, the Sunni's hate the Shia's and so on down the line. And they all come together to hate men of reason like Dawkins whom some of them would happily crucify. Beware crucifixion, you just never know where that might lead. Maybe all you can ever hope for in life is that we can live together in the spirit of tolerance on our own piece of earth, in our own garden. Heaven knows, and of this I am certain, if we cannot all live together with mutual respect then surely, "We will all go together when we go".

As Dave Allen might have said, "May your guardian angels and your sky-gods go with you", but do not tell me how to live my life or even dictate how I must end it. Nothing also ever gives you the right to oppress groups of people, especially women, and certainly not based on ancient scriptures or testaments written when we knew so little about our universe. If you are told that this is some form of divine law, laid down centuries ago, which gives you the right to subjugate, to suppress, to destroy, then have the guts to leave the temple. Just as in cricket, it is the spirit in which events are played out that is so fundamental. It is never about power itself but just what you choose to do with it. Maybe all you need is love. Naive and only ever part of the solution, of course, but it sure as hell goes a long way.

My only other wish is based on one of those wonderful old Danish toasts, as they danced vigorously round the horn, somewhere not a million miles away from Dane Park. To the cowards, bullies and tossers. You know who you are. If you will not or cannot reform, then may you travel through eternity with your very own personal cricket stump inserted neatly from the rear, the chant from a Christmas pantomime audience as your own sacred and permanent ring-tone. Maybe more Dan Leno than Grimaldi.

"It's-behind-you".

You'd better believe it.
To infinity and beyond,
with not a single celestial A&E in sight to ease the pain.

'Pyurs'!